AF682671

Boundaries of Loyalty

Talmudic legislation prescribed a penalty for a Jew testifying in a non-Jewish court, against a fellow Jew, to benefit a gentile – for breach of a duty of loyalty to a fellow Jew. Through close textual analysis, Saul Berman explores how Jewish jurists responded when this virtue of loyalty conflicted with values such as justice, avoidance of desecration of God's name, deterrence of crime, defense of self, protection of the Jewish community and the duty to adhere to law of the land.

Essential for scholars and graduate students in Talmud, Jewish law and comparative law, this key volume details the nature of these loyalties as values within the Jewish legal system, and of how the resolution of these conflicts has been handled. Berman additionally explores why this issue has intensified in contemporary times and how the related area of 'Mesirah' has wrongfully come to be prominently associated with this law regulating testimony.

Saul J. Berman is Professor of Jewish studies at Stern College of Yeshiva University and Adjunct Professor at Columbia University Law School, where he is the Rotter Fellow of Talmudic Law. As an Orthodox Rabbi in Berkeley, CA, Brookline, MA and at Lincoln Square Synagogue in New York, Berman was an early participant in the Soviet Jewry and Civil Rights movements. His research and teaching are focused on women in Jewish law, Jewish social and medical ethics, and the connections between law and spirituality, on each of which he has published articles.

Boundaries of Loyalty

Testimony Against Fellow Jews in Non-Jewish Courts

SAUL J. BERMAN

CAMBRIDGE
UNIVERSITY PRESS

CAMBRIDGE
UNIVERSITY PRESS

One Liberty Plaza, New York NY 10006, USA

Cambridge University Press is part of the University of Cambridge.

It furthers the University's mission by disseminating knowledge in the pursuit of education, learning and research at the highest international levels of excellence.

www.cambridge.org
Information on this title: www.cambridge.org/9781107090651

© Saul J. Berman 2016

This publication is in copyright. Subject to statutory exception and to the provisions of relevant collective licensing agreements, no reproduction of any part may take place without the written permission of Cambridge University Press.

First published 2016

Printed in the United States of America by Sheridan Books, Inc.

A catalog record for this publication is available from the British Library

Library of Congress Cataloging in Publication data
Names: Berman, Saul J., author.
Title: Boundaries of loyalty : testimony against fellow Jews in non-Jewish courts / Saul J. Berman.
Description: Cambridge, United Kingdom : Cambridge University Press, 2016. | Includes bibliographical references and index.
Identifiers: LCCN 2016021103 | ISBN 9781107090651 (hardback)
Subjects: LCSH: Informers (Jewish law) | Witnesses (Jewish law) | Conflict of laws (Jewish law) | Criminal jurisdiction. | Legal polycentricity.
Classification: LCC KBM2025 .B47 2016 | DDC 347/.066–dc23
LC record available at https://lccn.loc.gov/2016021103

ISBN 978-1-107-09065-1 Hardback

Cambridge University Press has no responsibility for the persistence or accuracy of URLs for external or third-party internet websites referred to in this publication, and does not guarantee that any content on such websites is, or will remain, accurate or appropriate.

Of the many gifts with which God has blessed me –
the greatest is my wife,
Shellee

מצא אשה מצא טוב

10 "justice" – a legal value outside of law is recognized

Contents

Acknowledgments

My parents, Rabbi Ephraim and Rose Berman, of blessed memory, taught me integrity, humility, the centrality of Torah study and the importance of striving for justice in an imperfect world. My parents in-law, Dr. Nathan and Rose Birn, of blessed memory, taught me to work hard, to stand up for principles, to live modestly and to never think that you have enough knowledge. The four of them modeled for their children love of Torah, of family and of God. The only way in which one can repay such a debt, which Shellee and I have attempted to do, is to pass on those same values and virtues to the next generation.

A select group of teachers have shaped my spiritual and intellectual life. Prime amongst them was Rabbi Joseph B. Soloveitchik, of blessed memory, whose intellectual brilliance and religious passion enlightened my mind and elevated my soul. Dr. Louis Feldman and Rabbi Emanuel Rackman at Yeshiva College, Professor Edmond Cahn of New York University Law School, Professor David Daube at the University of California at Berkeley, Justice Menachem Elon at Hebrew University Law School and Professor Aaron Kirschenbaum at Tel Aviv University Law School – each in his unique way empowered me to study Jewish legal texts not only as God's will, but as God's will for the governance of all of human society; which then allowed for and enriched the application of Halacha to contemporary reality, and the comparison between Jewish law and other legal systems. The teaching and writings of my friend Dr. Haym Soloveitchik demanded a level of precision and rigor in reading texts and in the analysis of ideas and of reality that enriched my thinking, teaching and writing in Torah. Each one of them contributed in important ways to my own attempt to tease out of Jewish law the underlying truths, virtues and values that are the spiritual underpinnings of legal and ethical decision making.

"Give me friendship, or give me death," said Choni HaMe'agel correctly (Ta'anit 32a), for in friendship there is unparalleled richness of life. I am blessed with friends, too many to mention, but in the interaction with whom the virtues and values expressed in this book came to be formed and sharpened as intellectual awareness, as spiritual devotion and as living forces. Childhood friends, and friends from Yeshiva Torah Vodaath, friends from Yeshiva College, and RIETS of YU, from Berkeley California and Brookline Massachusetts, from Murray Hill, Lincoln Square Synagogue and the Upper West Side in Manhattan – they and their children have accompanied us, as we them, through the challenges of a lifetime, the sorrows and the joys, the failures and the successes. We always remember the kindnesses and moments of mutual caring in those relationships that brighten our lives.

My earliest research on the subject matter of this book took place during my initial years as a faculty member and Chairman of the Department of Jewish Studies at Stern College, under the Deanship of Rabbi David Mirsky. He encouraged my desire to develop a series of courses in Jewish law and contemporary social and political problems, entitled The Individual and Society. By now over four decades of students at Stern College, and twenty years of students at Columbia Law School, have studied with me elements of the relevant values, ideas and sources embedded in this book, and I have been enriched by their ever-fresh insights and passionate ethical commitments as we have confronted the texts themselves and their struggle with competing loyalties.

In the academic year 2009–2010, I was honored to serve as the Berkowitz Fellow at The Tikvah Center for Law and Jewish Civilization at New York University School of Law. I am indebted to The Tikvah Fund for its sponsorship of the Center, and to Professors Joseph Weiler and Moshe Halbertal, both for their vibrant intellectual leadership of the Center, and for reading drafts of this book and making valuable recommendations that contributed to its final form. I am grateful for the collegiality of all of the extraordinary scholars who served as Tikvah fellows with me; and particularly to Professors Aharon Shemesh and Adiel Schremer whose breadth of knowledge and insight into primary and secondary sources in Jewish law enriched me enormously as I wrote this book. Rabbi Dr. Menachem Meier, a devoted friend, read much of the manuscript and recommended small and large changes from which the readers will benefit.

My thanks to Dr. Lewis Bateman of Cambridge University Press for his confidence in the merits of this book. Also to Cassi Roberts for shepherding the book through the process of being prepared for publication and Helen Flitton for her excellent editorial work on the manuscript. Special thanks to my daughter, Esther Lefkowitz, for her consistently outstanding work on every aspect of the preparation of the manuscript for publication and for the performance of technical skills which I could never have mastered.

Shellee, to whom this volume is dedicated, often wears a pin with the Hebrew word "bonayich," meaning "your builders," which at the end of Tractate Berachot is used in a play on the word "banayich," "your children," in Isaiah 54:13, "(you shall have) much wholeness (through) your children." Indeed, our children, their spouses and our grandchildren have been the builders of our wholeness and happiness. Gifts of God to us, they taught us the varied forms that depth of intellect, goodness of heart, sensitivity to justice, and humor can take. They have embodied the values and virtues of integrity, self-sacrifice, religious devotion, joy in life and kindness in uniquely configured proportions appropriate to each one's distinctive, autonomous identity. And so, I acknowledge them all: Shama and Rachel Berman, and Shoshi, Adira, Ephraim and Adiv (may God grant him healing and long life); Efrath and Gal Levy, and Natalie, Gabriel and Abigail; Akiva Berman; Esther and Rafi Lefkowitz and Ava. To all, with pride and love.

This will be reviewed in major Jewish studies journals by specialists

But JAAR wants works like this "mainstreamed" & not left to specialists

What larger truth in REST arises? or is suggested?

Introduction

I first became interested in the issue that is the subject of this volume in April 1975. At that time, the New York Special Prosecutor for Nursing Home Investigations, Mr. Charles Hynes, had empaneled a grand jury to hear evidence concerning Bernard Bergman, an owner and operator of nursing homes, who stood accused of various illegal acts. A woman employee of the Towers Nursing Home was subpoenaed to testify concerning allegations of financial improprieties affecting government reimbursement of nursing home expenses. She filed a petition to the court claiming that she should be exempt from the duty to testify on the grounds of her constitutional guarantee of freedom of religion. She claimed that under Jewish law she was forbidden to testify against a fellow Jew in a non-Jewish court, that to do so would constitute a violation of the Jewish law against *Mesirah*, "informing," and would subject her to effective excommunication from her Orthodox Jewish community. The court heard oral argument on the issue, including the testimony of experts in Jewish law, and rejected the plea, ordering the witness to testify.[1]

Reading the reports of these events in the newspapers raised a set of questions in my mind. On the one hand, the horror of informing against fellow Jews is a profoundly deep sensibility in Jewish life and literature. The central Jewish liturgical text of daily prayer, the *Amidah*, had been fixed containing eighteen blessings almost 2,500 years ago. Through that entire period of time, the only blessing added to it, making for nineteen blessings in the *Amidah*, was the special blessing requesting divine

[1] Marcia Chambers, "Ex-Bergman Aide Declines To Talk," *New York Times*, April 30, 1975, p. 81.

protection of the Jewish nation against informers.[2] Beyond that, Jewish law seemed to provide for the summary execution of informers without the usual standards of evidentiary process and other judicial procedures mandated in the protection of the lives of criminals.[3] And a Midrashic text says it all. When the Israelite nation lost the war against the city of Ai, Joshua challenged God to explain why the assurance of Jewish conquest of the Land of Canaan was not being fulfilled. God responded that a Jew had stolen from the proscribed booty of the city of Jericho. When Joshua, in the *Midrash*, asked God who had perpetrated the crime, God responds as in shock, "Am I then an informer?!"[4] Thus in this *Midrash*, God refuses to inform on a person whom He knows with certainty is a criminal, even to Joshua, the duly constituted head of government of the Jewish people, appointed by God Himself.

On the other hand, I asked myself, is it really conceivable that according to Jewish law actions by a citizen to bring a criminal to justice, or to prevent damage to another person, within a well-ordered judicial system could itself be considered a criminal action? Is Jewish law so viscerally opposed to the utilization of any system of law other than itself that it would prefer to have criminals and perpetrators of economic wrongs roam free rather than have Jews cooperate with a non-Jewish legal process? What in fact is the position of Jewish law on the question of testimony by a Jew against a fellow Jew in a non-Jewish court?

2 *Berachot* 28b, Rambam, *Mishneh Torah, Tefillah* 2:1; and end of *Sefer Ahavah*, *Seder Tefillot Kol Hashana, Nusach Birchot Hatefillah Vesidduran*, no. 12.

3 *Tosefta Bava Metzia* 2:33. *Rosh Hashana* 17a. Abraham A. Rapaport, "The Informer in Jewish Literature" (Until the End of the Geonic Period), unpublished doctoral thesis, May 1952, Bernard Revel Graduate School of Yeshiva University, New York, pp. 120–126.

4 The text is found in four separate locations in the *Midrash* and twice in the *Talmud*. *Midrash Tanchuma*, Warsaw, *Vayeshev*, sec. 2; *Yalkut Shimoni, Parshat Beshalach*, Joshua, ch. 7, and Ezra, ch. 8. *Sanhedrin* 11a and 43b.

1

The Use of Non-Jewish Courts: The *Tannaitic* Period

1.1 LITIGATION IN NON-JEWISH COURTS

Jewish law naturally favored Jewish courts and Jewish substantive and procedural rules, because it operated out of the conviction that the Jewish legal system, based on the divinely revealed Biblical text, would bring the best possible justice to the ordering of human affairs. There has always been a powerful sense of pride that Jews have taken in the distinctive nature of the ethical advances of *Torah* law over ancient and modern legal systems – the application of the crime of homicide to all persons, the virtual elimination of vicarious liability, the exclusion of confession as a basis for criminal conviction, the early reduction of the evils of slavery, the high demand of disclosure in commercial relations, the affirmative duty of rescue of life and so many other basic values embedded in Jewish Law This conviction led to two distinctive operational values, which could potentially be in conflict with each other. On the one hand stands the valuing of Jewish jurisdiction as an institutional interest, as the critical mechanism for achieving the valued aspiration. On the other hand stands the ultimate aspiration itself, the achievement of justice. What would happen under circumstances in which justice might best be actualized by the engagement of non-Jewish jurisdiction?

In consequence of the conviction of the distinctively just nature of Jewish law, early Jewish law deemed it impermissible for Jewish litigants to submit their conflict to non-Jewish courts. The *Beraita*[1] reports the teaching of Rabbi Tarfon in the mid-second century of the Common

[1] *Gittin* 88b.

Era, who understood this proscription to be *DeOraita* law, revealed law, based on an odd reading of Exodus 21:1:

it has been taught, Rabbi Tarfon used to say:
In any place where you find non-Jewish law courts,
even though their law is the same as the Jewish Law,
you must not resort to them, since it says,
'These are the judgments which thou shalt set before them,'
that is to say, before them (Jewish judges)
and not before non-Jews.[2]
Another matter, before them (Jewish judges)
and not before (Jewish) laymen[3]

A reasonable assumption to make is that this intense expression of the value of safeguarding exclusive Jewish jurisdiction would apply to all three phases of the judicial process:

(1) ascertaining the facts (fact finding);
(2) determining the rules applicable to those facts (judging); and
(3) ordering the enforcement of the appropriate outcome or remedy (execution of judgment).

Jewish law has distinctive rules and values related to each of these phases, and ought, presumptively, to seek the application of its own jurisdiction in relation to each of them. Surprisingly, such was not the case.

1.1.1 Fact Finding

Firstly, in regard to the fact-finding process, Talmudic law was distinctively open to the use of non-Jewish legal instruments as a means of establishing facts for further adjudication in Jewish courts. This is manifest already in the clarity with which *Tannaitic* sources accept the use of documents from Roman *Arkaot*. The term *Arkaot* in *Tannaitic* sources has to do exclusively with the archival functions of the legal system, and not with either litigation or testimony in non-Jewish courts. The relevant *Tannaitic* discussions refer to the Hellenistic institution of archives, not courts, and relate solely to the enforceability in Jewish courts of documents executed and deposited in those archives.[4] The role of the archive

[2] This interpretation is not found explicitly in the *Halachic Midrashim*, but is implied in *Mechilta*, *Nezikin* sec. 1 (Horowitz-Rabin edition, p. 246). The law is explicitly cited in *Midrash Tanchuma*, *Mishpatim*, sec. 3 (in Mantu edition, but not in Tanhuma Buber).

[3] *Gittin* 88b.

[4] Despite intense debate for over a century as to the precise meaning and legal role of the *Tannaitic Arkaot*, I will argue in a separate paper that the *Arkaot* of the *Tannaitic* period

was purely evidentiary as to the will of the parties expressed in the document. It provided a distinctive degree of certainty as to the "facts" of the agreement between the parties.

Instead of resistance to this incursion into the first stage of the judicial process, Jewish use of and participation in such "fact-finding" process by a non-Jewish institution, was, strikingly, held to be not objectionable. But the opposing value of preserving Jewish jurisdiction was upheld in two ways:

a. The substantive rules of law applied by the Jewish court in the course of litigation would be exclusively those of Jewish law;
b. Documents such as those of divorce and manumission, which required execution in consonance with substantive rules of Jewish law, execution not reflected on the face of the witnessed and archived documents, were excluded from recognition.

This set of rules is already manifested in *Mishnah Gittin* 1:5:

All legal documents on deposit in non-Jewish *Arkaot*,
even if their signatories are non-Jews, are valid;
except writs of divorce and of manumission of slaves.
Rabbi Shimon says, these also are valid –
they are mentioned only when they are drafted by laymen.

An unstated premise of the law of this *Mishnah* is the ineligibility of non-Jews as witnesses in Jewish law. The precise basis for this disqualification, as well as its status, came to be the subject of extensive debate amongst *Rishonim*.[5] Maimonides[6] asserts explicitly that the ineligibility is *DeOraita*, a matter of revealed law, while Rashi[7] suggests that it is of Rabbinic origin. While the relevant Talmudic passages indeed leave room for this debate,[8] the fact of disqualification itself is incontrovertible. *Tannaitic* texts already explicitly indicate the ineligibility of non-Jews as witnesses, without any indication of dissent.[9]

were neither governing bodies nor courts; they were archives. Every single *Tannaitic* text referring to the Arki, early and late *Tannaitic*, *Halachic* and *Aggadic*, *Mishnah*, *Tosefta* and *Beraita*, without exception, deals with the preparation, execution or storage of legal documents. In not a single instance was the Arki the setting for adjudication, nor for any other legal or governmental function.

5 For a summary of the various positions on this matter, see Rabbi Shlomo Josef Zevin, *Encyclopedia Talmudit*, vol. V, pp. 337–339.

6 Rambam, *Mishneh Torah*, Book of Judges, Laws of testimony 9:4.

7 Rashi to *Gittin* 9b, s.v. *Chutz*. His position is so understood by the Baalei HaTosafot in *Bava Kamma* 88a, s.v. *Yehei*, even though they dissent from that position.

8 See *Gittin* 9b, *Yevamot* 47a and *Bava Kamma* 14b–15a.

9 *Mishnah Bava Kamma* 1:3, *Tosefta Bava Kamma* 1:2.

Against this backdrop, our *Mishnah*, by saying, "even if their signatories are non-Jews," first implies that Jews might have been witnesses to the document, in which case the validity of the document would not be impaired by its having been executed and stored in the non-Jewish archive. That is, the *Arkaot* are not negative legal instruments, but may merely be neutral. But then the *Mishnah* raises the question of the status in Jewish Courts of legal documents found on deposit in the *Arkaot*, the signatories to which are non-Jews. Given the indicated ineligibility of non-Jews as witnesses, a general legal document signed by non-Jews, in the possession of one of the parties to litigation in a Jewish court, would be held to be unenforceable. Yet our *Mishnah* makes the radical assertion that was the very same document to have been executed and stored in the non-Jewish *Arkaot*, it would be held valid and subject to enforcement by a Jewish court.

The non-Jewish *Arkaot* serve to establish the validity of legal documents that would otherwise be considered invalid. The *Arkaot*, then, are not simply neutral, they are positive vehicles for the validation of documents. The Jewish court can place full faith and credit in a document on deposit in the Archive as a truthful embodiment of the agreement that had been arrived at between the parties now in litigation in the Jewish court. The non-Jewish legal instrument can be a perfectly valid means of establishing facts upon which the Jewish law litigation can then proceed.

As the *Mishnah* then goes on to note, excluded from this openness to the use of the non-Jewish Archive as a means of establishing facts are the instances of writs of divorce and manumission of slaves. In those instances, the contract is not merely the factual indication of the will of the parties, but is itself the legal means of causing change of legal status of the parties in Jewish law. Jewish witnesses remained essential in those circumstances.[10]

1.1.2 Execution of Judgment

Second, it is clear that Rabbinic insistence on litigation in Jewish courts did not preclude Jewish use of non-Jewish courts for the third stage of the judicial process, the enforcement of judgments. Again, the competing

[10] The varied texts of the Vienna versus the Erfurt manuscripts of *Tosefta Gittin* 1:4 suggest that there was a substantial history of *Tannaitic* debate about the precise rules to be applied to status-fixing Jewish documents executed and stored in the non-Jewish *Arki*. Comprehensive treatment of this issue is to be found in Saul Lieberman, *Tosefta Kifeshutah*, vol. VIII, Order Nashim, NY, 1973, at pp. 785–791.

value of preserving Jewish jurisdiction was upheld by insistence that such non-Jewish enforcement would be viewed as valid only in the implementation of a judgment already arrived at by a Jewish court in its usual application of Jewish law. The use of non-Jewish procedure in the interest of effectuating the rule of Jewish law was acceptable when Jewish procedures to achieve the same result were not available since, otherwise, justice could not be achieved.

This emerges clearly from the text of *Mishnah Gittin* 9:8 (88b):

> A *Get* given under compulsion by a Jewish court is valid;
> but by a non-Jewish court (the *Get*) is invalid.
> A non-Jewish court, however, may flog a person and say to him
> "Do what the Jewish court has ordered you," (and it is valid.)

The Rabbinic understanding of the description of the divorce procedure in Deuteronomy 24:1, "and he shall write her a bill of divorcement and deliver it into her hand" necessitated the husband's exercise of his free will in the issuance of a *Get* to his wife.[11] Despite the clarity of that *DeOraita* requirement, our *Mishnah* unequivocally supports the authority of a Jewish court to coerce a husband to issue the *Get*. The *Mishnah* in *Arakin* 5:6 (21a) offers the reconciling theory of a legal fiction to explain the basis of the legitimacy of such coercion in divorce cases; "they exercise force until he says 'I consent!'." The husband's verbal declaration of assent is the technical hook on which the validity of the *Get* is hung.[12] While the Talmudic Sages limited the situations in which such coercive methods would be used, they clearly recognized this as an essential tool in terminating marriages that the wife justifiably sought to end, but to which the husband refused to consent.[13]

But what then is to be done when due to lack of jurisdiction, Rabbinic courts cannot actually coerce the husband to even grant his verbal assent? It is to this situation that our *Mishnah* addressed itself by indicating that if a non-Jewish court on its own initiative were to coerce a Jewish man to issue a *Get* to his wife, the resultant *Get* would be deemed invalid by Jewish law. However, if a Jewish court had

[11] *Yevamot* 112b. Rambam, *Mishneh Torah*, *Hilchot Gerushin* (Laws of Divorce) 1:1–2.

[12] See Rambam, *Mishneh Torah*, *Hilchot Gerushin* 2:20 for his philosophical justification of this coercion by *Beth Din*, including the use of physical force, as not contradictory to the free-will requirement.

[13] For a detailed treatment of the circumstances under which a Rabbinic court would order coercion against a husband for the achievement of the issuance of a *Get*, see Irving A. Breitowitz, *Between Civil and Religious Law: The Plight of the Agunah in American Society*, Westport, CT, Greenwood Press, 1993, at pp. 5–40.

ordered issuance of a *Get*, had been unable to enforce its judgment, and a non-Jewish court stood ready and available to order the husband to comply with the demand of the Jewish court, then, even in the face of the coercive action undertaken by the non-Jewish court, the resultant *Get* would be deemed perfectly valid according to Jewish Law. The Jewish court would not relegate a woman to the status of an Agunah, a woman chained to a dead marriage, just because of its lack of jurisdiction – when they could utilize the services of a non-Jewish court for the enforcement of their judgment.

But here, as to execution of judgment, as in regard to the use of non-Jewish legal institutions for fact finding, the underlying value of the preservation of Jewish substantive law is clearly upheld. The only situations in which coercion as to issuance of a *Get* is acceptable is when a prior deliberation in a Jewish court has led to an order of issuance of a *Get* which lacks only enforcement tools to be effectuated.[14] Justice then demands the utilization of the value-neutral tool of the non-Jewish legal enforcement.

Thus, *Tannaitic* defense of Jewish jurisdiction against the inroads of non-Jewish legal institutions was subservient to the interest of the achievement of justice, but the dialectic between the two values was always manifest in the detailed modes of approval of utilization of the non-Jewish institutions. The Sages allowed for a significant role to be played by non-Jewish legal institutions in the determination of facts and in the enforcement of judgment, the first and the last of the three essential phases of the judicial process.

1.1.3 Judging

What then of the middle phase of these three, the direct application of the substantive rules of Jewish law by a Jewish court? Was there room here as well for the operation of this fundamental dialectic between loyalty to Jewish law and loyalty to justice? I will argue that the same pattern continues to manifest itself even in relation to this most central aspect of the Jewish judicial process. For example, where litigation in Jewish courts was not possible because one of the parties was a non-Jew, early *Tannaitic* law already recognized the need to participate, as either litigant or witness, in non-Jewish adjudication in order to achieve whatever justice could thereby be made available. The earliest explicit indication of

[14] See again *Rambam, Mishneh Torah, Hilchot Gerushin* 2:20, closing sentences.

the permissibility of the use of non-Jewish courts in such situations is to be found in *Tosefta, Avodah Zarah* 1:8:[15]

1. One may go to a heathen fair ... and buy from them[16]
2. houses, fields and vineyards, male and female slaves,
3. because it is like rescuing something from them;
4. and he may draw up contracts and deposit them in their Archives.
5. A *Kohen* [priest] may make himself ritually unclean for them
6. by testifying and adjudicating concerning them
7. outside the Land of Israel.

The first part of the *Tosefta* text quoted (lines 1–4), is a response to a general prohibition against engaging in business transactions with idolatrous non-Jews at a heathen fair.[17] Our text generates an exception to that constraint, allowing such transactions when there is an element of "rescue" in the purchase at that time, recognizing that the opportunity to restore Jewish ownership over land in Israel, and to purchase and liberate Jewish slaves from their idolatrous masters are interests of greater magnitude than the possibility of encouraging an idolator to worship his pagan deity.

The latter part of this *Tosefta* text (lines 5–7), makes an equivalent claim as to the power of these interests in "rescue" (restoring Jewish ownership over land in Israel and the liberation of Jewish slaves from their idolatrous masters) to override the Rabbinic restriction on a *Kohen* leaving the land of Israel which was the consequence of the Rabbinic declaration of the ritual uncleanness of all lands outside Israel.[18] The overriding nature of these interests would allow the *Kohen* to become impure so as to be able to participate as a litigant, or as a witness, or in some versions of our text also as an attorney, in attempting to achieve this "rescue."[19]

[15] The text of this law is also found with some variations in *Tosefta*, in *Gemara* of the Babylonian and Jerusalem *Talmudim*, and in the *Midrash*: *Tosefta Moed Kattan* 2:1; and (in whole or in part) in *Eruvin* 47a, *Moed Kattan* 11a, *Avodah Zarah* 13a, J. *Berachot* 3:1, J. *Nazir* 7:1, and *Semachot* 4:14 (Higger edition at p. 121.) It is also recorded in Genesis *Rabbah* 47:10.

[16] S. Lieberman in *Tosefet Rishonim* vol. II, p. 186, and in vol. I, p. 242, points out the scribal error in this text, adding the word "*ain*, " "may not," thereby incorrectly reversing the entire meaning of the passage, contrary to its grammar and context, as well as contrary to every other record of this text.

[17] For a full treatment of this issue see Gerald Blidstein, "Rabbinic Legislation on Idolatry," unpublished doctoral thesis, Bernard Revel Graduate School, Yeshiva University, 1968, particularly at pp. 122–130.

[18] *Mishnah Taharot* 4:5. For treatment of this general issue see G. Alon, *Mehkarim Betoldot Yisrael*, (Heb.), HaKibutz Hameuchad Pub. House, 1958, vol. II, pp. 121–147, and particularly at pp. 144–145.

[19] Also evidenced in J. *Berachot* 3:1 (23 a,b), *Semahot* 4:14 (Higger edition p. 121), and J. *Nazir* 7:1.

Interestingly, neither this *Tosefta* nor any other Talmudic text raises the question of whether such participation in non-Jewish courts would constitute a breach of the teaching of Rabbi Tarfon. The implication is that barring the concern with the impurity of a *Kohen*, participation in litigation with a non-Jew in a non-Jewish court would not fall within the restrictive position of Rabbi Tarfon and would be entirely permissible according to Talmudic Law.[20]

This implication is further strengthened by the recognition that the power of the "rescue" interests dealt with by the *Tosefta* were only of sufficient strength to override the Rabbinic prohibition of impurity, not to override *DeOraita*, revealed, laws.[21] But Rabbi Tarfon had asserted that his constraint against litigating in non-Jewish courts was based on an explicit verse of the *Torah*. If then his position also precluded litigation between a Jew and a non-Jew, the greater argument of the *Tosefta* would have been to contend that the power of the "rescue" interests could even override the *DeOraita* teaching of the prohibition against litigating in non-Jewish courts. The *Tosefta* would then not have had to introduce the issue of the *Kohen* at all, but could have taught us the even more extreme proposition that the "rescue" of land in Israel and of Jewish slaves from idolators was of sufficient power to even supersede the *DeOraita* prohibition against litigating in non-Jewish courts.

The combination then of the implication of the *Tosefta* and the Talmudic silence as to a contrary ruling suggests clearly that litigation between a Jew and a non-Jew may permissibly take place in a non-Jewish court. Why was this not a betrayal of the duty of allegiance to Jewish law? Were Jewish law to forbid such litigation, it would result in the general inability of Jews to achieve any justice in their economic relations with non-Jews. Non-Jews could then simply refuse to litigate in a Jewish court and would be assured immunity from legal process by the Jewish litigant, or be confident in victory in a hearing in the non-Jewish court in consequence of the non-appearance of the Jewish party. While the higher justice of Jewish law might be preferable, not being able to pursue one's

[20] In fact it is only in the early Gaonic period (seventh to ninth centuries C.E.) that the suggestion is first made that even in adjudication with a non-Jew, the Jewish party is obligated to attempt to convince the non-Jew to adjudicate in a Jewish court. See *Tanhuma*, *Shoftim*, sec. 1 (in mantua edition and in *Tanhuma Buber*.)

[21] This limitation to overriding only Rabbinic uncleanness is emphasized by Rambam in *Hilchot HaYerushalmi LehaRambam*, *Berachot* ch. 3, p. 27. See there the commentary of S. Lieberman at sec. 100.

legal rights and privileges at all is totally unacceptable – some justice is better than none.

Aside the issue of litigation, this *Tosefta* text provides us with the first indication of the position of Jewish law as to testimony by a Jew in a non-Jewish court.

1.2. TESTIMONY IN NON-JEWISH COURTS: ADVANTAGING TESTIMONY ON BEHALF OF THE JEWISH PARTY

Explicit in the *Tosefta* text is the ruling that testimony by a Jew in a non-Jewish court on behalf of a Jewish party, where the other party is a non-Jew, is permissible and that, in the interests of the two "rescue" transactions listed by the *Tosefta*, certain Rabbinic prohibitions will even be overridden. The further implication of the text is that when such litigation between Jew and non-Jew is permissible before a non-Jewish court, there being no violation of the law of Rabbi Tarfon, there is also no barrier to a Jew serving as a witness even on behalf of the non-Jewish party. However, the law will not supersede other Rabbinic prohibitions in order to effectuate such testimony by the Jewish witness – unless other vital Jewish interests are at stake, such as restoring Jewish ownership of land in Israel, or the freeing of Jewish slaves from non-Jewish ownership.

If our reading of the explicit and implicit rulings of this *Tosefta* text is correct, then we have before us a minor, but nevertheless distinctive, *Tannaitic* bias in favor of a Jewish party in his legal contest with a non-Jew before a non-Jewish court. It is minor in that its circumstances are limited to the following situation: where a Jew and a non-Jew are litigating in a non-Jewish court outside Israel and a potential witness is a *Kohen* residing in Israel. Under those limited circumstances, if the success of the Jewish party in the adjudication would result in land in Israel being returned to Jewish ownership, or in the manumission of Jewish slaves from their non-Jewish owner,[22] then the *Kohen* may leave Israel to testify on behalf of the Jewish party. The *Kohen* would not be permitted to violate the Rabbinic constraint against his leaving Israel to testify on behalf of the non-Jewish party whose victory in the litigation would not produce the desired "rescue" effects.

[22] S. Lieberman in *Tosefta Kifeshutah, Moed*, pp. 1241–1242 indicates that the *Amoraim* did not automatically apply this ruling to override any and all Rabbinic prohibitions, but only the ones made explicit in *Tosefta Avodah Zarah* 1:8.

Since this *Tosefta* text is the sole *Tannaitic* passage that deals with the issue of testimony in a non-Jewish court, any attempt to define the reason for the existence of this minor bias must remain largely speculative. However, it is valuable for us to briefly explore the possible reasons, to serve as a conceptual framework within which to see the subsequent developments in Jewish legal discourse on this matter.

1.2.1 To Achieve "Religious Rescue"

Firstly, it is possible that this bias is motivated by the magnitude of the religious imperatives to be achieved in these particular transactions – the settlement of the Land of Israel through the purchase from non-Jews of homes, fields and vineyards, and the rescue of Jews from submergence into idolatry through their purchase and manumission. Indeed, each of these religious imperatives functions elsewhere in Jewish law as legislative motive for the modification of other Rabbinic Laws.[23] It would be perfectly reasonable, therefore, to assume that the minor bias of the *Tosefta* was the byproduct of the intensity with which the *Tannaim* desired to achieve these two "religious rescue" goals. However, it appears that this very question may have been the basis of late *Tannaitic* and then Amoraic debate reflected in textual variants of our *Tosefta* text. In a singular instance, the *Tosefta* text quoted in *Moed Kattan* adds to the list of transactions the purchase of cattle.[24] On that basis, all Babylonian Amoraic citations of our *Tosefta* text include this third case as one in which the *Kohen* could leave Israel to testify on behalf of the Jewish litigant in the non-Jewish court.[25] The "religious rescue" motive is thereby weakened.

A further weakening of the "religious rescue" element is evidenced in Palestinian Amoraic sources, where a version of our *Tosefta* text is cited without reference to the situation of the Heathen Fair, and the exemption for the *Kohen* to leave Israel despite the presence of rabbinic impurity in other lands is broadened to include permissibility for all commercial purposes.[26] This broadening is further evidenced in the Babylonian *Gemara*, raising the possibility that even the purchase of non-Jewish slaves might

[23] As to legislation to promote the settlement of the Land of Israel, see *Gittin* 8b, *Bava Kamma* 80b, *Bava Metzia* 101a, *Menahot* 44a and *Tamid* 29b. For an interesting instance of legislation to prevent submergence into idolatry, see *Gittin* 88b.

[24] *Tosefta Moed Kattan* 2:1.

[25] *Eruvin* 47a; *Moed Kattan* 11a; and *Avodah Zarah* 13a and b.

[26] J. *Berachot* 3:1; J. *Nazir* 7:1 and *Semachot* 4:14.

be included in the exemption, a position which is confirmed in the citation of the position of the Palestinian *Amora* Rabbi Shimon ben Lakish, who argued that even in the purchase of such slaves there is a religious motive, of converting the non-Jewish slaves to Judaism.[27]

No wonder, then, that toward the close of the Amoraic period, Rav Ashi (c. 335–427 C.E.) was uncomfortable with the expansion of the list of circumstances in which the exemption was granted, and needed a new conceptualization to encompass them all, proposing that the underlying motive of this law was the desire to diminish the economic capacity of the non-Jewish community of Israel.[28] While the Amoraic treatment of this particular ruling then involved a broadening of its application far beyond the original two situations, there is still present the sense of the religious imperative for the Jewish settlement of the land of Israel. While attenuated from its original clarity, we can certainly still seriously consider the possibility of this motive of "religious rescue" as the basis for the bias in the *Tosefta*, allowing the *Kohen* to leave Israel to testify on behalf of the Jewish litigant, but not on behalf of the non-Jewish litigant, in their contest in the non-Jewish court.

1.2.2 Limits on the Duty to Testify

A second possible basis for the preferential treatment of the Jewish party in this *Tosefta* text may lie in the *Tannaitic* limitation of the *DeOraita* obligation to testify on behalf of a fellow Jew. The Biblical verse which serves as the basis of the positive obligation to testify as to one's knowledge of the facts of a case says as follows: "When a person (*nefesh*) sins, as when, having heard the declared curse (against one who fails to testify), he is able to testify, having seen or known, but does not testify as to the information he has, he is to bear guilt."[29] The verse itself does not explicitly distinguish between the need for testimony by a Jewish party as opposed to a non-Jewish party.[30]

[27] *Avodah Zarah* 13b.

[28] *Avodah Zarah* 13a and b.

[29] Leviticus 5:1.

[30] The *Midrash Halacha* does restrict applicability of this passage to Jews through interpretation of the word "*nefesh*," at *Sifra*, Leviticus 1, *Dibbura DeHova, Parshata* 1. on Lev.4:1. Since Lev. 5:1 also uses the word "*nefesh*," the *Midrash* concludes that it too, like Lev. 4:1, refers solely to Jews. However, this has to do with the question of who is obligated to testify, and therefore to bring a sin offering upon failure to fulfill the legal duty to testify. It bears no relationship to the question of the identity of the potential beneficiary of the testimony.

Nevertheless, when the *Tosefta* in *Shavuot* records the law that one who violates this commandment and fails to testify is not financially liable for the indirect injury he caused, it does, at least by implication, address the question of exactly who would have been the beneficiary of the testimony which was not offered. The *Tosefta* says:[31]

1. One who knows of evidence in favor of his friend (*chavero*)
2. but does not testify on his behalf,
3. is not liable to pay by law,
4. but is not forgiven by Heaven until he pays.[32]

The choice of the term *Chavero*, "his friend," seems, on the basis of other *Tannaitic* usage to imply the restriction of the Biblical obligation to testify to testimony on behalf of a fellow Jew.[33] This same limitation might be implied by the alternate source from which the obligation to testify is derived, the verse in Leviticus 19:16, "you shall not stand idly by the blood of your neighbor (*re'acha*)."[34] The term *re'acha*, "your neighbor," in Biblical usage, is almost universally understood solely as a reference to fellow Jews. Interestingly, while this limitation is not made explicit in Talmudic literature, the reference to *chavero* is preserved by the *She'iltot* of R. Hai Gaon,[35] and then by Rambam.[36] This was apparently sufficient

[31] *Tosefta Shavuot* 3:1–2; and as a *Beraita* in *Bava Kamma* 55b–56a.

[32] J.N. Epstein contends that this *Tosefta* text is a fragment of the *Halachic Midrash* of the School of Rabbi Ishmael to the Book of Leviticus, most of which was lost to us. "Fragments of Debei R. Ishmael to Leviticus," (Heb.) in *Festschrift for Samuel Krauss*, Jerusalem, R. Mass, 1936, pp. 19–35, at p. 25.

[33] For explicit indication that *chaver* means only fellow Jew, and not a non-Jew, see *Mechilta, Bo, Parasha* 9 (Horowitz – Rabin edition, p. 30, lines 19–21.) The fact that both *Mechilta* and the text of *Tosefta Shavuot* 3:1–2 are from the School of Rabbi Ishmael (as in note 32 above), might suggest that this position was exclusive to that School. However, there are no explicit counter-indications to this position, and conversely there are later undisputed Amoraic indications of the same limited understanding of the term *chaver*, as in *Hagiga* 26a.

[34] While the use of this verse as a basis for the obligation to testify is not preserved in the *Talmud*, it is recorded in *Sifra*, *Kedoshim*, *Perek* 4, sec. 8; and in Pseudo-Jonathan to Leviticus 19:16. For a fuller treatment of this source, see Aaron Kirschenbaum, "The Good Samaritan and Jewish Law," *Dinei Yisroel*, 7, 1976, at pp. 10–12, particularly notes 15 and 16.

[35] *She'iltot*, sec. 69.

[36] *Mishneh Torah*, Laws of Testimony 1:1. But Rambam neither uses the word *chavero*, nor does he otherwise indicate any exclusion of duty toward non-Jews in the relevant passage in *Sefer HaMitzvot*, Positive Precepts, no. 178. For an extraordinary exploration of the theory of the universality of the parallel Biblical term *Achicha*, see Adiel Schremer, *Brothers Estranged: Heresy, Christianity and Jewish Identity in Late Antiquity*, Oxford and New York, Oxford University Press, 2010, pp. 131–141.

to lead Rabbi Joshua Falk (Poland, circa 1555–1614) to make explicit the assertion that the *DeOraita* obligation to testify does not apply for the benefit of a non-Jewish party.[37]

If this limitation on the obligation to testify was in fact *Tannaitic* law, then the slight bias of the *Tosefta* would simply be a logical consequence of the permissibility of violation of the Rabbinic uncleanness law for the sake of fulfillment of the "greater" *DeOraita* obligation to testify on behalf of a fellow Jew; an overriding obligation which would not be present when the party expecting testimony by the *Kohen* is a non-Jew.[38]

However, this approach requires one further assumption, that the legal obligation to testify on behalf of a fellow Jew would be fully applicable even if the adjudication takes place in a non-Jewish court; so long as the matter is permissibly before that court rather than before a Jewish court, thus not in violation of the Law of Rabbi Tarfon.[39] This would mean that the duty to aid a fellow Jew achieve justice through judicial process would be applicable whether the litigation was taking place in a Jewish court or was taking place in a non-Jewish court as litigation against a non-Jew; or perhaps even as litigation against a fellow Jew under circumstances in which the litigation before the non-Jewish court was permissible even within the Law of Rabbi Tarfon. Indeed there are absolutely no Talmudic counter-indications to this assumption.[40]

[37] Rabbi Joshua Falk, *Sefer Meirat Einayim* to *Shulchan Aruch*, *Choshen Mishpat*, 28:2.

[38] I will address the issue of disparity in Jewish Law between duties to Jews and duties to non-Jews, somewhat more directly in Chapter 8, below.

[39] *Gittin* 88b.

[40] However, Rambam, possibly sensitive to precisely this issue, added, with logic but without apparent textual precedent, the specification that the obligation to testify pertains to testimony before a *Beth Din*. *Mishneh Torah*, Book of Judges, Laws of testimony 1:1; and *Sefer Hamitzvot*, Positive Precepts no. 178. Did he mean thereby to preclude the existence of a duty to testify in a non-Jewish court, or was he simply describing the most common context in which testimony would be obligatory?

2

Legislative Constraint on Testimony: The Amoraic Period

As in the period of the *Tannaim* (c. 70–200 C.E.), so in the literature of the *Amoraim* (c. 200–500 C.E.) there is only a single legal passage that addresses the issue of testimony by a Jew in a non-Jewish court. That brief text generated a minor response in the period of the Gaonim (c. 600–1000 C.E.), but a voluminous literature in responsa, codes and commentaries in the periods of the *Rishonim* (c. 1000–1600 C.E.) and the *Acharonim* (c. 1600 to present). Because of the centrality of this one text to later developments, we will, after presentation of the text itself, subject it to two separate, but vitally interrelated, levels of analysis. Firstly, we will examine the terminology and literary structures of the passage, for the purpose of establishing the original language of the legislation and the likely development of its current form. The second level of analysis will examine the possible underlying legal doctrines on which the Amoraic legislation might have been, or could not have been, based. These two layers of analysis should provide us with a vantage-point from which to examine the developments that later took place.

2.1 THE AMORAIC LEGISLATION

The Amoraic text is found in *Bava Kamma* 113b–114a,[1] and reads as follows:[2]

[1] The text is neither repeated elsewhere in the Babylonian *Talmud*, nor does it have any parallel in the Jerusalem *Gemara*, nor in any other Talmudic era literature.

[2] The text as presented is that which appears in the published Vilna *Talmud*. The numbering of the lines is my own and is purely for the convenience of references in the text and footnotes of this volume. Footnotes to this text itself will not cover material that is dealt with later in the book.

1. Raba, or others say R. Huna, proclaimed
2. to those who go up (to Israel) and those who come down (to Babylonia):[3]
3. If a Jew knows evidence for the benefit of a non-Jew,
4. but he did not summon him (to testify),
5. and he goes and testifies in a non-Jewish court against his fellow Jew,
6. he is to be excommunicated.[4]
7. What is the reason? Because they determine monetary liability on (the basis of) the testimony of a single witness.
8. We do not say this except when there is one (witness), but if there are two, it does not apply.
9. And even if there is one, we do not say this except in *Magista* courts,
10. but in *Dawar* courts, they too, if there is one (witness), impose an oath upon him (the defendant.)
11. R. Ashi said,
12. When we were at R. Huna's[5] academy,[6] we raised this question:
13. A prominent man (*Adam Chashuv*)[7] upon whom they would rely as two (witnesses),
14. since they will determine monetary liability on the basis of his testimony (alone), ought he not to testify –

[3] The full form of lines 1–2 appears only three times in the *Talmud*: in our text (B.K. 113b), in *Bava Kamma* 23b and *Bava Batra* 45a. In each case two *Amoraim* are referred to as the possible originators of the law, and in each the manuscripts offer alternate names to each of the passages (see Rabbinovicz, *Dikdukei Soferim*). The common elements are: (a) in each instance, the proclamation is ascribed to heads of Academies in different locations, Pumbedita and Mehoza, or Mehoza and Sura; (b) the only *Amora* common to all three texts is Rava; (c) the common legal issue may be that of liability for indirect injury. It may have been the attempt to insist on a common legal issue that led Rambam in *Nizkei Mammon* 5:1 to offer a reading of *Bava Kamma* 23b to which most other *Rishonim* objected (see commentaries to Rambam, *ibid.*).

[4] For a full treatment of the issue of excommunication in the Amoraic period, see Gideon Leibson, "Determining Factors in Herem and Nidui During the *Tannaitic* and Amoraic Periods," *Shenaton HaMishpat HaIvri*, vol. II, Jerusalem, Institute for Research in Jewish Law, 1975, pp. 292–342, (Heb.) A brief treatment of our passage, B.K. 113b–114a appears on p. 324. His identification of this passage as anonymous may be incorrect. See below at text preceding n. 57.

[5] All of the manuscripts and many of the *Rishonim* read here, "R. Kahana" in place of R. Huna. *Dikdukei Soferim* to BK 114a, at p. 281, n. 20. This reading seems logical since R. Ashi was a student of R. Kahana and often reported on discussions which took place at his academy in Pum Nahara. A listing of such instances appears in A. Hyman, *Toldot Tannaim VeAmoraim*, London, Express Printers, 1910, vol. III, at p. 847.

[6] The classic treatment of the term "*bei Rav*," is that of David M. Goodblatt, *Rabbinic Instruction in Sasanian Babylonia*, Leiden, E.J. Brill, 1975. The resultant controversy between Goodblatt and Yeshayahu Gafni as to the existence of academies during the Amoraic period was recently revisited in a reconciling manner by Jeffrey L. Rubenstein, "The Rise of the Babylonian Rabbinic Academy: A Reexamination of the Talmudic Evidence," *JSIJ* 1, 2002, pp. 55–68.

[7] See my article, Saul J. Berman, "Adam Hashub: New Light on the History of Babylonian Amoraic Academies," *Dine Israel*, 13–14, 1988, pp. 123–154, 174, 183.

15. or perhaps, since he is a prominent man
16. he cannot escape, and may testify?
17. The question remained undecided (*Teiku*).

2.1.1 The Authority of the Teaching: The Term *Machriz*

The Aramaic root *karaz*, meaning to proclaim, is found twice in the Biblical Book of Daniel in describing royal proclamations by the Babylonian King.[8] In an analogous usage, the Aramaic *Targumim* of the *Torah* use the word in relation to a public proclamation by Moses.[9] In *Tannaitic* literature, the word *Machriz* – "proclaimed," is used most frequently in relation to general public announcements, as for example in regard to the required announcement of lost property.[10] It is also twice used to describe a *Bat Kol*, a heavenly voice.[11]

The most significant *Tannaitic* usage of the term *Machriz* is as a description of a pronouncement of a Rabbinic Court. *Tannaitic* literature refers to only two such pronouncements: one, of the Court's intent to sell property belonging to orphans;[12] and second, when a court officer would invite additional evidence in regard to a criminal trial involving capital or corporal punishment.[13] This usage of *Machriz* as a reference to Court pronouncements of facts was expanded in Amoraic literature to include announcements of the sale of land by a widow,[14] the declaration of a woman as a rebellious wife,[15] an announcement of persons Rabbinically

[8] Daniel 3:4 and 5:29.

[9] As to Exodus 36:6, see *Onkeles*, ed. by A. Berliner, Berlin, 1884; and *Pseudo Jonathan*, ed. by M. Ginsburger, Berlin, 1903.

[10] In relation to lost property, see *Mishnah Bava Metzia* 2:1–8; *Tosefta Bava Metzia* 2:1–7, *Mechilta* to Exodus 23:4, *Mishpatim parasha* 20 (Horowitz-Rabin edition pp. 324–325). In relation to announcements by charity collectors, see *Tosefta Demai* 3:15–16. In regard to an announcement of the sale of a cow for slaughter, to avoid its offspring being slaughtered on the same day, see *Sifra* to *Emor*, *Perek* 8, sec. 9 (*Sifra de bei Rav*, Jerusalem, 1959, p. 104a).

[11] *Mishnah Avot* 6:2, and *Sifrei* to Deuteronomy *Piska* 357 (Finkelstein edition, p. 428).

[12] *Mishnah Arakin* 6:1; and *Tosefta Arakin* 4:1.

[13] *Mishnah Sanhedrin* 6:1; *Sifrei* Numbers *Piska* 137 (Horovitz edition p. 184) (echoed in *Kiddushin* 81a.).

[14] *Ketuboth* 98a.

[15] *Ketuboth* 63b. According to S. Lieberman, the original *Tannaitic* legislation found in *Tosefta Ketuboth* 5:7, involved only repeated private warnings by the court to the rebellious wife. This practice was continued in Israel during the Amoraic period, but the Babylonian *Amoraim* legislated a new practice, of public declarations. *Tosefta Kifeshutah*, *Ketuboth*, pp. 266–268.

disqualified from testimony[16] and a few other situations[17] – all involving pronouncements of facts to the public.

A crucial Amoraic development was the expansion of the term *Machriz* to a new context: the pronouncement of new laws. The Babylonian *Gemara* refers to eight instances of Amoraic legislation introduced by the word *Machriz*. Two of the instances appear to be the pronouncement of a binding final resolution of matters previously in debate.[18] The other six cases are new laws, without apparent precedent, responding to novel situations.[19] Each of these eight legislative acts are ascribed to one or more Heads of *Yeshivot*,[20] and it was, impliedly, by virtue of that position that they were the appropriate persons to "proclaim" the new legislation adopted by the Academy.

There are by contrast eight additional Amoraic instances of the use of the term *Machriz* to introduce a distinctively different set of teachings that clearly relate to ethical or health matters of a non-legal character in which the moral authority of leading scholars, primarily also heads of Academies, was called upon to shape the moral fiber of the people.[21]

But clearly, in regard to our passage constraining testimony against a fellow Jew in a non-Jewish court under certain circumstances, the use of the term *Machriz* suggests that we are not merely dealing with ethical counsel, but with a legislative act adopted in one or more of the Babylonian Academies, and "pronounced" by the Head of the Academy. And so indeed this passage has been treated as a legislative act throughout the rest of the history of Jewish Law.

2.1.2 The Legal Constraint on Testimony

What appears then to be the bottom line in this teaching is as follows:

(1) A Jew is subject to excommunication if he testifies in a non-Jewish court when **all** of the following conditions pertain:

[16] *Sanhedrin* 26b.

[17] See *Yevamot* 36a, and parallels at 41b and 119b. Also *Bechorot* 53a.

[18] (1)*Shabbat* 139a, and (2) 146b.

[19] (3)*Rosh Hashana* 21a;(4) *Bava Kamma* 23b; (5)*Bava Kamma* 113b;(6) *Bava Metzia* 107b; (7) *Bava Batra* 45a; and (8)*Sanhedrin* 26a. It is interesting that the latter four of these texts involve problems as to the ritual or financial obligations of Jews caused by either the intervention of non-Jews or the relationship to the non-Jewish society.

[20] (1) Rav of Sura; (2) Rav of Sura; (3) R. Jochanah of Tiberias; (4) Rav Joesph of Pumbedita, or Rabbah of Pumbedita, or Rava of Mehoza; (5) Rava of Mehoza, or R. Huna of Sura, or R. Joseph of Pumbedita; (6) R. Ami of Tiberias; (7) Rava of Mehoza or R. Papa of Naresh; (8) R. Yannai of Akhbara.

[21] *Berachot* 28a and *Shabbat* 31a–b relate to ethical guidance. *Shabbat* 129a and *Ketuboth* 77b relate to health advice. *Beitzah* 16b, *Kiddushin* 70b and 81a are factual announcements. *Avodah Zarah* 19b is a call to repentance.

(a) his testimony is against a fellow Jew,
(b) in the benefit of a non-Jewish litigant,
(c) the witness has not been subpoenaed,
(d) he is the sole witness, and
(e) the litigation takes place in a *Magista* court.

By contrast:

(2) This constraint would **not** apply if **any** of the following conditions were present:
(a) his testimony is in the benefit of a fellow Jew,
(b) the other litigant is also a Jew,
(c) the witness has been subpoenaed,
(d) there are two witnesses (even in a *Magista* court),
(e) the litigation is in a *Dawar* court (even as a single witness).

The inapplicability of the Amoraic constraint on testimony when one of the first two conditions apply, that is, where the testimony is in the benefit of the Jewish litigant, or where the other litigant is also a Jew, is self-evident based on the *Tannaitic* texts which we have previously seen. No early teaching in Jewish Law would prevent a Jew from being a witness in a non-Jewish court when a fellow Jew was the beneficiary of such testimony. What, however, is the role of subpoena in this deliberation? What is the difference between a *Magista* court and a *Dawar* court? And what is the critical nature of the number of witnesses in determining the permissibility of testimony? We need to turn to these issues to further clarify the foundations of the Amoraic legislation.

2.1.3 The Role of Subpoena

The presence of the fourth line in the above-cited legislation of Rava, "but he did not summon him (to testify)"[22] introduces a vital exemption from the general restriction. According to this language, were the non-Jewish party, or the non-Jewish court itself, to summon a Jew to testify against his fellow Jew in the non-Jewish court, he would be permitted to testify. Only voluntary testimony is constrained.

[22] The use of term *tava* in the sense of a summons to testify, already appears in *Sifra*, Leviticus, *Dibura DiHova, Perek* 16, sec. 5. The *Gemara* in *Shavuot* 31b does not preserve the term in its indication of the requirement of issuance of a summons as a basis for liability for refusal to testify. However, Rambam, Laws of Testimony 1:1, revives the use of the term from the *Sifra* for this purpose.

However, all manuscripts and printed editions of the *Talmud* prior to the middle of the sixteenth century lack this entire phrase.[23] Likewise, every quotation of this *Gemara* passage by Gaonim[24] and *Rishonim*[25] lack this exempting language, up to and including the responsa of Rabbi Moshe Isserlis.[26] The first appearance of the phrase "but he did not summon him" as an integral part of this text is in the Tractate *Bava Kamma* published in Basel in the month of *Tammuz* of 1578.[27] That printed edition of the *Talmud* was heavily censored by Cardinal Marco Marini,[28] which led R. Rabbinovicz to propose that the addition of this phrase was made by the Christian censor[29] in order to subvert Jewish law and to deceive Jews into more active participation as witnesses in non-Jewish courts, even against the interests of fellow Jews.

We will later explore another possible theory for the entry of this phrase into the Talmudic text, but whatever motivated its inclusion, it was certainly not an original element of the Amoraic legislation.

2.1.4 *Magista* Courts and *Dawar* Courts

These two terms, *Magista* courts and *Dawar* courts, describing apparently distinct judiciaries in Sassanian Iran in the fifth century of the Common Era, are shrouded in both historical and linguistic difficulties.[30] The primary historical problem is the fact that extant Babylonian records

23 Rabbinovicz, *Dikdukei Soferim* to *Bava Kamma* 113b, at p. 281.

24 The passage is cited only three times in extant Gaonic literature and the phrase is absent in all of them. *Sefer Halachot Pesukot* by Rav Yehudai Gaon, Codex Sassoon 263, ed. by S. Abramson, Jerusalem, 1971, at p. 82. Shimon Kayyara, (Behag-Baal Halachot Gedolot), *Sefer Halachot Gedolot*, Tel Aviv, 1962, sec. 43, at p. 177; and B.M. Lewin, *Otzar Ha-Geonim* to *Bava Kamma*, Jerusalem, 1943, at p. 100.

25 There are two apparent exceptions to this, but both are actually subsequent revisions of the text of a Rishon to make it conform to a later reading of the *Gemara*: (1) Rabbenu Asher to *Bava Kamma* 113b includes the phrase; but Rabbinovicz, *Dikdukei Soferim* to *Bava Kamma* at p. 281, note 8 indicates that the phrase is absent in the earlier manuscripts and printed editions; (2) Responsa of Rashba (Aderet) vol. VII, no. 160 contains the phrase in the Warsaw edition of 1868 (actually published in 1908). However, in the Rome edition of circa 1480 (reprinted Jerusalem, 1977) the phrase is absent. Also later in the text of that very responsum, Rashba explicitly rejects the possibility of an exemption based on summons by a non-Jew (as does Meiri to *Bava Kamma* 113b.)

26 Responsa of RaMA, no. 88, ed. by Asher Siev, Jerusalem, 1971, at p. 381.

27 Rabbinovicz, *Dikdukei Soferim* to *Bava Kamma*, and in *Dikdukei Soferim* to *Berachot*, Introduction, p. 101.

28 Rabbinovicz, *Dikdukei Soferim* to *Berachot*, Introduction, pp. 104–105.

29 Rabbinovicz, *Dikdukei Soferim* to *Bava Kamma* 113b, at p. 281, note 8.

30 Ezra Spicehandler, "*Bei Dawar* and *Dina D'Magista*: Notes on Gentile Courts in Talmudic Babylonia," *HUCA* 26, 1955, pp. 333–354 (hereinafter "Spicehandler").

never use either of these terms to describe courts of any kind.[31] Thus lacking any external sources for verification of the true nature of these institutions, we are thrown onto the Talmudic material itself, which is quite scant, and philological analysis is only of limited aid.

Firstly, as to the term בי דאור, *Dawar* court, Spicehandler agrees with and defends Kohut's identification of the word *Dawar* as derived from the Persian word meaning judge. Despite the absence of the word in Persian materials in any construct referring to a court, they contend that *Bei Dawar* is the courthouse over which the *Dawar*, the judge, presides.[32]

The three Talmudic instances of use of the term *Bei Dawar* provide us with some limited information. The implication is present that this was an official government institution, where the need to appear on time in response to a summons was perceived by non-Jews of sufficient urgency to justify the refusal to help a person in dire need.[33] Further, it was a court in which a Jew could fairly expect to recover even from a non-Jewish litigant, so that his failure to pursue a claim in the *Bei Dawar* is presumptive evidence of his abandonment of the property.[34] And, in our passage, the *Bei Dawar* is a court in which it is permissible for a Jew to testify against a fellow Jew in favor of the non-Jewish party, even if he is the only witness.[35] Certainly, a very positive attitude is reflected in these Talmudic passages.[36]

Can we date this usage? Other common Talmudic terms for non-Jewish courts are attested to specific *Amoraim* and therefore are subject to relatively precise dating and identification with specific Amoraic schools. So, for example, the term *Beit Din shel Ovdei Kochavim* ("Courts of Idolators") was apparently a school usage in Pumbedita by the students of R. Judah b. Ezekiel.[37] The term *Dina DeParsa'i*, ("Persian Courts") was apparently a school usage in Mehoza by the students of Rava.[38]

[31] Spicehandler, at pp. 344 and 351.

[32] Spicehandler, at pp. 341–344; A. Kohut, Aruch Completum *of Nathan ben Yehiel of Rome, (c.1035–1106)*, vol. III, pp. 31–32.

[33] *Avodah Zarah* 26a. The official character of this court is also reflected in *Tanhuma, Ekev*, sec. 11, where the judge is the bearer of official government documents.

[34] *Gittin* 58b.

[35] *Bava Kamma* 114a.

[36] We might add that a further suggestion of this positive attitude might be the very use of the term "*Bei*" which is otherwise reserved for the Rabbinic Academy itself. Cf. Abraham Shaul Amir, *Institutions and Titles in Talmudic Literature* (Heb.), Jerusalem, Mossad Harav Kook, 1977, pp. 18–37. Also, Goodblatt, *Rabbinic Instruction*, at n. 41.

[37] *Gittin* 28b and 29a; *Kiddushin* 14a.

[38] *Shavuot* 34b; *Bava Kamma* 58b; *Bava Metzia* 108a; *Bava Batra* 55a and 173b; *Avodah Zarah* 71a. In all of these instances, except that in *Bava Batra* 173b, the translation could either be Persian law, or law of the Persian Courts.

However, the term *Bei Dawar* appears only in what are, judging by their language and structure, apparently anonymous Stammaitic explanatory passages which are indeterminate as to date.[39]

Thus lacking both external evidence and precise dating for the Talmudic texts, it is not really possible to determine whether this positive attitude toward the *Bei Dawar* was a function of the general quality and integrity of those particular non-Jewish courts, or was reflective of a more positive attitude toward general non-Jewish courts in a particular Rabbinic school at a particular point in time.

In marked contrast to the attitude toward the *Dawar* court, the two Talmudic passages referring to *Magista* courts are both very negative. In our passage, the *Gemara* insists that Rava's restriction on testimony against a fellow Jew is distinctively and exclusively applicable in the *Magista* courts.[40] In the other instance, the *Gemara*, in a rhetorical question, contrasts the law of *Magista* courts with the law of *Torah* in a distinctly disparaging tone.[41]

Attempts to identify the actual historical legal institution that is described in Talmudic terminology as *Magista* courts have foundered until now on lack of sufficient data. Suggestions that the term describes either the people's assembly, or magistrates' courts or a travelling justice of the peace, are all rejected by Spicehandler on either philological or historical grounds.[42] He does, however, make one additional suggestion of an orthographic change which would allow the word *Magista* to be related to the Persian Magi, who are elsewhere in the *Talmud* identified both as low echelon officers of the Iranian government, and as crude and boorish people.[43]

[39] For indications of the late character of the *Bei Dawar* passages, note the following. As to *Shabbat* 19a, the sudden shift from Hebrew to Aramaic, and comments on that phenomenon by Shamma Friedman, "Perek HaIsha Rabba," in H.Z. Dimitrovsky (ed.), *Mechkarim U'Mekorot*, New York, Jewish Theological Seminary of America, 1977, pp. 275–441, at pp. 301–302; and B. DeVries, *Mechkarim Besafrut HaTalmud*, Jerusalem, 1968, at pp. 195–196. As to *Gittin* 58b, the passage begins with the phrase *Mai Ta'ama*, as does our passage in *Bava Kamma* 114a. Again, Friedman, *ibid.*, at pp. 303–304, 346 and 378 is inclined to see in that usage a late Stammaitic character. As to *Avodah Zarah* 26a, the usage appears as an alternate answer in the form of *Iy namei*, also seen as a late addition by E.Z. Melammed, *An Introduction to Talmudic Literature* (Heb.), Jerusalem, 1973, at pp. 435–436.

[40] *Bava Kamma* 114a.

[41] *Bava Metzia* 30b.

[42] Spicehandler, at pp. 345–351. Spicehandler does not cite an article by M. Wohlman, "Bet Mishpat Magista," in *Hamishpat*, vol. IV (1930–1931), pp. 114–116, arguing for *Magista* as a travelling justice of the peace. But the elments of Wohlman's position are indirectly dealt with and rejected in Spicehandler's treatment of other positions.

[43] Spicehandler, at pp. 353–354, citing *Shabbat* 139a and *Sotah* 22a.

The Gaonim did not appear to be concerned with the historical nature of the *Magista* courts, but they were clearly interested in understanding why the *Amoraim* had such a dismal view of those courts. While we will later address the way in which the Gaonim relate to the question of testimony in non-Jewish courts, we can take a moment now to note their understanding of the term *Dina D'Magista*. The picture that emerges under the prism of the Gaonic authorities is of a court which was at best inexpert,[44] probably corrupt[45] and possibly violent.[46] While the philological derivations they proposed as the bases of these theories were usually strained,[47] the criteria that emerged as tests of whether any court should be considered to be like a *Magista* court or not were quite unequivocal.

The contrast that emerges from the limited information available, then, is that the *Dawar* court is an established governmental institution that is trustworthy in its legal process, while the *Magista* court is inexpert and probably corrupt. Whether it is this contrast of general characteristics or the specific difference in evidentiary law that served as the basis for distinction in our passage as to permissibility of a single Jewish witness to testify against a fellow Jew to the benefit of a non-Jew in a *Dawar* court, contrasted with the impermissibility of his doing so in a *Magista* court, is an issue that we will explore in another section.

2.1.5 Literary Structure of the Passage

Analysis of the literary history of the passage under discussion is vital for an understanding of its legal content. The central question is: what precisely was the legislative language of Rava? We have already established that line 4, *velo t'va'o minei*, "but he did not summon him (to testify)," was a very late medieval addition. But what now of lines 7 through 10, containing the rationale of the law (line 7) and the two limitations on its

[44] Rabbenu Chananel ben Chusiel, in Commentary to *Bava Kamma* 114a, in Lewin, *Otzar Ha-Geonim* to *Bava Kamma*, part 2, p. 105. (Echoed in Rashi, *Bava Kamma* 114a, s,v, *D'Magista*.)

[45] Hai Gaon, in Lewin, *ibid.*, Responsa p. 100. Kohut, *Aruch Completum*, vol. V, pp. 78–79, suggests two separate derivations from Persian words which would substantiate this meaning. Spicehandler rejects them both, at pp. 349–350.

[46] Hai Gaon in *Sefer Hamekach Vehamemkar*, ch. 32, para. R, p. 67a. Here, too, Kohut's attempted derivation in *Aruch Completum*, vol. III, p. 386b, is rejected by Spicehandler at p. 347. Spicehandler at p. 351 likewise rejects a suggestion by Ginzburg of a Persian derivation to support this explanation. (Rashi echoes this suggestion that violence is the dominant characteristic of the *Magista* courts, in *Bava Kamma* 114a, s.v. *Chad amumsa shadu lei*.)

[47] See Spicehandler, pp. 345–351.

scope (lines 8–10), limited to a single witness, in a *Magista* court? Were these integral elements of the original decree, or were they later additions to and modifications of the initial legislation?

The clearest element of response to this question is in regard to the two limitations of lines 8 through 10. The form in which those restrictive clauses appear, *velo amaran elah ... aval ...*, "they did not proclaim this except ... but ...," is a relatively common Amoraic usage for limiting the applicability of a stated law to particular situations, while precluding its applicability to other circumstances.[48] The form is already attributed to the earliest Babylonian *Amoraim*, such as Samuel,[49] and continues in use through the Amoraic period. Indeed, Rava himself, the author of our law, is reported to have used this formula some sixteen times to limit an earlier law.[50]

However, there is not a single attestation of the use of this form by the author of a law in relation to his own law. The grammatical structure itself indicates that it is someone other than the original legislator who adds the limitation. The word *amaran*, "we say," is first person plural[51] and clearly does not identify the authors of the limitation with the author of the initial law being so limited. Thus, we would be led to conclude that lines 8 through 10, limiting Rava's law to testimony by a single witness, and even that, only within a *Magista* court, are not part of the original legislation, but are subsequent additions.

What, however, of line 7, which posits as rationale of the restrictive legislation the injury that would result to the Jewish party? If that was the reason offered by Rava himself, then our exploration of the legal basis of the legislation has an unequivocal starting point. But if it too was a subsequent Amoraic or even later addition, then we would need to explore whether Rava himself might have had some other motive in restricting testimony in non-Jewish courts.[52]

[48] The form is used in the *Talmud* more than 200 times. Cf. Chaim Josua Kasowski, *Thesaurus Talmudis*, vol. I, New York, Jewish Theological Seminary in America, 1954, pp. 121–125.

[49] E.g. *Eruvin* 29a and *Succah* 28a.

[50] *Berachot* 50b; *Shabbat* 12a, 23a, 62b, 129a; *Eruvin* 79a; *Pesachim* 6a, 76a; *Succah* 32a; *Megillah* 19a; *Ketuboth* 61a, 96a; *Kiddushin* 42b; *Bava Metzia* 74a; *Menachot* 35a; *Hullin* 50a.

[51] J.N. Epstein, *A Grammar of Babylonian Aramaic*, (Heb.), Jerusalem, Magnes Press, 1960, at pp. 61 and 63.

[52] There is a substantial literature on this pattern of separating between the initial law and its subsequent explanation. See Ch. Albeck, *Tarbiz* 9 (1938), pp. 163–178, and his *Mavo LaTalmudim*, Tel Aviv, Dvir Co., 1969, ch. 7, pp. 504–522. Further development of Albeck's thesis is found in a series of articles by Hyman Klein, in *J.Q.R.* 38 (1947), pp. 67–91; 43(1953), pp. 341–363; 50 (1959), pp. 124–146; in *Journal of Semitic Studies*

The language of the passage itself might be indicative, but is far from conclusive. The phrase which opens line 7, *mai ta'ama*, "what is the reason?" is such a commonplace in the *Talmud* as to defy precise dating.[53] Nevertheless it is worth noting that the words would be unnecessary if the rationale that followed were part of the original legislation.[54] Rava could quite smoothly have continued from the law to its rationale without the intervening question.[55] Similarly suggestive is the fact that the word *apumah*, literally "by the mouth of," appears in the sense of testimony only in passages which apparently post-date Rava himself.[56]

More significant than the terminology in this instance is the evidence of the logic of the passage itself. Line 7, as rationale for the law of Rava, is deeply deficient. Firstly, the initial formulation of the legislation does not specify its exclusive applicability to only one witness. Indeed, it is precisely that limitation which line 8 first propounds, without which we would have assumed that Rava forbad testimony in a non-Jewish court even for two or more Jewish witnesses. Why then should a rationale of the initial legislation be offered that does not adequately explain the full scope of the law? Secondly, if the rationale of line 7 is intended as the sole basis for restriction of testimony, then further justification of that as the criterion would certainly be expected, but is absent in the text, and is difficult to construct even as a pure matter of legal logic. If, on the other hand, the intent of the rationale in line 7 is intended simply as an illustration of an evidentiary rule that would produce a result different from that which would be produced by Jewish law, then why is not the latter made explicit – that is, why does the *Gemara* not directly state that the rationale of Rava's restrictive legislation is that the Jewish party would then be subjected to a legal outcome that varies from that which would result from an application of Jewish law?

3 (1958), pp. 363–372; and in *Tarbiz* 31 (1962), pp. 23–42. A fine summation of the state of the art is found in Friedman, "Perek HaIsha Rabba," pp. 283–321.

53 The phrase is used some 1,700 times in the *Talmud*. Cf. Kasowski, *Thesaurus Talmudis* vol. XV, pp. 228–251.

54 Cf. Friedman, "Perek HaIsha Rabba," at pp. 303–304.

55 Friedman, *ibid.*, does in fact at two points assign passages including the phrase *mai ta'ama* to the later *Stama DiGemara* rather than to the original *Ikkar haGemara*, at pp. 346 and 378. However, in neither case does he indicate that the term itself was the determinative factor in his dating.

56 It appears once ascribed to R. Papa in *Ketuboth* 23b. In all other instances, the word is part of an anonymous explanation of prior laws, including one other instance of explicating a statement of Rava, in *Gittin* 15a, b. See Kasowski, *Thesaurus Talmudis*, vol. XXXI, pp. 57–60.

As inappropriate as line 7 is as a rationale for the initial law of Rava (lines 3, 5 and 6), it is conversely perfectly appropriate as a rationale for line 8, the limitation of the law to a single witness. As to the question of why Rava's Law should apply solely to a single witness (line 8), the response that it is because non-Jewish courts will reach their decision based on the testimony of a single witness (line 7) is a perfect answer.

While still speculative, the legal and terminological elements in this passage could yield the following conclusions as to the development of the text before us:

Stage 1: The initial legislation of Rava, restricting any testimony against a fellow Jew in a non-Jewish court, under threat of excommunication (lines 3, 5 and 6) –

3. If a Jew knows evidence for the benefit of a non-Jew,
5. and he goes and testifies in a non-Jewish court against his fellow Jew,
6. he is to be excommunicated.[57]

Stage 2: The limitation of Rava's Law to where there is only a single witness and the rationale of that limitation is based on the fact that non-Jewish courts reach decisions based on the testimony of a single witness (lines 8 and 7) –

8. We do not say this except when there is one (witness), but if there are two, it does not apply.
7. What is the reason? Because they determine monetary liability on (the basis of) the testimony of a single witness.

Stage 3: The concretization of the rationale by indication that only *Magista* courts actually reach judgment based on a single witness, while *Dawar* courts do not; and therefore, testimony in *Dawar* courts is permissible even for a single witness (lines 9 and 10) –

9. And even if there is one, we do not say this except in *Magista* courts,
10. but in *Dawar* courts, they too, if there is one (witness), impose an oath upon him (the defendant).

Stage 4: The inversion of the sequence of lines 8 and 7 to connect the legislation with the rationale (albeit imperfectly), and to make for clearer continuity in the sequence of the two limitations which are built upon one another.[58]

57 I omit line 4 from the original legislation of Rava due to the late medieval origin of that line into the Talmudic text, as above in text related to notes 22–29.

58 For a perfectly analogous instance of this literary development see *Gittin* 77b, and its treatment by A. Weiss, *Mehkarim Betalmud* (Heb.), Jerusalem, 1975, pp. 225–226.

2.2 LATER AMORAIC/STAMMAITIC LIMITATIONS ON THE CONSTRAINT

2.2.1 Identifying the Original Legislation of Rava

Given these assumptions about the unfolding of the Talmudic text before us, Rava's original legislation consisted of the following (identified earlier as lines 3, 5, and 6):

If a Jew knows evidence for the benefit of a non-Jew,
and he goes and testifies in a non-Jewish court against his fellow Jew,
he is to be excommunicated.

This being the case, a number of additional issues require explication. First and foremost is the question of why Rava should have introduced such a broad constraint on testimony and what is the legal theory behind it. This original text of Rava's law provides no clue to its motive. While I leave for a later section a fuller exploration of this issue,[59] we need here to examine the tension between the legislation of Rava and the *Tosefta* text in *Avodah Zarah* 1:8, which we introduced earlier. Our prior analysis of that text left us with the clear impression that early Jewish law interposed no objection to the testimony of a Jew in a non-Jewish court when the litigation itself was justifiably before that court, as, for example, when one of the parties was a non-Jew. The underlying assumption of that analysis was that in a situation in which justice cannot be achieved through the medium of a Jewish court adjudicating by the substantive laws and procedures of Jewish law, then one is to go with the best possible alternative, and not simply abandon any hope of justice because the matter will be litigated in a non-Jewish court.

However, we need now to note that the explicit text of that *Tosefta* relates to testimony on behalf of the Jewish party, in opposition to the non-Jewish party. The testimony thus served to achieve one of the "rescue" purposes that would justify overriding the Rabbinic prohibitions against business transactions with idolators during their festivals, or the *Kohen* leaving Israel subjecting himself to the Rabbinic "impurity" of foreign lands. The implication of the *Tosefta* was that in the absence of the possible violation of some Rabbinic law, there would be no constraint at all on testimony, whether it was in favor of the Jewish party, or in favor

[59] See Chapter 3 below.

of the non-Jewish party. Such would certainly be the case in regard to testimony of a Jewish witness in litigation before a Jewish court in which one of the parties was a non-Jew. There has never been a suggestion in the literature of Jewish law that a Jew ought not to testify in a Jewish court in favor of a non-Jewish litigant. The legislation of Rava is thus not in explicit contradiction to the *Tosefta*. It created a constraint within a lacuna in *Tannaitic* law, which had, theretofore, never explicitly confirmed the permissibility of testimony by a Jew in a non-Jewish court in opposition to the interests of the Jewish party to the litigation.

The following two segments of the text that were added to the original legislation of Rava served to limit the breadth of the applicability of the constraint, and also may introduce us to what those later anonymous *Amoraim*, (or *Saboraim*, or *Stammaim*) thought about the motivation of Rava in this legislation.

2.2.2 The First Limitation and the Rationale of Rava

The first limitation attached by the *Gemara* text to the legislation of Rava (identified earlier as lines 8 and 7) was:

> We do not say this except when there is one (witness), but if there are two, it does not apply.
> What is the reason? Because they determine monetary liability on (the basis of) the testimony of a single witness.

This limiting interpretation of the legislation of Rava would allow the testimony of a Jewish witness in a non-Jewish court against the Jewish defendant where there were two witnesses. It leaves intact the constraint where the Jew was a sole witness. What is the meaning of this distinction? The text itself asks the question and seems to provide an answer. If there are two witnesses in favor of the non-Jewish plaintiff, then whether the litigation takes place in the non-Jewish court, or were to have taken place in a Jewish court, the outcome would be the same – judgment in favor of the non-Jewish party, whose position is supported by two witnesses. On the other hand, if the Jewish witness is the sole witness on behalf of the non-Jewish plaintiff, then while the non-Jewish court would still find in favor of the non-Jewish party, a Jewish court could not base its judgment solely on such testimony, and would therefore find in favor of the Jewish defendant.

According to this approach, the single Jewish witness testifying against the Jewish party in the non-Jewish court would be causing that party a loss, which he would not have suffered according to Jewish law. This disparity of outcome could well be the motivation of the legislation of Rava – that is, to prevent a Jew from causing economic injury to a fellow Jew through the medium of a non-Jewish court, which is not justified in the application of Jewish law. In fact, Rashi directly explains the restriction on such testimony by a single witness in exactly that manner, saying "with the result that he causes him loss not in accordance with the (Jewish) Law."[60]

The *Talmud* does not explore this position any further, leaving open to later *Rishonim* the opportunity to deal with the issue of substantive differences in the legal systems which would result in divergent outcomes even if there were two witnesses.[61] Nor does the *Talmud* here explain why – if the theory of Rava is the injury that would result to the Jewish litigant – the separate legislation was necessary. Why not just rely on normal Jewish law of financial injury and allow the injured Jewish litigant to sue and recover from the single Jewish witness who had testified against him in the non-Jewish court, and thus caused him to suffer financial injury? We will examine these and other questions about this theory of what underlies the position of Rava when we discuss the *Rishonim* in detail.

2.2.3 The Second Limitation and the Rationale of Rava

A further limitation on the legislation of Rava is the continuation of the Talmudic passage (previously identified as lines 9 and 10):

> And even if there is one (witness), we do not say this except in *Magista* courts, but in *Dawar* courts, they too, if there is one (witness), impose an oath upon him (the defendant).

By virtue of this addition, even the limitation on testimony by a single Jewish witness against a fellow Jew in a non-Jewish court would pertain only in the context of *Magista* courts; while being perfectly permissible in *Dawar* courts. Given the lack of internal Talmudic evidence as to the nature of the courts here referred to as *Magista* and *Dawar*, one logical approach would be to interpret the passage in consonance with the suggested rationale in the earlier passage and in terms of its final observation: that these two forms of courts differ in regard to their

[60] Rashi to *Bava Kamma* 114a, s.v. *Apuma dechad.*

[61] See, for example, Tosafot to *Bava Kamma* 114a, s.v. *Velo amaran elah chad.*

rules in instances where a plaintiff is able to produce only a single witness. Since the *Magista* court would then still find in favor of the non-Jewish plaintiff, the single Jewish witness would have caused loss to the Jewish defendant which he would not have suffered under the rules of Jewish law, and the witness is therefore subject to penalty. On the other hand, the rules of the *Dawar* court were apparently similar to those of Jewish law, providing that if the plaintiff can only provide a single witness, the court will exact an oath of the defendant that he is not liable, and will then dismiss the charges against him.[62] The outcome in the non-Jewish *Dawar* court could be identical to that which would have been arrived at in the Jewish court. The single Jewish witness would then have caused no loss to the Jewish defendant, and is therefore not subject to penalty under the terms of this second limitation on the legislation of Rava.

This approach would have us see perfect consistency between the first and second limitations on the position of Rava, reflecting a common assumption that Rava's initial legislation was motivated by the disparity of legal outcome as between a Jewish and a non-Jewish court, with Rava intending to penalize Jews who would cause economic loss (by standards of Jewish law) to fellow Jews through their testimony in non-Jewish courts.

2.3 THE GAONIC RATIONALE OF PROCEDURAL JUSTICE: SOME JUSTICE IS BETTER THAN NONE

However, a number of factors suggest the possibility of another understanding of how this latter passage views the rationale for, and therefore the application of, restrictions on testimony in non-Jewish courts. Two factors leap out at us in regard to this passage. Firstly, if the presumed determinant of penalty intended by Rava is non-conformity of outcome, then it is very strange that the passage focuses on a single evidentiary rule, rather than the more impactful substantive rules of law which could differentiate Jewish and non-Jewish courts, and which would result more directly in divergent outcomes of litigation. Certainly the *Amoraim* and later Babylonian Sages were aware of the fact that the substantive rules of Jewish law were different from those of Persian law.[63]

[62] See *Rambam, Mishneh Torah, Edut* 5:1; and *To'en venit'an* 1:2.

[63] Yaakov Elman, "Middle Persian Culture and Babylonian Sages: Accomodation and Resistance in the Shaping of Rabbinic Legal Tradition," in Charlotte Elisheva Fonrobert and Martin S. Jaffe eds., *Cambridge Companion to the Talmud and Rabbinic Literature*, Cambridge and New York, Cambridge University Press, 2007, pp. 165–197.

Why then focus on a single procedural rule related to how the system deals with the burden of proof in cases where there is only one witness?

Secondly, the introduction in this latter passage of the reference to different kinds of non-Jewish courts suggests that more was at stake here than just commonality of outcome. While neither Talmudic nor Middle Persian studies have been able as yet to resolve the historical question of what real-life Persian institutions were being referred to by the terms *Magista* and *Dawar* courts, it is not unreasonable to think that what is at stake here is the intimation that the use of a particular procedural rule is an indication of the more general commitment of certain courts to levels of procedural justice that warrant their utilization by Jews as a reasonable means of achieving justice; and that Jewish witnesses should not be penalized for participating in litigation in those kinds of court, even though the outcome might differ from what might have been arrived at in a Jewish court.

This alternative approach is directly suggested and elaborated in a singularly significant Gaonic responsum dealing with the question of testimony in non-Jewish courts. Since this responsum relates not only to this issue but to others that we will address later, it is valuable to introduce the entire text at this point. The responsum is ascribed to Rabbi Sherira Gaon and/or to Rabbi Hai Gaon,[64] and it reads as follows:[65]

64 Lewin, *Otzar Ha-Geonim* to *Bava Kamma*, sec. 291, at p. 100. The division of the text into numbered sentences is my own, purely for the convenience of referencing elements of the responsum. Tsvi Groner contends that all such responsa attributed to both R. Sherira Gaon and R. Hai Gaon, were actually authored by R. Hai Gaon and need to be viewed as part of his corpus of responsa. Tsvi Groner, *The Legal Methodology of Hai Gaon*, Chico, CA, Scholars Press, 1985, at pp. 118–119.

65 The text of this responsum appears in full in Sha'are Zedek, ed. by Hayyim Modai, Salonika 1792, at p. 846, no. 4 (part IV, Sha'ar 7, no. 4). Lewin reproduces this text in *Otzar Ha-Geonim* to *Bava Kamma*, sec. 291, at p. 100. The text appears again in Responsa of Adret (Rashba) of Rome 1470 (1473?), no. 137, reprinted in Jerusalem, 1976. (The table of contents incorrectly identifies this as no. 138.) The Adret version of this responsum is ascribed to Hai Gaon, while the Sha'arei Zedek version has no ascription of authorship. The Adret version is substantially identical to the Sha'are Zedek version in sentences 1 through mid-17 (except for three slight variations which I will note later on). However, beginning with mid-sentence 17 till the close of the responsum, the Adret version appears to be an intentionally abbreviated presentation of the Sha'are Zedek text. Both halves of the Adret version have been discovered in Genizah fragments and have been published. The first half, sentences 1 through 13, appears in Louis Ginzberg, *Genizah Studies in Memory of Dr. Solomon*

1. As to your question.
2. In a place where there is no official Judge and there is a Jew who has on deposit with his friend a loan, or a security deposit, or an inheritance, and (the latter) was brought before the Elders, the Students[66] and the Lay

Schechter (Ginzei Schechter), New York, J.T.S., 1929, vol. II, pp. 127–128, item no. 137. The second half of the Adret text, starting with the very next word after the Ginzei Schechter fragment, was published even earlier by D. Max Weisz in *Seridim Min HaGenizah*, Budapest, 1924, p. 29. Ginzberg takes Weisz to task, *ibid.* at p. 123, for failing to recognize that the fragment he had published was in fact from the Adret 1470 Responsa collection, and chides him for publishing, unawares, as if it were only then seeing the light of day, a text which had already been printed some 300 years earlier. Ginzberg, *ibid.* at p. 118, suggests that in fact the combined pages that he and Weisz published were the manuscript on which the Adret 1470 printing were based. He cites the three textual variations which his fragment and the Adret text have in common as the basis for his assertion. His case is substantially strengthened by the absence of an entire word, *lehatrot*, in mid-sentence 16 in both the Weisz fragment and the Adret version. Whatever the text history relationship is between the Adret 1470 version and the Genizah fragments, the overriding oddity remains the substantial identity of the Adret text with the Sha'are Zedek text in sentences 1 through mid-17, and then the sudden shift to an apparent synopsis in the last part of the Adret text. Lewin, in *Otzar Ha-Geonim*, publishes at the side of this responsum a text quoted by *Sefer HaIttur* of Isaac b. Abba Mari of Marseilles (c. 1120–1190), Warsaw, end of Part I, sec. 8, at pp. 32b-33a, which is apparently an abbreviation of the Sha'arei Zedek text. It is distinct, however, from the abbreviation in the second half of the Adret text, and in contrast to that text, ascribes the responsum to Sherirah Gaon. It is in all likelihood this text in *Sefer HaIttur* which served as the basis for a subsequent synopsis which appears in *Sefer HaTerumot* of Samuel b. Isaac Sardi (c. 1185–1256), Sha'ar 62, part I, at p. 342a. I am indebted to Dr. Neil Danzig for calling to my attention an article by Esriel Erich Hildesheimer, entitled "Die Komposition der Sammlungen von Responsen der Gaonen," in Joseph Wohlgemuth (ed.), *Judisce Studien*, Frankfurt am Main, 1928, pp. 177–269. Hildesheimer, in a chart at p. 196, reports a parallel manuscript text to Sha'are Zedek IV, 7, 4, in Montefiore Manuscript (Jews College) 98a, at 24 r.v., no. 134. Responsum 134 in that manuscript is largely identical to the Sha'are Zedek text, except for minor orthographic variations and a single instance of homoiolenton (hashmata al pi hadomot) resulting in the omission of an entire line (sentence 3.) In two details, the text of Adret 1470 bears greater similarity to the Montefiore manuscript than to the Sha'are Zedek version. After the last word in sentence 13, the Montefiore manuscript adds the word *tirgum*, which is preserved in Adret 1470; and in sentence 14, the word *mi'sevarah* (or *a'sevara*) is absent in the Montefiore manuscript as well as in Adret 1470.

66 Ginzberg, *Genizah Studies* at p. 124, note to line 15, claims that the term *Talmidim*, "students," in Gaonic responsa is equivalent to *Talmidei Chachamim*, "scholars." But see A.E. Harkavy, *Zichron la-rishonim*, vol. I, Berlin, 1887, reprinted under new title, *Teshuvot HaGaonim – Harkavy*, Jerusalem, 1966, no. 213, p. 111, where the term *Talmidei Chachamim* is used in contrast to *Zekenim*, "Elders." However, there is a single note of hesitancy sounded at the very end of the responsum when the Gaon limits the right of participation in the non-Jewish court to when the Jewish adjudication had taken place in an established Jewish court or before scholars (*Talmidei Chachamim*). By contrast, if the initial Jewish trial had taken place before unlearned judges, though

Leaders of the town, who found him liable to repay what he owed him according to the (Jewish) Law.

3. But he was unwilling (to pay) and he rebelled.
4. And they are unable to extract from him what he is liable for according to the Law.
5. There is in that location a non-Jewish *Dawar* court, which does not accept bribes, nor does it practice favoritism, and it accepts the testimony of a Jew against a fellow Jew.[67]
6. Ought those Elders and Students and those witnesses, to appear before the non-Jewish Judge, to testify against the guilty party, and to say that this one is liable to the other the following amount – so as to achieve the return of the money to its owner, and to rescue stolen property from a robber, and so that lawless people should not be taught to act with violence – lest thieves and robbers increase?

they be "worthy elders" of the community, then only the original witnesses should testify in the non-Jewish court. That is because there is the possibility that the Jewish "judges" had erred in their conclusions, and it would be inappropriate to represent to the non-Jewish court that the prior outcome is in fact what Jewish Law requires. The use of the term *Talmidei Chachamim* in this concluding passage of the responsum, in conjunction solely with the reference to the Bei Dina, the established Jewish court – in contrast to the term Zekenim Chashuvim ("worthy elders"), casts doubt on the suggestion by Ginzberg, *ibid.* at n. 111, that the term *Talmidim* in the responsum discussed above is in fact equivalent *to Talmidei Chachamim*. If in fact, as seems likely, both of these responsa were authored by Hai Gaon, then we may in fact be observing a systematic usage in distinguishing between the *Talmidei Chachamim* as scholars capable of adjudication inconsonance with Jewish Law, as opposed to *Talmidim* as students, uninitiates, who may join in courts of Hedyotot with elders of the community, but whose judgments are not to be invested with a presumption of true consonance with Jewish Law.

[67] A definitive historical study has not yet been done to establish the extent to which non-Jewish courts in the Gaonic period did accept jurisdiction over conflicts between Jews. While there is a substantial body of Gaonic responsa indicating recourse to such courts by Jews, our responsum of Rav Hai reflects almost a sense of exceptionality at the fact that this particular local Dawar court does accept such jurisdiction. The Genizah material is likewise filled with mixed indications as to the nature of the cooperation between Muslim courts and the Jewish community. See S.D. Goitein, *A Mediterranean Society*, vol. II, *The Community*, Berkeley, CA, University of California Press, 1971, at pp. 395–402. Cf. Joseph Schacht, *An Introduction to Islamic Law*, Oxford, Clarendon Press, 1964, p. 132. Schacht indicates the acceptability in Muslim courts of testimony by non-Muslims, "Dhimmis," exclusively in matters concerning other Dhimmis. Nevertheless, our responsum, as well as the one in Harkavi, Teshuvot HaGeonim, *ibid.*, no. 213, p. 111, cast some doubt on Schacht's assertion. Indeed, the latter responsum refers explicitly to a situation in which the non-Jewish court refuses to accept the testimony of the Jewish witnesses – although it would accept testimony from the Elders of the Community who had served as unofficial judges (arbitrators) in the initial Jewish adjudication of the case. Thus, the non-Jewish court would accept jurisdiction, but not necessarily accept as witnesses persons who would qualify to act as witnesses in the Jewish court.

7. Or do they not have permission (to appear)?[68]
8. This is how we see it: that they have permission, and it is a *Mitzvah*[69] to do so.
9. Even were the victim of the theft to have been a non-Jew,[70] and the thief a Jew, we would be permitted to testify against the Jew to non-Jews, at (the court of) a Judge who is not a violent robber.
10. Thus we say, (*Bava Kamma* 113b) Rava proclaimed, others say it was Rav Huna, (Let it be known to) those who go up to Israel, and those who descend to Babylonia, that if a Jew knows evidence in the benefit of a non-Jew, against his fellow Jew, and he goes and testifies in a non-Jewish court, he is to be excommunicated.
11. However, this was not taught except as to a single witness, but as to two witnesses, it was not taught.
12. And even as to a single witness, this was not taught except as to a "*Magista* court," but as to a "*Dawar* court," they impose an oath (on the defendant when there is a single witness against him).
13. The meaning of "*Magista* court" is "court of the platter," as similarly the phrase "*ka'arat keseph*" (Numbers 7:13) is (translated by Onkeles as) "*magista dich'saf*," (a silver platter).
14. That is, they issue judgment based on their momentary thoughts, and they are not (concerned with) details, and they accept bribes, so that whoever brings a "platter," they decide in his favor.
15. We also regularly order the Judges to do exactly this in regard to a person who rebels against the (Jewish) Law, and does not dread the Rabbinic excommunication.[71]

[68] The bias of the questioner could not be more clear than in this formulation of the alternative possible responses – expansively as to the first and with great brevity as to the second. The second posed alternative is even more de-emphasized in the *Adret* version, which here simply reads *Oh lo*?, "or not?" In the *Sefer HaIttur* synopsis, this quality is lost by the recasting of the entire responsum into declarative form and elimination of the separate presentation of the question in favor of integrating the preferred alternative directly into the response.

[69] Much of the force of the response is made evident in the Gaon's use of this phrase "and it is a *Mitzvah* to do so!" For a careful analysis of the multi-vocal term *Mitzvah*, see Benjamin DeVries, *Halachic Categories* (Heb.), *Bar Ilan Annual*, vol. II, 1965, pp. 77–83.

[70] The word non-Jew is absent in the Adret version and in the equivalent passage in the Genizah fragments found in *Ginzei Schechter*. Ginzberg notes this and correctly insists that it is a pure scribal error, *Genizah Studies*, vol. II, at p. 118. The obviously erroneous nature of this omission is not only because the word is present in every other version of the responsum, including the synopses, it is also because the responsum goes on to quote in support of his position in this hypothetical case the legislation of Rava in *Bava Kamma* 114a. That law is exclusively relevant to testimony in a situation in which one party is a non-Jew.

[71] On the basis of this passage, David E. Sklare, *Samuel Ben Hofni Gaon and his Cultural World*, Leiden, E.J. Brill, 1996, at p. 74, n. 24, makes a broad generalization that Rav Hai Gaon "had knowledge of the contemporary Muslim judicial system in Baghdad and approved of its trustworthy witnesses and justice." Perhaps this statement is a tad too broad.

16. However, it is necessary to warn him first in a public warning, and then if he does not accept (the Jewish Law judgment), we testify against him (in the non-Jewish court) and (thus) collect from him.
17. As for the Rabbinic teaching (*Gittin* 88b), "We were taught, Rabbi Tarfon said, In whatever place one finds the courts of non-Jews, even if their laws are the same as Jewish Law, you are not permitted to have recourse to them, as it says, (Exodus 21:1) "(These adjudications) you shall place before them (Jewish Judges)," not before non-Jews, for they are to be treated as "*hedyotot*," non-ordained (non-expert adjudicators.)
18. Thus in a place where you can collect the debt through Jews (adjudicating,) do not resort to them (non-Jews.)
19. And likewise, in a place where the (official Jewish) Judge is able to collect, do not resort to non-ordained (adjudicators), as the Rabbis taught, "before them" and not before non-ordained adjudicators.
20. But in a place where there is no official (Jewish, ordained) Judge, one should collect through non-ordained Jewish adjudicators, in accordance with the Law – and do not cause financial loss!
21. And in a place where the thief has no fear of Jewish scholars, the debt is to be collected through non-Jews – and do not cause financial loss!

This responsum contains many elements of significance to the legal analysis of the legislation of Rava. Most important is the way in which the Gaon understands the implications of the use of the terms *Magista* and *Dawar*. As we noted earlier, the Gaon understands these terms to refer alternatively to corrupt as opposed to honest courts. The responsum minimizes the significance of the evidentiary rule that in the presence of a single witness the court would require the defendant to take an oath. Rather than this single rule being the litmus test for the permissibility of testimony, it is no more than an indication of the integrity of that court. The ultimate determination as to permissibility to testify is not a single procedural rule, but the broad character of the particular non-Jewish court: is it honest, does it have standard procedures, does it treat Jews fairly? If the answers to those questions are positive, then according to the Gaonim, it is permissible even for a single Jewish witness to testify in such a non-Jewish court in favor of a non-Jewish plaintiff, against the interests of the Jewish defendant.

The determinative test is not the particular outcome and its comparability to the outcome that would have been produced in a Jewish court. The crucial test is whether justice can be served in that court. Indications of a just court are its integrity (avoidance of bribery), the regularity of its procedures and its fairness to all litigants (including Jews.) The reverse qualities in the judiciary are indications of the presence of injustice,[72] which would necessitate avoiding participation so as not to become complicit with inflicting injustice on the Jewish litigant.

[72] See Edmond N. Cahn, *The Sense of Injustice*, New York University Press, 1949, pp. 11–27, where at p. 24 Cahn argues that people by nature "regard injustice to another as personal aggression."

3

Rejected Rationales for Testimonial Restriction: The Gaonic Period into the Period of the Rishonim

The product of all of that we have looked at so far is the text that we have before us in the *Gemara Bava Kamma* 113b–114a. However, we are no further enlightened as to the motive of the legislation of Rava. Indeed, the question is now sharpened, since we have established, with a reasonable degree of probability, that the original legislation was even broader than we might have thought, providing no exemption for persons subpoenaed, no distinction between a single witness or multiple witnesses, and no distinction related to the kind of court in which the testimony would take place. The restriction appears to have been severe and unequivocal, consisting of the three lines (3, 5 and 6) cited earlier:

3. If a Jew knows evidence for the benefit of a non-Jew,
5. and he goes and testifies in a non-Jewish court against his fellow Jew,
6. he is to be excommunicated.

What precisely was the legal foundation for this intense prohibition? Over the course of the succeeding centuries, since the time of Rava, distinct approaches to this question have been considered. We will examine each of the possible approaches through the lens of the legal literature of the Gaonim and *Rishonim*.

3.1 AS EXTENSION OF THE BAN ON LITIGATION – *LIFNEIHEM*

The simplest way to understand the legislation of Rava would have been to view it as an extension of the law of Rabbi Tarfon, prohibiting recourse by Jews to non-Jewish courts.[1] However, as we have demonstrated earlier, that law relates only to adjudication between two Jews. Indeed, the sole *Tannaitic* text which relates to testimony in a non-Jewish court, the *Tosefta* in *Avodah Zarah*,[2] seems clearly to indicate the inapplicability of this restriction to the circumstances of adjudication between a Jew and a non-Jew, and certainly indicates its inapplicability to potential witnesses in such instances.

3.1.1 Rejection of the Theory by R. Nissim

Was Rava consciously reversing the law of the *Tosefta* by extending the applicability of the Law of Rabbi Tarfon even to testimony in a case where one party was a non-Jew? While this proposition sounds feasible, it finds almost no echo in all of Rabbinic literature and is expressly rejected by R. Nissim, b. Reuven of Gerondi (c. 1310–c. 1375) in a brief Responsum.[3] The inquiry related to adjudication between two Jews in a non-Jewish court, which the questioner attempted to justify on the grounds that the Jewish parties had consented to that non-Jewish forum, and that, therefore, the law of Rabbi Tarfon would not constrain them. The questioner further attempted to argue that since the law of Rabbi Tarfon was not applicable, the Law of Rava restricting testimony against a fellow Jew in a non-Jewish court, would also be inapplicable – thus reading the law of Rava as an extension of *Lifneihem*, the law of Rabbi Tarfon. Rabbi Nissim, in a curt response, dismisses the latter contention and indicates that *Lifneihem* is unrelated to the issue of testimony. He says,

I don't understand your contention.
There (in the case of Rava), the Jewish friend testifies in favor of a non-Jew,
when that non-Jew (the plaintiff), sued the Jew (the defendant) in his own (non-Jewish) court.
Then, even if the Jew does testify,
he does not thereby violate "Thou shalt not place,"
for the *Torah* thereby (*Lifneihem*) prohibits only placement (of cases by litigants in non-Jewish courts)
While this (testimony) is not related to *Lifneihem*.
This is simple.

[1] *Gittin* 88b. See text and related footnotes at 1.1.

[2] *Tosefta*, *Avodah Zarah* 1:8.

[3] Responsa of R. Nissim b. Reuven Gerondi (RaN), no. 73, Koenigsberg, 1831, final paragraph. (Earlier in that section, the reference to Rashba is an obvious typographical error for Rashbam, and is so corrected in the later edition of Ran's Responsa published in Warsaw in 1882.)

Why indeed was it so "simple" and clear to R. Nissim that the Biblical prohibition of *Lifneihem* bears no relevance whatsoever to the situation of testimony in a non-Jewish court as raised in the law of Rava? Why was this so self-evident that in all Rabbinic discussion of the legislation of Rava, through the periods of the Gaonim and the *Rishonim*, the possibility of its being based on *Lifneihem* is not even mentioned? The following factors were apparently determinative in excluding *Lifneihem* as the basis of the legislation of Rava.

3.1.2 Basis of the Inapplicability of *Lifneihem*

3.1.2.1 Permissibility of Litigation Between Jew and Non-Jew in Non-Jewish Courts

Firstly, until well into the Gaonic period there is not the slightest hint of any hesitation as to adjudication in a non-Jewish court when one party is a non-Jew. As we had seen earlier, the *Tosefta*, *Avodah Zarah* 1:8 had clearly indicated that where litigation in Jewish courts was not possible because one of the parties was a non-Jew, early Jewish law had already recognized the need to participate, as either litigant or witness, in non-Jewish adjudication in order to achieve whatever justice could thereby be made available.[4] Interestingly, neither this *Tosefta* nor any other Talmudic text raises the question of whether such participation in non-Jewish courts would constitute a breach of the teaching of Rabbi Tarfon. The implication is that barring the concern with the impurity of a *Kohen*, participation in litigation with a non-Jew in a non-Jewish court would not fall within the restrictive position of Rabbi Tarfon and would be entirely permissible according to Talmudic law.

When the issue is eventually raised in the early ninth century in a Midrashic text,[5] the hesitation is merely advisory, suggesting that the Jewish party should attempt to have the matter adjudicated in a Jewish court. The passage in *Midrash Tanhuma*[6] reads as follows:

How do you derive
that if a Jew and a non-Jew have some matter (of litigation) between them,

[4] See 1.2.

[5] *Midrash Tanhuma* is dated by Zunz in the first half of the ninth century. Zunz, *Haderashot BeYisrael* (Heb.), ed. by H. Albeck, Jerusalem, Mossad Bialik, 1947, at p. 111. S. Buber does not disagree with that dating, *Tanhuma Buber*, Vilna, 1885, reprinted 1946, New York, Sefer Press, at pp. 9–10.

[6] *Tanhuma*, *Shoftim*, sec. 1, Stettin, 1865, p. 324a. The text is virtually identical in *Tanhuma Buber*, *Shoftim*, sec. 1, Vilna, 1885, p. 14a; and in the Mantua manuscript of *Tanhuma*.

that it is forbidden for the Jew to say to the non-Jew
"Go with me to your courts (*arkaot*)."[7]
And that he would (thereby) violate a prohibition – as it says,
"He hath not dealt so with any nation, and as for His laws, they have not known them. *Halleluyah*." (Psalms 147:20)

The legal form of the passage and its firm language might almost lead one to think that the *Midrash* is in fact positing the existence of a Biblical prohibition against the behavior described. However, it is vital to note that the *Midrash* does not suggest the involvement of the prohibition of *Lifneihem*, of which it is clearly aware.[8] Rather, the *Midrash* cites a passage in Psalms which suggests the inferiority of non-Jewish law to divinely revealed law. Indeed, the behavior the *Midrash* finds objectionable is not the actual adjudication in non-Jewish courts, which is the subject of *Lifneihem*, but rather is the encouragement offered by the Jew to adjudicate in that venue. It appears that the *Midrash* is suggesting the moral impropriety of a Jew who might have the possibility of litigating with his non-Jewish opponent in a Jewish court – leaping at the opportunity to adjudicate in the non-Jewish court.[9] He has thus abandoned the wisdom and goodness of the Divine law in favor of the inferior non-Jewish law.

But this moral urging of the *Midrash* in defense of the dignity and honor of the divinely revealed Jewish law never matures into a substantive restriction regarding litigation between a Jew and a non-Jew. Thus, Rava, dealing with the question of testimony in litigation between Jew and non-Jew in a non-Jewish court, is clearly outside the framework of the law of Rabbi Tarfon. The idea that *Lifneihem* might apply to a witness under circumstances where it is clearly not applicable to the litigants has neither logic nor Rabbinic source to substantiate it. This is clearly one element in the thinking of RaN in excluding the applicability of Rabbi Tarfon's law to the situation of witnesses in a non-Jewish court.

[7] Dating in the early 800s would make this the earliest attested Gaonic usage of the term *Arkaot* as referring to non-Jewish courts.

[8] See *Tanhuma*, *Mishpatim*, sec. 3, at p. 124b. (However, in *Tanhuma Buber* this *Mishpatim* passage is absent.)

[9] A. Gulak, *Le-Heker Toledot ha-Mishpat ha-Ivri bi-Tekufat ha-Talmud*, Jerusalem, Ha-Sifriyyah ha-Mishpatit, 1929, at p. 58 suggests that this passage in *Tanhuma* is a reflection of Rabbinic opposition to the use of the non-Jewish archive for the deposit of documents when the Romans did not require such deposit. However, the passage clearly is unrelated to deposit of documents, the issue at stake is adjudication – the application of one or the other legal system for the resolution of conflict between the parties.

3.1.2.2 *Permissibility to Testify in Honest Non-Jewish Courts*

Secondly, we have previously introduced a significant Gaonic responsum, variously ascribed to Rabbi Sherira Gaon and or to Rav Hai Gaon, dealing with the question of testimony in non-Jewish courts. That responsum does incorporate discussion of the Law of Rabbi Tarfon – *Lifneihem*. In regard to our current concern, whether the legislation of Rava was simply an extension of the prior teaching of R. Tarfon, we should note the sharp differentiation that was made by Rav Hai Gaon between the legislation of Rava and the law of R. Tarfon. The former is introduced into the responsum not in relation to the query which was actually submitted, but rather in response to the hypothetical case of theft by a Jew from a non-Jew. R. Hai attempts to use that hypothetical case as the foundation for an *a fortiori* argument that will reinforce his conclusion as to the permissibility of going to the non-Jewish court in adjudication between two Jews, one of whom refuses to submit to the jurisdiction of the unofficial judges of the Jewish community. Thus, sentences 9 through 14 of the responsum relate to the application of the law of Rava to the hypothetical case propounded by R. Hai himself. Then, at sentence 15, R. Hai reverts to treatment of the question submitted to him, the focus of which is not on testimony per se, but on the question of whether the entire matter may be permissibly brought before a non-Jewish court. It is within this latter context that R. Hai treats the law of R. Tarfon – indicating the existence of an exception in dealing with a party who refuses to submit to the authority of the local Jewish tribunal.[10]

In an even less complicated context, another Gaonic responsum, probably also penned by R. Hai Gaon, affirms unequivocally in a situation in which one party refuses to submit to the judgment of a Jewish court, and the resultant trial in a non-Jewish court is therefore authorized by Jewish Law, that there is absolutely no objection to the original Jewish witnesses proceeding to testify in that non-Jewish court. This much is taken as obvious, while the responsum needed to proceed further because the non-Jewish court would not accept the testimony of the Jewish witnesses, but would accept testimony from outstanding members of the Jewish community.[11]

[10] The earliest reference to such an exemption is in a responsum ascribed to Rav Paltai Gaon (Pumbedita c. 842) recorded by Rabbenu Asher to *Bava Kamma* 92b. The responsum is quoted in Lewin, *Otzar Ha-Geonim* to *Bava Kamma* 92b, at p. 69; and see notes 5 and 6 there. In the final event, it is unclear whether Rav Paltai was the author only of the legal principle, or also of the striking figurative interpretation of the Talmudic passage.

[11] Schacht, *An Introduction to Islamic Law* at pp. 192–195, and Goitein, *A Mediterranean Society*, vol. II, at pp. 86 and 367–368, discuss the Muslim legal procedure of the *udul*,

The Gaon proceeds to deliberate on the question of whether the judges of the original Jewish adjudication would be permitted to represent themselves as witnesses in the non-Jewish court since they heard the original testimony of the witnesses. The Gaon does not allow such misrepresentation, but expresses no hesitancy whatsoever as to the full participation of the Jewish judges to testify in the non-Jewish court as to the outcome of the original Jewish adjudication.[12]

Again, in all of this, there is not the slightest consideration given to the possibility that the witnesses might be constrained from testifying in litigation which is permissibly before the non-Jewish court, on grounds of violation of the law of Rabbi Tarfon, the law of *Lifneihem*.

3.1.2.3 Absence of Challenge from the Tosefta *Text*

Thirdly, what might have served for Rabbi Nissim as the most decisive element of evidence to establish that Rava did not base his prohibition on *Lifneihem*, and did not intend to reverse the clear implication of the *Tosefta*,[13] is the very fact that the *Tosefta* text is not quoted in conjunction with Rava's legislation in the Talmudic passage itself. Had Rava himself, or the later *Amoraim*, *Saboraim* or *Stammaim* understood the restrictive legislation that way, we would certainly expect some Talmudic indication of, and resolution of, the conflict between the new legislation and the older *Tosefta* law.

However, aside the intrinsic weakness of such an argument *ex silentio*, there are further weaknesses in the evidence in this particular situation. Without entering into the substantial scholarly debate as to whether our entire *Tosefta* text was even known, or to what degree it was known, by Babylonian *Amoraim*,[14] there is in fact no evidence to indicate that Rava

the use of "officially certified witnesses of good reputation." This practice restricted the acceptance of testimony unless the persons were certified to be reliable and of good character. Our responsum suggests, albeit neither Schacht nor Goitein refer to it, that a similar procedure was applied by the Muslim courts to the qualification of Dhimmi (non-Muslim) witnesses. It could be for that reason that the questioner indicated that the non-Jewish court, not willing to accept the testimony of the witnesses who had appeared in the Jewish litigation, would be willing to accept testimony from the Jewish judges and other outstanding members of the Jewish community – who would thereby be recognized as equivalent to *udul* witnesses. Was this procedure itself an indication to the Gaonim of the integrity of those non-Jewish courts? But see Goitein, *ibid.*, p. 607, n.25, for indications of accusations of false testimony even by *udul*.

12 The Gaon makes short shrift of this possibility and simply indicates that it is prohibited because it is lying.

13 *Tosefta, Avodah Zarah* 1:8, as at 1.2.

14 Yaakov Elman, *Authority and Tradition: Toseftan Baraitot in Talmudic Babylonia*, New York, Yeshiva University Press, 1994, pp. 275–281.

(or Rav Huna for that matter) was aware of this particular *Tosefta* law. While his contemporary Abbaye does at one point seem to respond to the last part of this *Tosefta* text, even there it is possible that he is not responding to the text itself but rather to the report of a comment by Rabbi Jochanan as to what the accepted position is. Indeed, Prof. Saul Lieberman goes so far as to suggest that the bulk of this *Tosefta* text was not known at all to the Babylonian *Amoraim*.[15] This element, as a possible source for the position of Rabbi Nissim, remains inconclusive.

Nevertheless, taken together, the clarity of the implications of the *Tosefta* text – and the explicit Gaonic refusal to ascribe any relevance to the law of Rabbi Tarfon in regard to testimony – serve as a strong foundation for the unequivocal assertion by Rabbi Nissim that the legislation of Rava is not founded on the law of *Lifneihem*. We must look elsewhere then for the legal basis of the prohibition legislated by Rava against testimony in a non-Jewish court against a fellow Jew.

3.2 THE LAW OF *MESIRAH* (HANDING OVER/COLLABORATION)

Is it possible that the underlying legal basis of the Law of Rava is that such testimony against a fellow Jew would be viewed as a form of *Mesirah* – a form of "handing over" or collaboration with oppressors? To understand the foundation of the uniformly negative response to this question in the period of the *Rishonim* and early *Acharonim*, we must first explore the law of *Mesirah* itself.

3.2.1 *Mesirah* in Biblical Narratives

There is no explicit discussion of a law of *Mesirah* in the *Torah* itself. However, in the Prophetic books there are three narratives in which a Jew or Jews hand over a fellow Jew for apparent summary execution.

3.2.1.1 The Case of Samson

The first instance is in Judges chapter 15 where Samson, furious over the fact that his wife had been given by her father to another man, burnt down the fields of the Philistines. They retaliated by executing the wife and her father, to which Samson responded by killing many Philistines.

[15] Lieberman, *Tosefet Rishonim* vol. II, p. 186, and vol. I, p. 242.

The Philistine army then pursued Samson into the territory of the tribe of Judah, at which point the narrative continues as follows:

9 Then the Philistines went up, and pitched in Judah, and spread themselves against Lehi. 10 And the men of Judah said: "Why are ye come up against us?" And they said: "To bind Samson are we come up, to do to him as he hath done to us." 11 Then three thousand men of Judah went down to the cleft of the rock of Etam, and said to Samson: "Knowest thou not that the Philistines are rulers over us? what then is this that thou hast done unto us?" And he said unto them: "As they did unto me, so have I done unto them." 12 And they said unto him: "We are come down to bind thee, that we may deliver thee into the hand of the Philistines." And Samson said unto them: "Swear unto me, that ye will not fall upon me yourselves." 13 And they spoke unto him, saying: "No; but we will bind thee fast, and deliver thee into their hand; but surely we will not kill thee." And they bound him with two new ropes, and brought him up from the rock.[16]

The prophet offers no condemnation of the men of Judah for having handed over Samson for apparent execution by the Philistines. On the other hand, Samson himself consented to the collaboration, and, in the continuation of the narrative Samson is not killed, but rather kills two thousand Philistines with the jaw bone of an ass. Of course, the men of Judah did not know in advance that Samson was capable of rescuing himself, so was their handing him over to an oppressive force for execution an illicit act of collaboration in murder, or was it justified by the apparent concern that the failure to do so would result in war with the Philistines at the expense of many other lives? Or did they view his likely execution by the Philistines as legally justifiable? The Prophet remains silent about these questions.

3.2.1.2 *The Case of Sheva ben Bichri*

The second such narrative is found in II Samuel chapter 20. A rebellion against the authority of King David is initiated by Sheva son of Bichri of the tribe of Benjamin, and all of the tribes other than Judah are drawn into support of Sheva. King David sends his army under the leadership of Joab to pursue Sheva. After an eventful pursuit, they discover that Sheva was hiding in the town of Abel, and the army besieges the town. The narrative continues as follows:

15 And they came and besieged him in Abel of Beth-maacah, and they cast up a mound against the city, and it stood in the moat; and all the people that were with Joab battered the wall, to throw it down. 16 Then cried a wise woman out of the city: "Hear, hear; say, I pray you, unto Joab: Come near hither, that I may speak with thee." 17 And he came near unto her; and the woman said: "Art thou

[16] Judges 15:9–13. JPS 1917 translation.

Joab?" And he answered: "I am." Then she said unto him: "Hear the words of thy handmaid." And he answered: "I do hear."
18 Then she spoke, saying: "They were wont to speak in old time, saying: They shall surely ask counsel at Abel; and so they ended the matter.
19 We are of them that are peaceable and faithful in Israel; seekest thou to destroy a city and a mother in Israel? why wilt thou swallow up the inheritance of the LORD?"

20 And Joab answered and said: "Far be it, far be it from me, that I should swallow up or destroy.
21 The matter is not so; but a man of the hill-country of Ephraim, Sheba the son of Bichri by name, hath lifted up his hand against the king, even against David; deliver him only, and I will depart from the city." And the woman said unto Joab: "Behold, his head shall be thrown to thee over the wall."
22 Then the woman went unto all the people in her wisdom. And they cut off the head of Sheba the son of Bichri, and threw it out to Joab. And he blew the horn, and they were dispersed from the city, every man to his tent. And Joab returned to Jerusalem unto the king.[17]

Here too the Prophet remains silent as to the justification of the conduct of the "Wise Woman of Abel." By contrast to the case of Samson, Sheva is being "handed over" to Joab, the duly constituted authority appointed by the rightful King of Israel. But is it the expectation that Sheva will receive a just trial pursuant to which he will be punished, or will Joab simply summarily execute him? If the latter action by Joab is expected and is unjustified, is the wise woman's conduct justified by her fear that the entire town of Abel will be destroyed if they resist? Why does she not just hand over Sheva rather than decapitate him and throw his head over the wall? Is she simply afraid that even opening the gates to transfer Sheva alive would result in an attack on the town? Is she fearful of handing over Sheva alive lest he reveal who in the town had collaborated to hide him, who might then also be executed as co-conspirators with Sheva himself? None of this is explored in the Biblical narrative, the prophet, here too, remained silent about the handing over of Sheva.[18]

3.2.1.3 The Case of the Seven Sons of Saul and the Gibeonites

The most extreme Biblical narrative of a Jew handing over other Jews for summary execution is the account of the conduct of King David in II Samuel chapter 21. The text speaks best for itself:

[17] II Samuel 20:15–22. JPS 1917 translation.

[18] The extreme oddity of this case becoming in Rabbinic literature, as we shall see, the paradigm instance for the laws of *Mesirah*, despite the fact that the "handing over" is to a duly constituted Jewish authority, is compounded by the absence of any Rabbinic reference in this context to the singular parallel instance in the *Torah* itself where the Jewish

1 And there was a famine in the days of David three years, year after year; and David sought the face of the LORD. And the LORD said: "It is for Saul, and for his bloody house, because he put to death the Gibeonites." **2** And the king called the Gibeonites, and said unto them – now the Gibeonites were not of the children of Israel, but of the remnant of the Amorites; and the children of Israel had sworn unto them; and Saul sought to slay them in his zeal for the children of Israel and Judah – **3** and David said unto the Gibeonites: "What shall I do for you? and wherewith shall I make atonement, that ye may bless the inheritance of the LORD?" **4** And the Gibeonites said unto him: "It is no matter of silver or gold between us and Saul, or his house; neither is it for us to put any man to death in Israel." And he said: "What say ye that I should do for you?" **5** And they said unto the king: "The man that consumed us, and that devised against us, so that we have been destroyed from remaining in any of the borders of Israel, **6** let seven men of his sons be delivered unto us, and we will hang them up unto the LORD in Gibeah of Saul, the chosen of the LORD."

And the king said: "I will deliver them." **7** But the king spared Mephibosheth, the son of Jonathan the son of Saul, because of the LORD'S oath that was between them, between David and Jonathan the son of Saul. **8** But the king took the two sons of Rizpah the daughter of Aiah, whom she bore unto Saul, Armoni and Mephibosheth; and the five sons of Michal the daughter of Saul, whom she bore to Adriel the son of Barzillai the Meholathite; **9** and he delivered them into the hands of the Gibeonites, and they hanged them in the mountain before the LORD, and they fell all seven together; and they were put to death in the days of harvest, in the first days, at the beginning of barley harvest ... **14** And they buried the bones of Saul and Jonathan his son in the country of Benjamin in Zela, in the sepulchre of Kish his father; and they performed all that the king commanded. And after that God was entreated for the land.[19]

In this narrative the prophet is extremely careful not to ascribe to God the counsel of putting Saul's two sons and five grandsons to death. God only indicates that the nation is suffering a famine due to the slaughter of the Gibeonites by King Saul; He does not indicate how national atonement for this cruelty can be achieved. David takes the initiative in consulting with the Gibeonites about how their forgiveness can be gained, and, shockingly, he agrees fully to their terms despite its involving handing over seven innocent persons to summary execution. The prophet withholds any comment on the conduct of David.[20]

What in fact could David have been thinking? Did he consider it to be the case that the danger to the entire Israelite nation was so great that the national interest demanded the sacrifice of admittedly innocent persons

people, having come upon a fellow Jew violating the Sabbath, "bring him" to Moses and Aaron and the Elders. Numbers 15: 32–33.

19 II Samuel 21: 1–14. JPS 1917 translation.

20 Cf. II Samuel 12:7–12. (Where was the prophet Nathan when he was so needed?)

for the greater national good? Did he think that God was hinting to him that this course of action was justifiable in the light of the wrong to the Gibeonites? Is it clear that he was not motivated also by the opportunity to eliminate a potential threat to his own heirs to the throne that might eventually have derived from the descendants of his predecessor, Saul? Yet the passage ends with the indication that Divine atonement had been achieved – was that because of or despite the conduct of David?

These three narratives reflect elements that are strikingly common, and other elements that are quite diverse. Note the following five elements:

1. In all three instances the handing over of one or more persons is apparently motivated by the desire to rescue a larger group that is in danger – a tribe, a town or the entire Israelite nation.
2. In all three instances it is clear that the fate of the person handed over is to be death.
3. However, while in two of the cases the person demanded is identified as an individual by name (Samson and Sheva), in the third, the persons are identified only by class (offspring of King Saul), and the number demanded, seven, is less than the entire class. This is emphasized in the text by the indication that David himself made the selection and specifically did not include the offspring of Jonathan amongst those to be handed over.[21]
4. Further, in one instance (Sheva), the person handed over had in fact committed a capital crime according to Biblical law, the crime of rebellion against the authority of an anointed king.[22] In the case of Samson, he had unquestionably committed an initial crime, that of destruction of the Philistine fields, which might well have been a capital crime according to their law, but was certainly not a capital crime according to the Bible, which never utilizes capital punishment as penalty for a crime against property.[23] In the final case, the offspring of Saul had committed no crime at all – they were rather to be put to death for the crime of their father or grandfather, conduct which the Bible had explicitly denied to the Israelite

[21] II Samuel 21:7.

[22] Rambam, *Hilchot Melachim* 3:8.

[23] The Rabbis went to great lengths to demonstrate that the single instance that appears to involve justification of taking life to protect property, Exodus 22:1–3, is in reality a situation of presumed threat to life in which case the householder is acting in justifiable self-defense. See *Sanhedrin* 72. Even in that Biblical statute death is not a judicially imposed penalty, and would not be if the criminal is later apprehended for his crime of robbery by breaking and entering.

judiciary,[24] but which had been left as apparently justifiable as a form of direct divine action.[25]

5. Finally, Sheva was being handed over to the duly empowered military general of the Israelite monarchy to be punished according to Israelite law. By contrast, Samson was essentially being extradited to a foreign government, the Philistine authorities, for the commission of a crime on their territory, for which they desired to punish him, possibly in accordance with their law. In the case of the offspring of Saul, they are handed over to the Gibeonites, a tribe with which the Israelites under Joshua had entered into a pact allowing them to continue to reside in the land of Israel,[26] but whose plan to execute the seven offspring of Saul is not even presented by themselves as in pursuit of any just law, but is purely a matter of tribal revenge for the wrong done to them in the past.[27]

These three Biblical narratives and the problematic of the five elements we have identified serve as the backdrop to virtually all later Rabbinic discourse on the issue of *Mesirah*, even when they are not explicitly referenced.[28]

3.2.2 *Mesirah* in the Talmudic Era

3.2.2.1 Mishnah and Tosefta

The essential *Mesirah* texts in the early Talmudic period are a related set, a pair of teachings in *Mishnah*[29] and a third in *Tosefta*,[30] all three of which were probably originally a single text.[31] The *Mishnah* texts have to do with the questions of whether a Jew confronted by oppressors is

[24] Deuteronomy 24:16. "Parents shall not be put to death for (crimes of their) children, nor (shall) children be put to death for (the crimes of their) parents, a person shall be put to death only for his (/her) own crime."

[25] Exodus 34:7. "yet He does not remit all punishment, but visits the iniquity of parents upon children and children's children, upon the third and fourth generations." JPS Tanakh translation, 1985.

[26] Joshua chapter 9, particularly at 9:15.

[27] II Samuel 21:4–6.

[28] See Rapaport, "The Informer in Jewish Literature."

[29] *Mishnah Terumoth* 8:11–12.

[30] S. Lieberman, *Tosefta, Seder Zeraim, Terumot* 7:20.

[31] See David Daube, *Collaboration with Tyranny in Jewish Law*, London, Oxford University Press, 1965, at pp. 18–27 and 69–83. (I had the honor and privilege of studying under Professor Daube at the University of California at Berkeley, Department of Political Science, at the time of publication of this short but extraordinary volume.)

permitted to hand over a single loaf of *Terumah* for ritual defilement in order to rescue the rest of the loaves; and whether a group of Jewish women are permitted to hand over one woman to be raped by oppressors in order to rescue the rest of the group from a like fate. The following is the *Mishnah* text:

> If one was passing from place to place with loaves of *Terumah* in his hand and a gentile said to him:
> "Give me one of these and I will make it unclean; For if not, I will defile them all,"
> Let him defile them all, and not give him deliberately one to defile.
> But R. Joshua says: he should place one of them on a rock.
> Similarly, if gentiles say to women:
> "give us one of you that we may defile her,
> and if not, we will defile you all,"
> Then let them all be defiled
> Rather than hand over to them one soul from Israel.

The *Tosefta* text carries the issue a critical step further by raising the question of whether it is ever permissible to hand over a single person to oppressors for summary execution in order to rescue the rest of the group of which he is a part. The *Tosefta* text reads as follows:[32]

1. A caravan of persons to whom non-Jews said, "hand over to us one of you to be killed, and if not we will kill you all": let them all be killed, but they should not hand over to them one soul from Israel.
2. But if they had designated him to them, as they had designated Sheva son of Bichri, they should deliver him to them and they should not all be killed.
3. Rabbi Judah said, "When is this taught, when he is within and they are outside, but when he and they are inside, since he will be killed and they will be killed, they should hand him over to them and should not all be killed. And such is said, "And the woman came before the entire people in her wisdom," she said to them, "since (if we resist) he will be killed and you will all be killed, hand him over to them and do not all be killed."
4. Rabbi Shimon says, this is what she said to them, "Anyone who is a rebel against the monarchy of the house of David is capitally liable."

Confronting the tragic moral dilemma of whether to collaborate with an oppressor in the achievement of his evil intent in order to avoid an evil of even greater quantitative magnitude, the laws of the opening statements of all three cases, possibly the original majority opinions, represent a common approach of total resistance. In the first case of the *Mishnah*, as

[32] Lieberman, *Tosefta, Seder Zeraim, Terumot* 7:20. (The division into four paragraphs is my own.)

to loaves of *Terumah*, the majority position would disallow any collaboration despite the resultant desecration of all of the loaves. In the second case, of threatened rape of a group of women, the *Mishnah* is equally unequivocal that a single Jewish person may not be handed over for rape despite the dire consequences to the entire group. And finally, the opening statement of the *Tosefta* is identically unequivocal as to the impermissibility of handing over a single person for execution despite the presumed resultant death of the entire group. Yet in each of the three cases, the drive toward the preference of limited collaboration in the interest of partial rescue manifested itself in varying degrees.

In the first case of the *Mishnah*, Rabbi Joshua proposed a moderate step, not directly handing the loaf to the pagan since that would constitute directly causing the loaf to become impure, but depositing the loaf on a rock, allowing the pagan to fulfill his evil intention without its actually being done by the Jew. In the second case there is no *Tannaitic* record of equivocation, but the *Amoraim* of Israel, without elaboration, suggest that "this is not reasonable if she/it was already impure; this is not reasonable if one was a slave,"[33] suggesting that such a woman might be given up in order to spare the rest of the group. However, this text itself and its meaning are unclear and became the subject of extensive debate amongst the *Rishonim* as to whether such an allowance of collaboration actually existed according to Jewish law. Rambam recorded no such exemption from the duty of resistance in the case of threatened rape.[34] Rashba denied entirely that this was the intent of the Jerusalem *Talmud*, and insists that a woman's prior conduct or personal status have no impact on the duty of protection owed to her.[35] Meiri considers the possibility, although he does not clearly so conclude, that if there is a prostitute amongst the women, that she could be handed over in order to rescue the rest of the group.[36]

33 Jerusalem *Talmud* (JT) *Terumot* 8:10, at 46b.

34 Rambam, *Mishneh Torah*, *Hilchot Yesodei HaTorah* 5:5, records the law of the *Mishnah* in this regard, mandating no collaboration, and makes no reference whatsoever to the apparently exclusionary language of the *Gemara Yerushalmi*.

35 Rashba, Responsa, cited in *Kesef Mishneh* to Rambam, *ibid*. He read the first clause of the *Gemara* teaching as a reference to a loaf of *Terumah*, not to a woman having been "impure." The meaning in fact hinges on whether the word in the text is "*kevar*" or "*kikar*," i.e. whether the middle letter of the word is a *Bet* or a *Cof*; Rashba insists on the latter reading. Early manuscripts of this passage are in fact unclear. But Rashba insists that a woman's prior conduct, even as an unrepentant professional prostitute, does not justify subjecting her to rape, even in order to spare other women from that same fate.

36 Meiri, *Sanhedrin* 72b (at page 271.) His reluctance to conclude permissibly in the situation of the prostitute is that "perhaps she engaged in repentance in her heart." *Ibid*.

The most complex development of a partially accommodating position is to be found in regard to the third case, that presented in the *Tosefta* text, related to the threat to the lives of an entire group of persons if they fail to hand over a single victim. To return then to the *Tosefta* in *Terumot*, the opening statement, (paragraph 1) is an unequivocal position of resistance to the oppressor. The following anonymous statement (paragraph 2), provides an opening for rescue of the group through handing over an individual who was specifically named by the oppressor, as Sheva ben Bichri had been named by Yoav. Interestingly, the case of Samson might have served in this *Tosefta* as an even better model for the permissibility of handing over a designated person since there it involved clearly handing him over to an oppressive regime – the Philistines. However, the case of Sheva is a richer instance which could serve as textual basis for each of the three accommodationist positions (subparagraphs 2, 3 and 4). Other than the Biblical precedent of Sheva ben Bichri, this text offers no rationale as to why the victim's being named by the oppressor should lessen the community's duty to protect him. There is room for much speculation on this issue, and it may very well be the case that the following two limitations on this general exemption are actually reflective of two alternative approaches to precisely this question.

The following two positions in the *Tosefta* text, those of Rabbi Judah (in paragraph 3) and Rabbi Shimon (in paragraph 4), are presented as limitations on the previously stated accommodation (paragraph 2). However, the position of Rabbi Judah is particularly opaque.[37] The clearest reading is that Rabbi Judah takes the following position: There could be a full duty of resistance, despite paragraph 2, even when a single person has been named.[38] When would that be the case? When the designated person is "within" – meaning that he is definitely trapped and will probably be killed, but the rest of the group is "outside" – meaning that they could still have the opportunity of escape. Then, the group should resist as much as it can until the hopelessness of the situation is clear and then as many as possible of the group should escape while the named person is captured and killed by the oppressor. However, Rabbi Judah continues to assert, in this approach, that if to begin with it is clear that

[37] Extensive treatment of this issue is found in Daube, *Collaboration with Tyranny in Jewish Law*, and in S. Lieberman, *Tosefta Zeraim*, *Terumot* 7:20, at pp. 148–149, and *Tosefta Kifeshutah*, *Seder Zeraim*, *Terumot* 7:20, at pp. 420–421, Jewish Theological Seminary of America, New York, 1955.

[38] The weakness of this approach is that this is not the stated position of either the *Tanna Kamma*, or the anonymous author of the exemption in the case of the designated victim, but is some odd combination of the two.

both the designated victim and the rest of the group are all "within" – meaning that in resistance there is no possible escape for anyone, then the group should hand over the named individual, as was done by the Wise Woman of Avel – better that one named person should be handed over than that all should meet definite death.

Thus, according to Rabbi Judah, the reduction of duty to protect the named individual has nothing to do with his personal conduct, but may have to do purely with the fact that his fate is knowable. If it is clear that he cannot be saved and that the attempt to rescue him will simply result in the additional massacre of the rest of the community, then he is to be handed over to at least protect those whose lives can still be saved. On the other hand, if there is a possibility that he could escape, there would be no justification in handing him over to be killed in order to save the lives of any other person or even of the entire group.

But an alternative possible reading of Rabbi Judah is that he was originally responding to the *Tanna Kamma* of the *Tosefta* (paragraph 1), and in fact is positing the most lenient possible position – that even without designation, if all would otherwise be killed, the group should select a single person to be handed over.[39] There is no comment on how that selection might be done.

This harder line taken by Rabbi Judah is further intensified by the subsequently cited position of Rabbi Shimon (paragraph 4), who maintains that, in any case, even when resistance would be hopeless for all involved, it is not permissible to hand over even a designated individual unless that person is, like Sheva ben Bichri, *Chayav mitta* – capitally liable. (Or, even more narrowly, Rabbi Shimon might maintain that the named individual can only be handed over if he was capitally liable on a charge of treason against the Jewish government, as was Sheva ben Bichri.) For Rabbi Shimon it is clear that the only possible justification for reduction of the duty of protection owed to any single individual is that such an individual is in any case someone whose life is forfeit (an outlaw) due to his own conduct – either according to the law of the government seeking his death, or possibly only according to Jewish Law. If his life is not forfeit, then the group is never justified in handing him over according to Rabbi Shimon, even if the consequence will be that they will all be killed, including the person named and sought.

39 Such is the approach preferred by Professor Leiberman in *Tosefta Kifeshutah*. For a fascinating historical elaboration of this possibility see Daube, *Collaboration with Tyranny in Jewish Law*, at pp. 28–39.

3.2.2.2 *Jerusalem* Gemara

The four positions expressed in the *Tosefta* (paragraphs 1, 2, 3 and 4) are replicated in a *Beraita* in the Jerusalem *Talmud*,[40] albeit with the latter two positions cited not in the names of the *Tannaim* referred to in the *Tosefta* itself, but rather in the names of the two leading *Amoraim* of Israel during the second half of the third century:

We were taught:

a. A caravan of persons who were traveling on the road, whom non-Jews came across and said, "hand over to us one of you and we will kill him, and if not we will kill you all": even if they will all be killed, they should not hand over one soul from Israel.
b. But if they had designated one to them, like Sheva son of Bichri, they should deliver him and should not all be killed.
c. Rabbi Shimon ben Lakish said, "That is only if he is capitally liable like Sheva ben Bichri."
d. and Rabbi Yochanan said, "Even if he is not capitally liable like Sheva ben Bichri."

Each of the positions expressed, except for the first, seems to particularly reflect one of the Biblical narratives that we have previously explored. This *Beraita* begins with the position of the *Tanna Kamma* of the *Tosefta* (paragraph a), requiring complete resistance to the demand of the oppressor, even at the price of the entire group being killed. Interestingly, this position is not embodied in a single Biblical narrative. The *Beraita* then records the anonymous position allowing handing over if the victim is specifically named (paragraph b). This is parallel to the story of the men of Judah handing over Samson to the Philistines. The third position reported is that of Rabbi Shimon in the *Tosefta* (paragraph c), who allows the handing over only if the named person was capitally liable, albeit in the *Beraita* this is reported as the position of Rabbi Shimon ben Lakish. This position is parallel to the story of Sheva ben Bichri.[41] The fourth position reflected is that of Rabbi Judah in the *Tosefta* (paragraph d), but here in the *Beraita* it is reported as the position of Rabbi Yochanan, and comes closest to offering justification for the behavior of King David in handing over the sons and grandsons of Saul to the Gibeonites – that is, the group to be handed over had been designated, had committed no

[40] JT *Terumot* 8:10, at 47a. (The division into four subsections is my own.)

[41] It is also reflected in I Samuel 23:12, where God indicated to David that the people of the town of Keilah would hand him over to King Saul if the latter were to attack the city demanding that they hand over David.

crime, but David believed that it was only by handing them over that the rest of the nation could be saved from the famine.[42]

There are then two disparate ways of understanding the debate between Rabbi Shimon ben Lakish and Rabbi Yochanan. In both approaches, they each utilize the case of Sheva ben Bichri as the model for when a single person can be handed over to rescue a group. In the more restrictive approach, Resh Lakish requires that the designated person be capitally liable according to Jewish Law (like Sheva ben Bichri was); while Rabbi Yochanan requires only that he be viewed as capitally liable according to those who are making the demand (as Samson was.) In the more accommodationist approach, Resh Lakish maintains that the person designated must have been viewed as capitally liable by those making the demand (like both Samson and Sheva ben Bichri); while Rabbi Yochanan requires only that the individual has been specifically identified by those making the demand (as were the offspring of Saul), even if they were guilty of no crime whatsoever.

The *Beraita* cited in the Jerusalem *Talmud* offers no explicit resolution as to which of these understandings of the debate between Rabbi Shimon ben Lakish and Rabbi Yochanan is intended. Nor does it offer an explicit indication as to how the law is ultimately to be decided as between these two authorities. However, the immediately following narrative in that *Gemara* provides an instance of the actual application of these legal principles in Talmudic times, which might be the *Gemara*'s way of offering its resolution. It tells as follows:[43]

Ulla bar Koshev was sought by the (Roman) government.
He fled and went to Lod to Rabbi Joshua ben Levi.
They(the Romans) came, surrounded the city and told them,
"If you do not hand him over to us, we will destroy the city."
Rabbi Joshua ben Levi went to him (to Ulla), persuaded him, and handed him over.
Elijah, may his memory be a blessing, was wont to reveal himself to him,
but he no longer revealed himself –
so he (Rabbi Joshua) fasted some fasts, so he (Elijah) revealed himself to him.
He (Elijah) said to him, (explaining his absence),
"am I to reveal myself to ones who hand others over (*Moserot*)?!"
Said he to him, "Did I not act according to the Law (*Mishnah*)?"
Said he (Elijah) to him,
"Is this then the Law for the Righteous (*Mishnat HaChassidim*)?!!"

[42] This is clearly the understanding of this position offered by Rabbi Joseph Karo, in *Kesef Mishneh* to Rambam, *Hilchot Yesodei HaTorah* 5:5, at s.v. *Vechen im amru lahem*. He quotes the position of Rabbi Yochanan without its closing words, simply as, "Even if he is not capitally liable."

[43] JT *Terumot* 8:10, at 47a.

Without our having any further information about Ulla, we can only say that Rabbi Joshua ben Levi appears to have handed over to the Romans a person whom the Romans considered to be deserving of death, but who may not have committed any crime according to Jewish law. The prophet Elijah clearly objects to his having done so, but Rabbi Joshua defends himself by asserting that he had in fact acted precisely according to the teaching of the *Mishnah*. Elijah does not dispute Rabbi Joshua's consonance with the law, but nevertheless objects to his conduct on grounds of supra-legal standards of righteousness. Strikingly, while Rabbi Joshua could be understood as having acted in accordance either with Resh Lakish, in the more accommodationist paradigm of the debate, or with Rabbi Yochanan in the more restrictive paradigm of their debate, he cannot be understood as having acted in consonance with the most lenient position of Rabbi Judah who allowed handing over purely on the basis of the individual having been designated. That is, both Resh Lakish and Rabbi Yochanan are construed by this narrative as having decided in accordance with the *Tanna* Rabbi Shimon, against the *Tanna* Rabbi Judah. The open models are Shimshon and Sheva ben Bichri, but not the offspring of Saul.

It is in this manner that Rabbi Joshua ben Levi could lay claim to having acted in accordance with the *Mishnah*, that is with the rigorous position of the *Tanna* Rabbi Shimon in the *Tosefta*, albeit without its requiring that Ulla be guilty of a capital crime according to Jewish law. The response of Elijah is that there is an even more rigorous position available which demands even greater protection of Jewish life and which a *Chassid*, a pious person, such as Rabbi Joshua, should have maintained.

3.2.3 The Approach of Rambam: Distinction between Religious Oppressor, Violent Criminal and Government

This explains why Rambam, while clearly deciding the law in consonance with the position of the *Tanna* Rabbi Shimon, against the *Tanna* Rabbi Judah, apparently leaves open the question of whether the proper understanding of the position of Rabbi Shimon requires that the designated individual be guilty of a capital crime according to Jewish law, "like Sheva ben Bichri," or just be guilty of a capital crime according to those who are demanding that he be handed over, more similar to Samson, but also subject to being described as "like Sheva ben Bichri" in his being a criminal who was designated by name. Thus, Rambam's closing phrase, "But if he is not capitally liable, let them all be killed but should not hand over to them a single Jewish soul." Here he omits the emphasis which Resh Lakish placed on "capitally liable like Sheva ben Bichri."[44] Rambam goes on to indicate that the position of the prophet Elijah must also be taken into account as a timing constraint – that is, the people should not immediately be told that the person demanded can be permissibly handed over. Thus, Elijah's position continues to resonate as a *Midat Chassidut*, an especially righteous standard of conduct, while still confirming that in the final event the *Halacha* remains in conformity with the conduct of Rabbi Joshua ben Levi.

3.2.3.1 Mesirah *and* Kiddush Hashem

Rambam codified the laws of *Mesirah* in two separate locations, first in *Hilchot Yesodei HaTorah*.[45] There Rambam codifies the law of *Kiddush Hashem*, Sanctification of the Divine name, which requires resistance to religious oppression as a manifestation of loyalty to God and His commandments.[46] However, this requirement is balanced against the Biblical duty of preservation of one's own life.[47] Thus, if an oppressor of the Jewish religion demands of a Jew that he violate a commandment of the *Torah*, or be put to death, the Jew would be obligated to violate the commandment in order to preserve his life. However, there are two circumstances in which a Jew would not be permitted to violate the law, but would be required to resist to the point of death.[48]

The first circumstance relates to the nature of the demanded action; if the oppressor demanded that the Jew violate one of three "cardinal" crimes: idolatry, homicide or adultery/incest, then the law of *Kiddush Hashem* would override the duty to safeguard his own life.

The second circumstance relates to the intent of the oppressor plus the context: if the oppressor was motivated specifically by the desire to coerce Jews to violate Divine law (rather than his own personal benefit or

[44] Rambam, *Hilchot Yesodei HaTorah* 5:5 This is one possible response to the question posed by *Hagahot Maimuniot*, *ad loc.*, as to why Rambam apparently decides against the position of Rabbi Yochanan, contrary to the usual canons of *Pesak halacha*. See, by contrast, Nahum Rakover, *Mesirut Nefesh* (Sacrificing Life: Giving Up One to Save the Many) (Heb.), Jerusalem, The Library of Jewish Law, 2000, at p. 25.

[45] At 5:1–5.

[46] Based on Leviticus 22:32, *Venikdashti betoch Benei Yisrael*. See Rambam, *Sefer Hamitzvot*, Positive Commandments, No. 9.

[47] Based on Leviticus 18:5, *vechay bahem*.

[48] This particular formulation in terms of the requirement of resistance, rather than the usual expression of the requirement of giving up one's own life, follows the analysis by Rabbi Abraham Isaac Hakohen Kook, in Responsa *Mishpetei Kohen*, Responsum no. 144, sec. 15–16, at pp. 336–340.

pleasure), and the violation would be done in the presence of ten other Jews, then the Jew would be obligated to resist the violation of any law of the *Torah* in fulfillment of his duty of Public Sanctification of the Divine Name. The failure to resist when such was his duty would constitute violation of the prohibition against the desecration of the Divine name; or if done in the presence of ten other Jews, violation of the even more severe public desecration of the Divine name.

An essential element then of this treatment by Rambam is the indication of the general principle that the law against homicide may not be violated even in the attempt to rescue one's own life. However, if one were to directly kill an innocent person in order to save one's own life from a threatening oppressor, one would not be culpable of the act of homicide since one had acted under duress. The failure to resist to the point of losing one's own life, but instead actually taking the life of an innocent person, would not constitute violation of the crime of homicide, but would be violation of *Chillul Hashem*, the desecration of the Divine name.[49]

What then if the oppressor does not demand that the Jew directly take the life of an innocent victim, but only demands that the Jew hand over another person whom the oppressor will slay? Or if the oppressor does not demand that the Jew actually rape a married woman, but only demands that he hand over a married woman to be raped by the oppressor? These situations, which are the fact patterns of the *Mishnah* and *Tosefta* in *Terumot*, are integrated by Rambam into this section of the code, indicating that given the coercive nature of the circumstances, that is that the Jew was not acting volitionally, there would be no criminal liability even for aiding and abetting in the commission of the resultant crimes of homicide or rape. However, Rambam is informing us that the *Moser*, directly handing over to an oppressor someone who is then killed as a consequence of that handing over, would be in violation of the law of *Chillul Hashem* if the occasion was such that the person was under a duty to give up his life rather than allow the life of the other to be taken. But we had previously indicated that there were only two circumstances under which a duty to resist to the point of death was present; into which do these cases fall? They cannot fall into the first circumstance, because they do not actually call upon the Jew to commit an act of homicide or adultery. They must then fall only into the second circumstance where the intent of the oppressor is specifically to undermine the observance of

[49] Rambam, *Hilchot Yesodei HaTorah* at 5:4.

God's laws, and the breach would be done in the presence of ten or more persons. That would explain for Rambam why the *Mishnah* in *Terumot* co-joined the case of the demand for a woman to be handed over for rape with the case of the demand to hand over loaves of *Terumah* so that they would be made *Tameh*. This latter case is one in which clearly the intent of the oppressor is not to satisfy his own pleasure or benefit, but simply to coerce a Jew to violate the Divine law. That is also why the case of rape is situated not in the context of private conduct, but in the situation of a group. And that is also why the case of a demand for a single person to be handed over for summary execution is described by the *Tosefta* as being not in a private confrontation between two Jews and an oppressor, but in the situation of a caravan.

Thus, for Rambam, the two cases of demand for the handing over of persons for rape or to be killed are part of his second exception, not of the first. That is, they are situations in which the demand being made is for violation of Biblical law, but not of the three cardinal crimes – rather of the crime of aiding and abetting the commission of a crime by another. However, since the circumstances are such that the oppressor is motivated by the desire to get Jews to violate the Divine law, and it is a public situation, there is a duty resting upon the Jews to resist even such lesser violation of *Torah*, even to the point of death, based on the law of *Kiddush Hashem*.

3.2.3.2 Mesirah *and the Law of Damages*

The other context in which Rambam treats this law is in laws of assault and personal injury.[50] There, in regard to the handing over of property, Rambam indicates two fundamental conditions for violation of the law of *Moser*, first that the action is in response to a violent criminal (an *anas*), be he non-Jew or even Jew. Second, that if the action of the *Moser* was under duress, he would not be liable to the injured party unless he personally took the property of his fellow Jew, not under the direct supervision of the violent criminal, and delivered it directly into the possession of the *anas*. In that latter situation, Rambam implies, the *Moser* is actually personally performing the act of theft from the other Jew, in order to rescue himself or his own property from an eventual threat, and is therefore liable.[51] But, if the element of duress is present and immediate, then

[50] Rambam, *Hilchot Chovel Umazzik* 8:1–11.

[51] See *Bava Kamma* 117b.

in fact the *Moser* is not liable, since he is merely acting as the instrument of the *anas*, clearly not of his own will.[52]

As Rambam then moves from the constraint of handing over property to that of handing over a person, he strikingly does not postpone that element of the law to the next section of his code that deals with homicide. In regard to the entire subsequent passage in the *Mishneh Torah*, Rambam seems to be primarily basing his analysis upon a lengthy narrative passage in *Gemara*.[53] In that passage, we are told of Rabbi Eleazar the son of Rabbi Shimon (bar Yochai), who, due to his brilliant practical logic in the matter of singling out criminals, was appointed by the Roman court as a police officer, and in that capacity he arrested Jewish thieves who were then tried, and if convicted were punished in the Roman courts. The passage continues:

Thereupon, Rabbi Joshua son of Karcha[54] sent word to him,
"Vinegar, son of Wine! How long will you deliver up the people of our God for slaughter!"
Back came the reply (from Rabbi Eleazar): "I weed out thorns from the vineyard."
Whereupon Rabbi Joshua retorted: "Let the owner of the vineyard Himself (God) come and weed out the thorns."

The sharp response of Rabbi Joshua to the accommodating conduct of Rabbi Eleazar, is deeply reminiscent of the Jerusalem *Talmud*'s record of the response of the prophet Elijah to the accommodationist position of Rabbi Joshua ben Levi we discussed above. In fact the Babylonian *Talmud* itself makes the association in a subsequent passage by ascribing the precise words of Rabbi Joshua to the prophet Elijah in a parallel case, as follows:[55]

A similar occurrence befell Rabbi Ishmael ben Yossi
(that he was designated by the Roman government to arrest Jewish criminals).
Elijah met him and said to him, "How long will you deliver up the people of our God for slaughter?!"[56]
He replied, "What can I do, it is the royal decree."
Said he (Elijah) to him, "Your father fled to Asia, you can flee to Laodicea."[57]

[52] Compare the different analysis but identical conclusion arrived at by Rabbenu Asher ben Yechiel in *Asheri to Bava Kamma*, ch. 10, paras. 27–28, based partly on his reconciliation of the Bavli with the *Gemara Yerushalmi* on this point.

[53] *Bava Metzia* 83b.

[54] An older colleague, and friend of Rabbi Eleazar's father, Rabbi Shimon bar Yochai – thus the reference to the latter as "wine," as it were, the sins of the son not to be imputed to the father.

[55] *Bava Metzia* 83b–84a.

[56] The precise words spoken by Rabbi Joshua to Rabbi Eleazar.

[57] As in the preceding narrative, here too Elijah offers a comparison to the more righteous conduct of the father.

But, whereas in the Jerusalem *Talmud*, the prophet Elijah has the last word, in the Babylonian *Talmud*, the challenge by Rabbi Joshua is followed by a story which vindicates the behavior of Rabbi Eleazar ben Shimon. The story is as follows:[58]

> One day a Fuller met him (Rabbi Eleazar) and referred to him as "Vinegar son of Wine." Said the Rabbi to himself, "Since he is so insolent, he is certainly a criminal." So he gave the order to his attendant: "Arrest him! Arrest him!" When his anger cooled, he went after him to secure his release, but did not succeed. Thereupon, he applied to him (the Fuller) the verse, "He who watches his mouth and his tongue, saves himself from many troubles." (Proverbs 21:23). Then they (the Romans) hanged him, and he (Rabbi Eleazar) stood under the gallows and wept. They (his disciples) said to him, "Master, do not grieve; for he and his son seduced a betrothed maiden on the Day of Atonement." (On hearing this) he laid his hand upon his heart and exclaimed: "Rejoice my innards, rejoice! If matters on which you are doubtful are thus (accurate), how much more so on those which you are certain!"

This narrative served multiple purposes in enabling Rambam to arrive at an understanding of the final position of the *Talmud*. Why does Rambam in reference to the case of Rabbi Joshua ben Levi give the final word to the prophet Elijah, urging restraint in collaboration even when the person demanded is designated as was Sheva ben Bichri;[59] while in the matter of Rabbi Eleazar ben Shimon (and Rabbi Ishmael ben Yossi) Rambam makes no reference to the restraining words of Rabbi Joshua ben Karcha (and those of Elijah to Rabbi Ishmael)?[60] The distinction is clearly based on the identity and purpose of the "oppressor." The series of cases dealt with in the *Tosefta* and the Jerusalem *Talmud* are codified by Rambam in *Mishneh Torah, Sefer Madda, Hilchot Yesodei HaTorah* in the course of his treatment of the laws of *Kiddush Hashem*, for they deal exclusively with the relationship to violent oppressors (*anasim*) who are presumptively intent on destroying the Jewish people and their obedience to *Torah*. It is precisely for that reason that resistance to their orders, sometimes even to the point of giving up one's very life, is deemed to be an act of sanctification of the Divine name. Conversely, the failure to resist, or collaboration with the oppressor, could constitute the desecration of the Divine name, a criminal offense according to Jewish law even when it is in the service of the protection of one's life, and even when there is present a level of coercion which would exempt the collaborator from

[58] *Bava Metzia* 83b–84a.

[59] Rambam, *Hilchot Yesodei HaTorah* 5:5

[60] Rambam, *Hilchot Chovel Umazzik* 8:11.

criminal punishment. The virtue of resistance under such circumstances is manifested in the support of the position of the prophet Elijah, calling for procrastination in cooperating with the violent religious oppressor, even when the technical conclusion of the law would allow some degree of collaboration. This is the law of criminal collaboration with anti-Jewish oppressors which threatens the very survival of the Jewish people, and the honor and sanctity of God, which we are duty bound to uphold.

By contrast, the majority of discussions in the Babylonian *Talmud* related to *Mesirah* deal not with religious oppressors, but with violent criminals (*anasim*) who are simply after the property of Jews, but who will take the lives of their victims in order to appropriate their wealth. Such criminals are not out to coerce Jews to violate the *Torah* or to threaten the survival of the covenantal relationship between God and the Jewish people. They may specifically target Jews, but that is only because the Jews are defenseless and easy targets. Under these circumstances, a Jew who cooperates with such violent criminals, verbally by informing against them, or behaviorally by collaborating in the taking of property, is not only endangering the property of fellow Jews, but is putting their very lives at risk.[61] The relationship to such criminals is therefore codified separately by Rambam, in *Sefer Nezzikin, Hilchot Chovel Umazzik*.[62] These laws have nothing to do with the principles of sanctification of the Divine name, and therefore are not distinguished by whether the action takes place publicly or privately. These laws have to do with property damages, and the possibility of creating a risk to life through an act of collaboration with or informing criminals who would not refrain from taking life in order to obtain the property they wanted.

Rambam carefully codifies the laws applicable to such informers, or collaborators with violent criminals, with appropriate legal nuances related to: (1) the intent of the perpetrator, (2) the precise action that he performs and (3) the degree of coercion used against him by the criminals. He offers a dual conclusion to this discussion: firstly, given the indirectness of the criminal behavior of the collaborator, he offers a spiritual threat to deter such conduct: "Anyone who hands over the person of a Jew or his property to an idolator, has no portion in the world to come."[63] But then, in recognition of the possible threat to the life of the Jew whose property is being indicated to the violent criminal, Rambam adds that the

[61] Rambam recognizes the distinct character of this group of oppressors even in *Hilchot Yesodei HaTorah* 5:2.

[62] Chapter 8, Laws 1–10.

[63] *Ibid.*, 8:9.

informer in such a case is forfeiting his life by creating that threat to life, and his own life may therefore be taken by another Jew to prevent him from executing his threatened act of informing to violent criminals.[64] The concluding law in this sequence, Chapter 8, Law 11, is of critical importance; it consists of four clauses, and reads as follows:[65]

(a) If the *moseir* carried out his threat and informed on a fellow Jew, it appears to me that it is forbidden to kill him, unless he has made it an established pattern to inform. In such an instance, he should be killed, lest he inform on others.
(b) In the cities of the west, the common practice is to kill the *mosrim* who have made an established pattern of informing with regard to people's property, and to hand the *mosrim* over to gentiles to punish them, beat them and imprison them, according to their wicked ways.
(c) Similarly, one who causes difficulty and irritation to the community may be handed over to the gentiles to be beaten, imprisoned and fined. It is, however, forbidden to hand over to gentiles a person for causing irritation to one individual.
(d) It is forbidden to destroy property belonging to a *moseir*, although it is permitted to destroy his life. The reason is that his money is given to his heirs.

The first clause of Law 11, paragraph (a) above, is a logical continuation of Law 10. If the *Moser* had already committed his crime, then the deterrent purpose for killing him is no longer applicable – unless he is an habitual informer, in which case he can still be killed in defense of his certain future victims, despite the fact that the next victim is currently unknown. The second clause, paragraph (b) above, starts by simply confirming that the authority to take the life of the habitual *Moser* was in fact the common practice of Jewish communities of North Africa. However, the concluding phrases of that clause are deeply confusing and disconcerting. Who exactly are these "gentiles" (*Goyim*) to whom a Jewish criminal informer may be handed over to be beaten, punished or imprisoned as penalty for his crimes? Rambam had previously introduced us to *Goyim* who were religious oppressors.[66] He had also introduced us to *Goyim* who were violent criminals.[67] But who are *Goyim* who would be acting

[64] *Ibid.* 8:10.
[65] *Ibid.* 8:11. Trans. by Eliyahu Touger.
[66] *Hilchot Yesodei HaTorah* 5:5, based on the precise language of the *Tosefta Terumot* 8:20.
[67] *Hilchot Chovel Umazzik* 8:9 as in Rome edition and in Frankel edition.

in the interest of protecting the Jewish community itself to deter habitual informers by punishing those informers?

This question becomes even more intense as we pass into the third clause of Law 11, paragraph (c) above. Beyond the permissibility of handing over the *Moser* to non-Jews for criminal punishment, this clause provides that the Jewish community may itself use the non-Jewish criminal legal system to enforce order amongst Jews by handing over to *Goyim* Jews who threaten the good order of the Jewish community itself. In this clause Rambam is clearly basing himself on the passages from the Babylonian *Gemara* we have viewed above, the narratives related to the conduct of Rabbi Eleazar ben Shimon, and of Rabbi Ishmael ben Yossi, both of whom served the non-Jewish government in a policing capacity – handing over Jewish criminals for punishment by the non-Jewish authority. It is precisely the "Fuller case" involving Rabbi Eleazar ben Shimon that enables Rambam to then indicate that the authority to hand over Jewish suspects to a non-Jewish authority is not justified by the fact that the suspect personally offended an individual, but only if his offense rose to the level of offending or creating some threat to the community. Thus, Rabbi Eleazar was correct in regretting his having ordered the arrest of the Fuller on the grounds of the personal offense, but was vindicated by the discovery that the Fuller had in fact committed a crime that warranted capital punishment according to Jewish law. The fact that that same punishment could not have been administered by a Jewish court at that time did not make its implementation by the Roman courts unjust, or impermissible for Rabbi Eleazar to have enabled. The act of *Mesirah*, of handing over a fellow Jew to non-Jews for punishment, as performed by Rabbis Eleazar and Ishmael, were not criminal acts because the non-Jews involved were neither religious oppressors nor violent criminals, they were an ordered non-Jewish government that shared with Jews the responsibility for maintaining the good order and communal values of the Jewish population subject to non-Jewish governance.

3.2.4 Is *Mesirah* Based on the Duty of Rescue? Limits on Loyalty to Life

Earlier in this section we had explored three *Tannaitic* texts: the *Mishnah* concerning a demand made to hand over a woman; the *Tosefta* concerning a demand made of a caravan to hand over a person; and the Jerusalem *Talmud*'s case concerning Rabbi Joshua ben Levi being commanded to hand over Ulla bar Koshev. Through all of those texts, even when brought together in the *Mishnah* and *Gemara Yerushalmi*, there was no explicit indication of the legal basis of the constraint against handing over. In fact the question of the legal basis of the prohibition was raised and not clearly resolved in the *Talmud* and remained a problem into the period of the *Rishonim*. But actually, that lacuna may be filled by the narrative in the Jerusalem *Gemara*, which immediately follows upon the story of Rabbi Joshua ben Levi and the comment of the prophet Elijah.[68] That passage reads as follows:

> Rabbi Immi was taken captive in a dangerous place.
> Rabbi Yochanan[69] said, "Prepare to wrap his body in shrouds."
> Rabbi Shimon ben Lakish said, "I would rather kill or be killed. I will go and rescue him by force." He went and persuaded them, and they handed him over.

This particular Palestinian Amoraic debate between Rabbi Yochanan and Rabbi Shimon ben Lakish did not attract much Rabbinic attention until the twentieth century, when it became a central textual source for the discussion of the permissibility of a person being a live organ donor.[70] In that context, the recognition emerged that central to this Amoraic debate was the question of the legal extent of the duty of rescue incumbent upon Jews in their relationships to fellow Jews based on the Biblical verse in Leviticus 19:16, "you shall not stand idly by the blood of your neighbor."

The background to this issue is found in the famous passage in the Babylonian *Gemara* related to the situation in which two travelers in the desert find themselves still distant from a fresh source of water.[71] One of the travelers has sufficient water to enable him to survive until he arrives at the next well. The other could not survive on the water remaining to him alone. Nor could either of them survive if the first traveler shared his water with the second. What is the first traveler to do? Ben Petura maintained that, "It is right that they both should drink and die, and that one should not see (be complicit through his inaction in) the death of his

[68] JT *Terumot*, Venice edition 8:10, at 46b; Vilna edition, 8:4 at 47a, lines 16–19.

[69] Both Venice and Vilna editions read here, "Rabbi Yonatan," but both editions, in the continuation of the narrative, have Rabbi Shimon ben Lakish return to Rabbi Yochanan. Since the entire sequence of narratives in this section deal with a common debate between Rabbi Shimon ben Lakish and Rabbi Yochanan, it appears that this is just a copyist's slip. Rabbi Moshe Margalit in his commentary, *Mareh Hapanim*, *ad loc.*, s.v. *Tani*..., recognizes the uncertainty of the identification of the named parties in this passage as a way of dealing with the unusual phenomenon of Rambam deciding the *Halacha* in accordance with Rabbi Shimon ben Lakish against Rabbi Yochanan.

[70] Madeline Kochen, *Organ Donation and the Divine Lien in Talmudic Law*, Cambridge University Press, 2014, at p. 196, note 53, and p. 200.

[71] *Bava Metzia* 62a.

friend." The implication of the position of Ben Petura is that the legal duty of rescue, which cannot allow even the omission of action resulting in loss of life of another, is applicable even if the consequence would be loss of the life of the rescuer. At any moment in which the other's life is at risk, standing by, failing to act to rescue, as by failing to share his water, would place the potential rescuer in the position of having breached his duty to rescue the life of his fellow. However, Rabbi Akiva subsequently taught that the duty of rescue is limited by the duty to preserve one's own life, based on exegesis of Leviticus 25:36, "that thy brother may live with you." The words "with you" served for Rabbi Akiva as indication that you have no duty, or that it is impermissible, to rescue another at the expense of your own life. In this passage, it is, strikingly, Rabbi Yochanan who reports that the *Halacha* remains in accordance with Rabbi Akiva.

Reverting now to the debate between Rabbi Yochanan and Rabbi Shimon ben Lakish in the Jerusalem *Gemara*, we can understand how two divergent approaches to their debate could emerge. In one approach, Rabbi Yochanan informs his students that it is not permissible for them to risk their lives in order to rescue Rav Immi. Resh Lakish, on the other hand, says that there is simply no duty to do so, but he is entitled to choose to do so of his own volition – that is, such action is not mandatory, but it is permissible/discretionary.[72] An alternative approach is that Rabbi Yochanan told his students to prepare shrouds because he maintained that there was no duty to put themselves at risk under the duty of rescue; while Resh Lakish differed and maintained that given his belief that he might be able to rescue Rav Immi, that he was in fact duty bound to do so, so long as the result was not certain death for himself.[73] We could chart the possible positions in the following manner:

	Assur: Forbidden	*Reshut*: Discretionary	*Chiyuv*: Duty
Analysis 1	R. Yochanan	Resh Lakish	
Analysis 2		R. Yochanan	Resh Lakish

Pursuant to this recognition, deciding the *Halacha* in accordance with Rabbi Yochanan could mean that one is forbidden to put one's own life

[72] This is the approach of Rabbi Aryeh Grossnass in Responsa Lev Aryeh, London, 1973, vol. II, no. 39. In consequence of this understanding, Rabbi Grossnass, in accord with the view of Rabbi Yochanan, views being a voluntary organ donor as an impermissible act – the act of a *Chassid Shoteh*. See Kochen, *Organ Donation*, at pp.195–201.

[73] This approach to the debate is taken by Rabbi Eliezer Waldenberg in *Responsa Tzitz Eliezer*, vol. XIII, no. 101, Jerusalem 1985. In consequence of this understanding, the

at risk in order to rescue another person; or it could mean that one is not duty bound to do so, but that such possibly self-sacrificial action is permissible. On the other hand, deciding the *Halacha* in consonance with the position of Resh Lakish could mean that such possibly self-sacrificial action is discretionary; or it could mean that one is in fact duty bound to act in this manner. What exactly would be the source of the duty that Rabbi Yochanan precludes, but which Resh Lakish might well support? Clearly, that duty could only be the legal duty of rescue generated by the verse, "thou shalt not stand idly by the blood of your neighbor." (Leviticus 19:16). This distinctive Biblical legislation, which criminalizes the failure to rescue the life of a person at risk, does not detail the extent to which the potential rescuer must endanger himself in order to achieve the rescue which he is duty bound to perform. The earlier debate we discussed between ben Petura and Rabbi Akiva pertained only to the limited issue of whether the putative rescuer was obligated to rescue even when the result would certainly be the loss of his own life. Ben Petura contended that even then the law required rescue of a fellow Jew. Rabbi Akiva maintained that the duty of rescue leaves intact the overriding duty of an individual to safeguard his own life.

However, the acceptance of the position of Rabbi Akiva within that debate fails to clarify the more subtle further question of what degree of risk the rescuer might or must undertake short of certain death to himself. It is this issue that may very well be the heart of the debate between Rabbi Yochanan and Resh Lakish. In our analysis charted above, Rabbi Yochanan maintains either that taking any risk is forbidden, or that taking some risk might be permissible, but is certainly not mandated by the legal duty of rescue. On the other hand, Resh Lakish may be expressing the position that minimally some risk is permissible, but that it might very well be the case that significant risk, up to but not including certain death (in consonance with the position of Rabbi Akiva), is actually mandatory under the law of duty of rescue.[74]

Why did the *Gemara Yerushalmi* report this fascinating case and debate between Rabbi Yochanan and Resh Lakish, immediately following the

halacha remaining in accordance with Rabbi Yochanan, is that while there is no duty to do so, it is permissible for one to be a voluntary organ donor despite the existence of some risk to the life of the donor.

[74] For a fuller discussion of the *Halachic* issues involved in the question of risking one's life in order to save another, albeit making no reference to this particular text in the *Gemara Yerushalmi*, see Kirschenbaum, "The Good Samaritan and Jewish Law," Dinei Israel, 7, 1976, pp. 7–85, particularly at pp. 28–59.

record of the *Tosefta* of the caravan case, and the related case of Rabbi Joshua ben Levi, both of which have to do with the question of handing over a person to save a group or a community? It is possible that the *Gemara Yerushalmi* is here attempting to provide the answer to an obvious question raised by the former two cases – what is the legal basis of there being a constraint against handing someone over to an oppressive force in order to save oneself? After all, the degree of criminal offense in handing someone over for possible execution by an oppressive force is rather minor, it is abetting a crime, no more than a *Gerama*, an indirect cause, but it is clearly not the commission of the crime of homicide. In which case, the duty to protect one's own life should have priority since it does not actually involve the commission of any of the three cardinal crimes. The response of the story of Rabbi Immi and the debate between Rabbi Yochanan and Resh Lakish is that the issue at stake is not the crime of homicide at all, but rather the existence of an affirmative legal duty of rescue and the need to define the parameters of that duty.

To put the matter differently, the *Gemara* may be suggesting that the entire discussion of *Mesirah* and the constraint against handing over a person to relatively certain death is not premised on the assertion that in doing so the *Moser* would be in violation of some form of the crime of homicide. Rather it is suggesting that in being *Moser*, the one handing over would stand in violation of his duty to rescue his fellow Jew, that is, in violation of his special duty of loyalty to the life of his fellow Jew. It is on that basis that we could well understand the position of Rabbi Judah in the *Tosefta* arguing that the critical issue is not designation but rather the practical question of whether the other person could realistically be saved anyway. We could also then understand why in the final event the prophet Elijah does not disagree with the legal judgment of Rabbi Joshua ben Levi in handing over Ulla bar Koshev, but only pleads for more procrastination, or for having the act of handing over being done by others rather than by Rabbi Joshua ben Levi himself. The underlying assumption of these positions is that the act of handing over, in the final event, does partake of the criminal offense of homicide, albeit only as a non-punishable *Gerama*; but it is a justifiable action when the special loyalty to fellow Jews demanded by the duty of rescue has been exhausted because that duty does not require the giving up of one's own life.

This approach provides us with a further way of understanding why Rambam supported the position of Resh Lakish in preference to that of Rabbi Yochanan in regard to the caravan case, holding that handing over the designated person is only permissible when the designated person was "capitally liable like Sheva ben Bichri."[75] If the essential duty of not handing over even at some risk your own life is based on the affirmative duty of rescue, as is implied by the position of Resh Lakish in the Rabbi Immi case, then it is reasonable for Rambam to maintain that such a duty may be suspended when the individual involved, like Sheva ben Bichri, has become capitally liable, that is, he has become an outlaw – has forfeited his entitlement to the protection of the community through his debased behavior.

Thus, in the position of Rambam, in any given situation, in order to determine whether there is a constraint against *Mesirah*, it is vital to examine both the standing of the non-Jewish authority to whom the person would be handed over – i.e. to which category of *Goyim* that particular person or group belongs – and the status of the person to be handed over – to determine whether the duty of rescue owed to him is intact, or whether by virtue of his conduct he has forfeited that privilege.

3.2.5 Inapplicability of *Mesirah* to Testimony in Non-Jewish Courts: *Rashba* and *Rambi*

While infrequent in the long history of the literature related to testimony in non-Jewish courts, there are occasions in the literature of the *Rishonim* when scholars seemed to suggest that such testimony might constitute a breach of the Jewish law related to *Mesirah*. A primary instance of such apparent mingling of the two concerns appears in a responsum by Rabbi Solomon ben Abraham Adret, the Rashba (c. 1235–1310 Barcelona.) The text is as follows:[76]

> You additionally ask about Reuven who informed concerning Shimon
> that he had been paid by a non-Jew twice.
> He then testified to this effect and caused him financial loss.
> Is his law like that of a *Moser*, to pay him the loss that he had caused him,
> and to excommunicate him, or what is the (applicable) judgment?
> He answered, and this is his language:
> God forbid, Jews should not be suspected of such (actions).
> But, if he did so, he should be excommunicated.
> It is simple that he is subject at least to excommunication,
> for even had the non-Jew subpoenaed him,
> there are not two witnesses – and according to our Law

[75] Rambam, *Hilchot Yesodei HaTorah* 5:5.

[76] Rabbi Solomon ben Abraham Adret Rashba, *Teshuvot She'elot LeHaRashba, First Edition, Rome, circa 1470*. Introduction by Shlomo Zalman Havlin, Responsum no. 160, Jewish National and University Press, Jerusalem, 1976, responsum no. 160.

a party cannot be ordered to pay unless there are two witnesses,
while non-Jewish courts coerce and imprison in matters such as this
even based on a single witness –
and the Jew will then have to redeem himself from prison.
Thus this one through his testimony causes financial loss to the other.
This is not less than that which was taught in Hagozel Batra,[77]
"Rava, or others say R. Huna, proclaimed
to those who go up (to Israel) and those who come down (to Babylonia):
If a Jew knows evidence for the benefit of a non-Jew,[78]
Against his fellow Jew,
and he goes and testifies in a non-Jewish court,
he is to be excommunicated.
What is the reason? Because the non-Jews determine monetary liability
on (the basis of) the testimony of a single witness."
Therefore, he is to be excommunicated.
But beyond that, I say that this one is actually a *Moser*,
and he is not less (criminal) than one who insists that he will inform,[79]
for this one reported entirely of his own free will.
Thus he "pointed out" (endangered) the person and property of the other,
For in their courts he would be held liable for this crime
in both body and property.
Beyond even that, he made himself subject to the death penalty,
for a Jew once having fallen into the hands of a non-Jew
is like an antelope trapped in a net,[80]
as is explicated in *Hagozel Batra* (*Bava Kamma* 117a.)

In his response, Rashba clearly distinguishes between two separate actions on the part of the accused, and the penalty which attaches to each of those actions. Firstly he deals with the fact that the accused testified against a fellow Jew, in favor of the non-Jewish plaintiff, in a non-Jewish court, to the effect that the defendant had collected a debt twice from the non-Jewish plaintiff. In regard to that action, Rashba holds the witness to be liable to excommunication based directly on the legislation of Rava recorded in *Bava Kamma* 113a–114b. Rashba points out, without

[77] *Bava Kamma* 113b-114a.

[78] Note here the absence of the phrase "and he did not subpoena him." But not only is the phrase absent, but this is the first time that one finds, as Rashba states a few lines above, the explicit converse of the phrase which was later inserted into the text. That is, Rashba explicitly indicates that, even if the non-Jew had summoned the Jewish witness to testify, the same restrictions would apply to him according to the legislation of Rava. See above, 2.1.3.

[79] See *Bava Kamma* 117a.

[80] The image is based on Isaiah 51:20, and is explicated thus in the *Gemara*, *Bava Kamma* 117a: "Just as when an antelope falls into a net, no one has mercy on it; so with an Israelite, as soon as even his property falls into the hands of heathen oppressors, no mercy is shown towards him."

explicitly using the term *Dina de'Magista* that this was a non-Jewish court in which the testimony of a single witness would be sufficient to lead the court to order payment on the part of the Jewish defendant. It is precisely this action which the *Gemara* identifies as that which warrants excommunication according to Rava. Strikingly, however, Rashba does not suggest that the loss to the Jewish defendant which warrants the excommunication of the witness is the judicial determination by the non-Jewish court of the defendant's liability to the non-Jewish plaintiff to repay the doubly collected debt. In fact it appears that Rashba accepts that the witness was testifying truthfully and that the Jewish defendant was liable to repay his non-Jewish debtor.[81] Rather, here echoing the suggestion of the Gaonim, Rashba contends that the critical issue is that the court itself is violent and corrupt, that beyond coercing him to pay that which he properly owes the plaintiff, it will imprison the defendant and then demand payment for his redemption from his imprisonment. While such testimony in a corrupt court is punishable under the legislation of Rava by excommunication, Rashba is careful not to use the term *Moser* to describe any aspect of the wrongfulness of this testimonial conduct by the accused.

By contrast, in the last paragraphs of the responsum, Rashba addresses the allegation that the Jewish accused had actually caused the initiation of the action against the Jewish defendant by informing against him concerning the alleged double collection of the debt. It is this allegation that raises the question of whether the accused should be deemed a *Moser*. Rashba identifies three factors that lead him to the conclusion that such informing does result in the accused being liable as a *Moser*. Firstly, the accused had informed purely voluntarily. Rashba is clearly setting this up in contrast to the explicit point that he had made in regard to the testimony element, where, even had the witness been subpoenaed, he insisted that it would not have been permissible for him to testify in a *Magista* court in a manner that would result in unjust economic loss to the Jewish defendant.[82] By contrast, in regard to the act of *Mesirah*, the law had

[81] This impression is supported by the fact that Rashba, in his *Commentary to Bava Kamma* 113a, s.v. *Ha d'amrinan bebar Israel*, quotes the full text of the commentary on this passage by Ravad (which we will deal with in the next chapter), in which the certainty of the accuracy of the testimony of a witness even in a *Magista* court would relieve him of any liability to repay the Jew who suffered no actual loss and was only required to repay what he had attempted to take by fraud. Here, in the case of Rashba, the loss is created by the corruption of the court in its demand for payment to release the defendant from wrongful imprisonment.

[82] See *ibid.* at note 187.

clearly established, and Rambam had codified, that coercion which was not accompanied by direct action by the informer would exempt the informer from liability.[83] Therefore, Rashba here needs to assert that the accused had in fact informed of his own free will.

The second element that Rashba emphasizes is that the "pointing out" of the property of the fellow Jew results not only in potential monetary liability, which the Jewish defendant might well be liable for even by the standards of Jewish law, but also results in the endangerment of his "body and property." This assertion is vital to Rashba because the avoidance of rampant bodily mutilation was an essential reason that the Jewish communities in Spain at his time struggled to gain autonomy in criminal law matters from the Spanish courts. Rashba himself authorized Jewish courts to utilize forms of corporal punishment which had never previously been used in Jewish law. He states, for example:

> Therefore if these chosen judges, seeing the need and the requirement of the period, sentence one either to corporal punishment or to pay a fine in order to reform society, it is in accord with the law of the *Torah*. This is certainly true should they have authority from the King as was the case of Rabbi Eleazar the son of Rabbi Shimon.[84]

His successor, Rabbi Asher ben Yechiel (Rosh) clearly indicated that the use of such punishments by Jewish courts was intended to demonstrate to the Spanish government that Jewish courts were not "easy" on Jews who committed crimes. "Also the community judges with intent to save, as much more blood would be spilled if they were to be judged by the Arabs."[85] The disparity of penalties would not be sufficient in and of itself to classify as *Moser* a Jew who cooperates with the non-Jewish criminal legal system, as is indicated by the reference made by Rashba to the Talmudic case of Rabbi Eleazar son of Rabbi Shimon, whose role as police officer for the Roman government was approved by the *Talmud*,[86] and by Rambam,[87] despite unequivocal disparities in the penal system. However, when that disparity is combined with a third factor, namely

[83] Rambam, *Mishneh Torah, Hilchot Chovel Umazzik* 8:2.

[84] As cited by Rabbi Joseph Karo in *Beit Yosef* to Tur, *Choshen Mishpat*, Laws of Judges, sec. 2.

[85] Zev Farber, "Extra-Legal Punishments in Medieval Jewish Courts," in Yamin Levy (ed.), *Mishpetei Shalom, A Jubilee Volume in Honor of Rabbi Saul (Shalom) Berman*, New York, Yeshivat Chovevei Torah Rabbinical School, with Ktav Publishing House, 2010, pp. 191–232, at pp. 216–217.

[86] *Bava Metzia* 83b.

[87] Rambam, *Hilchot Chovel Umazzik* 8:11.

hatred and antagonism toward Jews that eliminates all justice and mercy and allows unlimited violence to be utilized toward them – then the handing over of a Jew even over a monetary matter results in a direct threat to life, and would constitute the informer as a *Moser*. It is for this reason that Rashba moves immediately from the danger to "body and property" to the citation of the *Gemara* which asserts that a *Moser* would himself be capitally liable if he informs to violent persons who view Jews as "an antelope trapped in a net," whose lives are therefore virtually certain to be taken.

Having already established that the accused in the case before him was subject to excommunication because of his testimony in the *Magista* court, what need did Rashba have to carry the matter further to denominate the accused also as a *Moser*?

To clarify this matter we need to examine an approach of a contemporary of Rashba, Rabbi Meir ben Isaac (Rambi) of Carcassonne,[88] a student of Ravad, whose position we will have occasion to examine further in dealing with the role of *Chillul Hashem* in the permissibility of testimony in non-Jewish courts. According to Rambi, testimony against a fellow Jew in a *Magista* court, a corrupt court, bears the penalty not only of excommunication, but also of monetary liability for any possible damage caused to the Jewish party through his singular testimony asserted to be false. On what basis does he assert the presence of monetary liability?

Rambi refers to testimony in corrupt courts to be "like unto *Mesirah*." He clearly understands that the parameters of the law of *Mesirah* would not allow its actual application in such a situation, as we have seen above, and in particular as has been explicated in the position of Rashba; which is why the term *Moser* rarely appears in the entire literature on the question of testimony in non-Jewish courts. But given the unique position of Rambi, who maintains that there is a moral constraint even against testimony in an honest non-Jewish court, his use of figurative language staining a witness who breaches Rabbinic counsel, if not Rabbinic law, with the accusation of being "like a *Moser*"[89] when he testifies in a corrupt non-Jewish court, is quite shocking.

[88] Cited in Betzalel Ashkenaze, *Shita Mekubetzet* to *Bava Kamma* 113b, s.v. *VehaRam za"l Misarkesta*.

[89] He uses the term twice in this passage, once in the form of *Umikra masur*, and then in the form *kemoser dami*. The latter usage is one illustration of a general Rabbinic pattern of the use of analogy to intensify the negative attitude toward actions which are otherwise

But even for Rambi, the analogy to *Moser* is used only as a basis for his argument that the single witness in a corrupt court is not only subject to excommunication, but can actually be held monetarily liable for the injury he caused to the Jewish defendant by his allegedly false testimony. In this regard, Rambi's position is not significantly different from that of Mordechai ben Hillel, who likewise used the analogy to *Moser* to establish the possibility of financial liability on the part of a single witness in a *Magista* court, based on a subsequent finding by a Jewish court, founded on the testimony of two witnesses, that the Jewish defendant in the non-Jewish court had been damaged unjustly through the testimony of his co-religionist. For both Mordechai ben Hillel and Rambi there is intense opposition to testimony by a single Jewish witness in a corrupt court when a fellow Jew could be unjustly fiscally injured as a consequence of the proceeding. Such untoward action could, according to them, result in a subsequent lawsuit in a Jewish court in which the Jewish witness could be held liable despite the indirectness of the injury which he caused. The analogy to *Moser* simply empowered the Jewish court to impose liability for such indirect injury – it did not constitute a declaration that the witness was in fact by Jewish law a *Moser*.[90] While some other *Rishonim* also struggled to preserve some limited possibility of monetary liability for the single witness in a corrupt court,[91] for the vast majority, such liability was not possible due to the indirect nature of the injury and the absence of specific Talmudic provision which might have moved this instance over from *Gerama*, indirect injury for which there is no liability, to *Garmi*, for which standards of strict liability pertain despite the indirectness of the causation.[92]

Rashba was apparently utilizing the *Moser* designation for the same purpose, to assert the presence of monetary liability for the accused in the case before him. But in contrast to Rambi, and to Mordechai ben Hillel, Rashba clearly did not want to muddy the waters of the legislation of Rava with the designation of even "being like a *Moser*." For Rashba, the legislation of Rava restricting some testimony in corrupt non-Jewish courts would only be punished by excommunication. It would only be in

not particularly serious violations. The broader Talmudic usage of this sort is the term *ke'ilu*.

90 See above 3.2.3.

91 RaMaH, Maharam Mintz and RaMA. For RaMaH see below 4.4. For Maharam Mintz see below 5.1. For RaMA see below 5.3.

92 Rashba, Rabbenu Tam and R. Yosef Karo. For Rashba see earlier in this section. For Rabbenu Tam see below 4.4. For R. Yosef Karo see below 5.2.

a case in which the accused could independently be charged with other action sufficient to establish him as a *Moser*, that monetary or other liability for that separate crime could be imposed. Thus in the case before him quoted above, Rashba found sufficient grounds to deem the accused to be a *Moser*, not on the basis of his testimony, but due to the conjunction of the three factors which he considered to be essential for a change of *Mesirah* to be upheld – a voluntary informing, to a corrupt and violent court, in which hatred of Jews could result in the summary execution of the Jew who came under their jurisdiction due to the charge against him on an economic matter made by a fellow Jew.

3.2.6 Summary of the Elements of the Crime of *Mesirah*

Within the framework of the position of these and other *Rishonim*, as they understand the central relevant Talmudic passages, we need to be clear as to why testimony against a fellow Jew in a non-Jewish court could not be considered to be an act of *Mesirah*. There are multiple elements necessary to constitute the crime of *Mesirah*, each of them containing essential terms or conditions which are subject of diverse understanding, and therefore of divergent legal standards and communal practice. The definition of the crime is that: If a Jew (1) **acted,** (2) **voluntarily,** in such a manner as to (3) **cause** a fellow Jew to be subjected to the jurisdiction or power of (4) **an oppressive authority** which would act in a disproportionally violent manner against the person or property of the victim, (5) including the likelihood of escalation of violence to death of the victim; then he has violated the crime of *Mesirah*.

There is certainly room for debate about the precise nature of what would satisfy the very first definitional condition, "action"; is speech sufficient, or is a physical act necessary such as pointing, or does it actually require taking into possession and handing over in order for this condition to be satisfied? It is obvious that there would be debate about the nature and degree of voluntariness, and the degree of coercion that would exempt an actor from liability for his conduct; is it only physical coercion, or also threat of injury, or implied threat to property, or threat of future injury? The third element, that the voluntary action had to cause the fellow Jew to be made subject to an oppressive authority or power, also leaves room for much debate; for example, what if the oppressor will definitely capture and execute the accused, no matter what resistance is offered by others? The fourth element is in some ways the most complex – how does one define an oppressive authority or power? It was clear to the *Rishonim* that this was not just a simplistic matter of Jew versus non-Jew. A Jewish group might be criminal in nature, and a non-Jewish group might be just. What then is the measure of "oppressive"? Is it that the violence they would utilize does not conform with the violence utilized in the Jewish penal or civil system, or is there some more general concept of justice that would yield the conclusion that the measures taken are indeed unjust? What if, for example, the non-Jewish authority is a government which is acting in the common interest of all of its citizens, both non-Jewish and Jewish, but it utilizes forms of criminal penalty, such as imprisonment, which are not present in the Jewish criminal law system? Would that government, for that reason, be considered "oppressive," or would the shared interest be determinative despite the disparate nature of the penalties? Would discriminatory policies specifically against Jews be a more likely basis for considering a non-Jewish government to be "oppressive" than a general degree of violence in its policies addressed equally to all citizens? Despite all of this room for refinement and debate, the essential elements of the crime of *Mesirah* are clearly established.

As Rashba points out in the responsum studied above, informing against a fellow Jew could constitute *Mesirah* if it meets the test of voluntariness, and if it meets the other conditions. But, if the fellow Jew is already subject to the jurisdiction or power of the non-Jewish, or Jewish, oppressive authority, whether for trial or for summary judgment, then testimony by another Jew in that matter cannot constitute *Mesirah* because then a primary element of the crime, element (3) above, would be absent. The action of testimony might be wrongful, as Rava legislated, but it could not be *Mesirah*. This position of Rashba, maintaining a sharp distinction between the act of testimony, and the act of *Mesirah* – informing or handing over – formed the basis for the next 750 years of Rabbinic discourse.

4

The Creation of a Duty to Testify Against Fellow Jews in Non-Jewish Courts: The Period of the *Rishonim*

By the end of the period of the Gaonim, and the entry into the early period of the *Rishonim* (the eleventh century) the issue of the juridical foundation of the Law of Rava had certainly not been resolved. On the other hand, the practical rules resulting from that early legislation were reasonably clear. The broad general constraint on testimony against a fellow Jew in a non-Jewish court had been whittled down to the situation in which a single Jewish witness would be testifying against a fellow Jew, in favor of a non-Jew, in a fundamentally dishonest non-Jewish court. Only in that situation would there be application of the penalty of excommunication. The issue of whether the excommunication would be accompanied by any form of monetary liability had not yet been raised since the explicit statutory language of Rava had made no direct reference to the possibility of monetary liability to an injured party.

However, the resistance to the Law of Rava had not yet fully played itself out. Over the course of the following centuries in the period of the *Rishonim* in each of the major centers of Jewish legal scholarship, the narrowed applicability of the restraint on testimony was affirmed, while a newly emerging notion grew – that there might be circumstances under which it would actually be mandatory according to Jewish law for a witness to testify in a non-Jewish court against a fellow Jew in favor of the non-Jewish litigant. We will examine five different approaches taught in the period of the *Rishonim* to demonstrate that such a legal duty could actually exist.

4.1 TO AVOID *CHILLUL HASHEM* (DESECRATION OF GOD'S NAME)

Rabbi Abraham ben David of Posquieres (Ravad) (1125–1198) presents one such approach in his commentary to *Bava Kamma* 113b.[1]

1. That which we say concerning a Jew who knew evidence in favor of a non-Jew against his fellow Jew, and went and testified against him (in a *Magista* court), that we excommunicate him.
2. It appears to me (that this would apply only) where the Jewish defendant had a valid legal argument (for his position) according to Our Law [as a result of which he would be held not liable,] while by Their Law he would be ordered to pay.
3. But if the testimony of the witness was such that the Jewish defendant would have no valid legal argument – for example, if the defendant confessed directly to the witness and invited him to testify on his behalf, and said to him,
4. "I intend to deny my liability and (if you support me) we can divide the money between us; or (at least) you should remain silent, because of your love for me, and I will keep the debt for myself."
5. And the witness did not leave the company of the defendant, so that the defendant could not claim that he had paid the plaintiff after that time.
6. So that the witness is certain that the (subsequent) denial of liability by the defendant is a claim which has no truth to it.
7. I say that this is a *Chillul Hashem*,[2] (a desecration of God's name), and the witness has a legal duty (to testify in order) to prevent him from executing the crime.
8. And even were this a case of *Hafka'at Halva'ato*, (a denial of liability to a loan for which he might in fact be found not liable according to Jewish Law), in an instance where there is a *Chillul Hashem*, it is forbidden.
9. And most certainly in a court in which they would require him[3] to take an oath (the witness has a duty to testify), lest he come to make a false oath.

The most striking element in this passage by Ravad is the move from the discussion of Rava's Law of prohibited (*Assur*) testimony, through the circumstances where such testimony would be permitted (*Muttar*), all the way across the legal spectrum to the discovery of a circumstance in

[1] *Sefer Chiddushe HaRavad al Masechet Bava Kamma*, ed. by Shmuel Atlas, 2nd edition, Jerusalem, Feldheim Pub., 1963 at p. 313.

[2] See Rambam, *Mishneh Torah, Hilchot Yesodei HaTorah* 5:10. See also Zevin, *Encyclopedia Talmudit*, vol. XVII, entry *Chillul Hashem*, columns 340–360.

[3] See below for exploration of the question of who is the subject of "him," the defendant or the witness?

which the testimony would actually be a legal duty (*Chayyav.*) Ravad, if he was aware of the position of Rav Hai, was not satisfied with the situation in which the testimony would be advisable, albeit still discretionary. Ravad uncovered two separate legal instruments which enabled him to construct a case for the existence of a duty to testify against a fellow Jew in favor of a non-Jew in a non-Jewish court. Let's examine these in turn.

4.1.1 The Biblical Texts of *Chillul Hashem*

A full explication of the law and concept of *Chillul Hashem*, the desecration of the Divine name, is beyond the parameters of this work. However, certain essential elements of both the concept and its function in Jewish law are necessary in order to understand the nature of the position of Ravad and others on the matter of when testimony in a non-Jewish court would be mandatory.

In a short series of five chapters in the middle of the Book of Leviticus, chapters 18–22, there is a codex of six verses recording the prohibition against desecrating the Holy name of God. One of them, the last in the series, Leviticus 22:32 is the most general of the statements:

You shall not profane my Holy name,
that I may be sanctified in the midst of the Israelite people –
I am the Lord who sanctifies you.

The balance between the first clause of the verse forbidding profanation of the Divine name, and the second clause, mandating sanctification of the Lord, led the Sages to the understanding that in any situation in which sanctification was mandated, the failure to perform it constituted profanation of God's name. Thus the *Talmud* reasonably concludes that in a situation where giving up one's life to resist the evil order of an oppressor is mandated as sanctification of the Divine name; failure to do so would constitute profaning God's name.[4] While this specific association of desecration of the Divine name with failure to sanctify His name is strong in the verse itself, it is worth noting that the immediately preceding verse, Leviticus 22:31, mandates the observance of all of God's laws:

You shall faithfully observe My commandments, I am the Lord.

[4] *Sanhedrin* 74a–b.

The other five verses all describe the profanation of the Divine name as being in consequence of the violation of a specific law. Two of them are specific to idolatry. Thus, Leviticus 18:21:

Do not allow any of your children to be offered up to Molech,
and do not profane the name of your God,
I am the Lord.

Interestingly, the bulk of chapter 18 deals with sexual crimes, as in verses 6 through 20 and then again in verses 22 and 23. Verse 21 seems to interpolate the crime of idolatry, and its attendant desecration of the Divine name, into the midst of the prohibitions against all forms of sexual crimes. This association of idolatry with sexual crimes is particularly significant given the power of the Rabbinic association of the two of them as fundamental laws for which one would have to give up life rather than submit to coerced violation. It is further worth noting that the conclusion of the passage, verse 26, commands the Jewish people to observe all of God's laws:

But you must keep My laws and My rules,
and you must not do any of those abhorrent things,
neither the citizen nor the stranger who resides amongst you.

Leviticus 20:3 is the second verse which specifically refers to an idolatrous act, again the worship of Molech, as constituting desecration of the Divine name:

And I will set My face against that man
and will cut him off from among his people,
because he gave of his offspring to Molech
and so defiled My sanctuary
and profaned My holy name.

Here, too, the paragraph discusses idolatry in verses 2 through 7, then sexual crimes in verses 8 through 21. And again, the passage concludes in verse 22 with a general demand for the observance of all God's laws:

You shall faithfully observe all My laws and all My regulations,
lest the land to which I bring you to settle in spew you out.

A third verse in which the desecration of the Divine name is associated with a specific criminal act is Leviticus 19:12:

You shall not swear falsely by My name,
profaning the name of your God,

I am the Lord.

While this prohibition against false oaths in the name of God is itself presumed to be an element of the third commandment, the powerful addition here of the explicit desecration of the Divine name clearly magnifies the significance of the prohibition. Again, looking at the passage in its entirety, we note that verses 2 and 31 of the passage deal with the prohibition against idolatry, verses 20 and 29 deal with sexual crimes, and again the passage concludes in verse 37 with an admonition to observe all of God's commandments: "You shall faithfully observe all My laws and all My rules, I am the Lord."

We have thus far seen a single verse entailing a general prohibition against the profanation of the Divine name; and three separate verses implicating this same prohibition in the performance of specific crimes, those of idolatry and false oath. In the passages in which all four of these verses are contained there is special emphasis on the duty of the entire Jewish people to be obedient to all of the Divine commandments; and in the latter three passages there is special emphasis on the horror of the crimes of idolatry and sexual wrongdoing.

The remaining two verses that identify actions constituting profanation of the Divine name are addressed only to the *Kohanim*, rather than to the entire Jewish people.

The beginning of Leviticus chapter 21 records the special prohibition against *Kohanim* coming into contact with dead bodies except those of his seven close relatives in whose burial he may participate. Leviticus 21:6 then informs us that becoming ritually impure would constitute a violation of the holiness of the *Kohen*, and a profanation of the Divine name:

They shall be holy to their God
And not profane the name of their God;
For they offer the Lord's offerings by fire, the food of their God,
And so must be holy.

It seems striking that even here, the profanation of the Divine name is surrounded by references to idolatry – pagan mourning rituals – in verse 5; and to sexual restrictions – constraints against marriage of a *Kohen* to a divorcee, to a prostitute or to one born of an illicit marriage – in verse 7.

The further verse which is addressed distinctively to *Kohanim* is Leviticus 22:2, which says:

Instruct Aaron and his sons to be scrupulous about the sacred donations

Which the Israelite people consecrate to Me,
Lest they profane My holy name, I am the Lord.

The continuation of the passage makes clear that the scrupulous behavior demanded of the *Kohanim* is that they must not handle or eat of sanctified foods when they are in a state of ritual impurity through any cause.[5] Indeed this restriction was implied already in the previous verse cited, Leviticus 21:6, where the motive clause which explained why the *Kohanim* were not permitted to become ritually impure through contact with dead bodies was precisely this fact – that they eat the Lord's offerings.

4.1.2 Rambam on *Chillul Hashem*

We can now understand the way in which Rambam, both in the *Sefer HaMitzvot*[6] and in the *Mishneh Torah*,[7] divides the prohibition of *Chillul Hashem* into three separate sets of actions. The first set, applicable to all Jews, says Rambam in *Sefer HaMitzvot*, is:

> Anyone of whom a demand is made (by an oppressor) during a period of persecution (against the Jewish religion), to violate any law of the *Torah* ... or, even not at a time of persecution, one of whom it is demanded that he violate the commands against idolatry, sexual crimes or homicide – is duty bound to give up his life to be killed rather than violate the law. And if he violated the law to save his life, he has profaned the Divine name, in violation of this prohibition.

This element of the crime of *Chillul Hashem* is based on the verse in Leviticus 22:23, which is the most general of the verses we saw. The power of this special application of *Chillul Hashem* resides precisely in the balance of the verse. "You shall not profane my Holy name, that I may be sanctified in the midst of the Israelite people." Since in these situations one is duty bound to risk life in order to sanctify the Divine name, the failure to do so constitutes its opposite, an act of profaning the Divine name.

We should note that the special application of this principle of *Chillul Hashem* to the instances of idolatry and sexual crimes is already intimated in the *Torah* itself in the fact that in four of the six instances of

[5] Doing so involves a double profanation, that of the Divine name, as in Lev. 22:2; and that of the sanctified food itself, as in the later verses, Lev. 22:9 and 15.

[6] Rambam, *Sefer HaMitzvot*, Negative Commandment no. 64.

[7] Rambam, *Mishneh Torah*, *Hilchot Yesodei HaTorah* 5:1, 10 and 11.

the appearance of the prohibition, the broader passage seems to be focused particularly on those two kinds of crime. In fact, the *Talmud* itself seems to recognize the absence of any Biblical connection between *Chillul Hashem* and homicide, and so argues that homicide belongs in the set because of its explicit association with the sexual crime of rape,[8] where the *Torah* authorizes killing of an attempting rapist in third-party self-defense by a comparison with the existence of that right in the case of a threatened homicide.[9]

Analytically, we could describe the situation in the following manner:

a. There is a legal duty not to violate any *Torah* law.
b. There is a legal duty to protect one's own life.
c. How is one to act when these two principles are in conflict?
d. Rescue of one's own life has priority over other duties, including the duty to not violate *Torah* law, except for:
   1) the legal duty to not perform acts of idolatry, incest or homicide; and
   2) the duty not to submit to systematic religious persecution against Judaism expressed in a demand to violate any Divine law (even privately); and
   3) the duty not to submit to an individual who, even motivated by personal benefit or pleasure, demands violation of any Divine law in public (i.e. in the presence of ten other Jews).
f. In these three instances, there is a legal duty to sanctify the Divine name by risking death (through resistance of the oppressor) to avoid violation.
g. Failing to undertake the risk, violating one of these laws to rescue one's own life without resistance is violation of *Chillul Hashem.*

Thus, in this first set of actions, the law of *Chillul Hashem* is an additional prohibition, added as a secondary crime to intensify the severity of the already criminal behavior which the actor is being coerced to perform.

The second set of actions, which is general in nature, that is, involves violation of the prohibition of *Chillul Hashem* when performed by any Jew Rambam describes as follows:

Also, when a person violates a prohibition in which there is neither sexual pleasure nor any benefit, but rather he shows through his action disdain (towards) and not

[8] *Sanhedrin* 74a.

[9] Deuteronomy 22:26.

being bound (by God's Laws) – he thereby profanes the Divine name and warrants lashes. This is why the verse says, "You shall not swear falsely by My name, profaning the name of your God." (Lev. 19:12).

Here, Rambam is apparently basing himself on the proposition that the frequent use of the Biblical injunction against profaning God's name suggests that the individual instances, such as false oath, are no more than illustrative of a global principle which is actually applicable to all laws of the *Torah*. This awareness is intensely suggested in the text of *Torah* itself through the fact that in five of the six instances of reference to this prohibition in *Torah*, as we noted above, the broader passage makes specific reference to the duty to observe all of God's commandments. This approach is already suggested in the *Midrash Halacha* to Chapter 19 in Leviticus, in its application of the law of *Chillul Hashem* to the content of a later verse in the same chapter, Leviticus 19:15.[10] The *Sifra* argues that a judge who falsifies a judicial outcome and a merchant who falsifies his weights are both in violation of the law of *Chillul Hashem*, as propounded in the earlier verse, Leviticus 19:12.

In this second set of actions through which the law of *Chillul Hashem* is violated, as in the first set, the action itself is forbidden, be it the false oath, the judicial falsification of judgment, or the merchant utilizing fraudulent weights and measures. The crime of *Chillul Hashem* constitutes an additional criminal charge to the charge related to the action being intentionally performed. This additional charge can be leveled, according to Rambam, only in a situation in which the behavior of the criminal manifested distinctive elements of rebelliousness against the authority of God, where the criminal act was not motivated by personal pleasure or profit, but rather by elements which reflect an especially negative attitude toward the law and the legislator. In *Sefer HaMitzvot* those elements are "disdain" and "rejection of Divine authority"; in *Mishneh Torah* the elements are identified as "a spirit of derision, to arouse Divine anger."[11] By contrast, in the first set, the additional element was simply the behavior – the refusal to act in a manner reflective of *Kiddush Hashem* (sanctification of the Divine name). There, it was the behavioral negative reflection on God's identity that justified the additional criminal charge, not the subjective motivation of the action. However, in both sets,

[10] *Sifra Kedoshim*, *parsha* 2, *perek* 4; and *parsha* 3, *perek* 8.

[11] *Sefer HaMitzvot*, Negative Commandments, no. 63. *Mishneh Torah*, *Yesodei HaTorah* 5:10.

the underlying action to which the additional criminal charge of *Chillul Hashem* was added was clearly a violation of a legal duty to refrain from certain behavior.

The third set identified by Rambam is radically different from the first two sets in two ways. Firstly, the concern does not relate to all Jews, but only to a special class of Jews. Secondly, the underlying behavior may even be actually permissible, but would be made forbidden by the attachment to it of the crime of *Chillul Hashem*. Rambam describes this set as follows in *Sefer HaMitzvot*:

> The segment related to special persons is: A person reputed to be especially righteous and of great integrity who does some act which appears to the populace to be sinful and to be an act of a nature that a righteous person such as he should not perform it – even though the act is actually permissible – has profaned the Name.

In *Mishneh Torah*, Rambam draws on the Talmudic exposition[12] of this set to provide the following concrete examples of situations in which "a person of great *Torah* stature who is renowned for his piety" would be in violation of *Chillul Hashem* even though the act itself is permissible according to Jewish law:

> For example, a person who purchases [merchandise] and does not pay for it immediately, although he possesses the money, and when the sellers demand payment he pushes them off; a person who jests immoderately; or who eats and drinks near or among the common people; or whose conduct with other people is not gentle and he does not receive them with a favorable countenance, but rather contests with them and vents his anger; and the like. Everything depends on the stature of the sage; he must be careful with himself and go beyond the measure of the law.[13]

The Talmudic material never clarifies precisely how this category is derived from the Biblical laws which refer to *Chillul Hashem*. We should consider the possibility that this set is derived by analogy from the two instances in which the *Torah* forbids to *Kohanim* actions that are permissible to the rest of the Jewish people. As is indicated explicitly in Leviticus 21:6, the motive of the special restriction against a *Kohen* becoming ritually impure, resides in his special relationship to God (he offers the food of the Lord), and the distinctive demand that he be Holy. Therefore, if

[12] Yoma 86a, and other sources cited in Joseph ben Ephraim Karo, *Kesef Mishnah* to Rambam, *Hilchot Yesodei HaTorah* 5:11.

[13] Rambam, *Mishneh Torah*, *Yesodei HaTorah* 5:11, trans. by Eliyahu Touger.

the *Kohen* performs an act permissible to the rest of the Jewish people, becoming ritually impure, then he will have profaned the Divine name. Of course, once the *Torah* forbids this act to all *Kohanim*, the analytic model shifts, and this instance becomes just like the prior elements in which a forbidden act becomes doubly criminal by the addition of the sin of *Chillul Hashem*.

However, based on this model, it appears that the Sages constructed a form of *Chillul Hashem* which was applicable beyond the *Kohanim*, to persons whose distinctive holiness, righteousness, integrity and scholarship made them embodiments of the honor of God Himself. Therefore, for such persons to act in a manner which reflected badly upon themselves, even if the action itself was perfectly permissible, would result in disgrace to God Himself – and therefore, *Chillul Hashem*. This is analogous to the Rabbinic position that in regard to the duty of honor owed to scholars and elders, there is a basic level which cannot be waived by the scholar or elder, because that level of honor due to him is in reality the honor due through him to *Torah*, or to God Himself. The waiver of that honor consequently would result in disgrace to *Torah* or to God, which would not be tolerable.[14]

What is it then that constitutes *Chillul Hashem* according to Rambam? It is the failure to recognize that there are values which transcend the value of one's own life, and instead, acting to protect one's life by directly breaching those superior values. What are those breaches that necessitate resistance to the point of death?

1. The primary breach is the repudiation of the Covenant between God and the Jewish people, in order to rescue one's own life. This repudiation can take three forms:
   a. An act of idolatry, in which the very nature of God is repudiated.
   b. In times of religious persecution, encouraging the enemy to believe that he can use the primacy of life to defeat the preservation of Judaism, thus enabling the repudiation of God's very presence through the Covenant.
   c. Demoralization of a Jewish community (an *Edah*) by submission to an individual oppressor who is an antagonist of God, thereby repudiating God's authority over the Jewish people within the Covenant.

[14] See Rambam, *Mishneh Torah*, *Talmud Torah*, end of 7:13 and comment of Karo, *Kesef Mishneh* to Rambam, *Hilchot Yesodei HaTorah*, 5:11.

2. The second form of *Chillul Hashem* is the breach of the sexual boundaries of the Covenant of Family in order to save one's own life. The breach of those boundaries within one's own family would be manifest through an act of incest; or the breach of the boundaries of other families would be through an act of adultery.
3. The third form of *Chillul Hashem* according to Rambam would be the breach of the Covenant formed by God between all human beings by their being common bearers of the Image of God (*Tzelem Elokim*). This breach, repudiating God as Creator, and thus denying the essential equality of all human beings, would be manifest in an individual choosing to directly take the life of another innocent person in order to protect his own life.

The way Rambam constructs his presentation of the law of *Chillul Hashem* both in the *Sefer Hamitzvot* and in the *Mishneh Torah*, the essential forms of Covenantal breach are fully spelled out in the context of the situations of the duty to resist evil demands threatening one's own life. The next two sets of instances of *Chillul Hashem* echo the earlier ones in non-life-threatening situations. Thus the second set, which involves the intentional violation of any law of the *Torah*, requires that the intention be specifically to deny Divine authority. As noted above, in *Sefer HaMitzvot* those elements are "disdain" and "rejection of Divine authority"; in *Mishneh Torah* the elements are identified as "a spirit of derision, to arouse Divine anger."[15] This means that the second set is just a less dramatic instance of an individual acting in a manner which reflects the repudiation of Divine authority.

The third set of actions constituting *Chillul Hashem* are of particular importance to us. They reflect the greater demands placed on *Kohanim* because of their special holiness, that is, because they are the executors of the Divine worship in the sanctuary. It is striking that the two areas of special demand placed on them in the Biblical passage relate to idolatry and marital conduct. They, in their special covenantal relationship to God, are not to engage in actions which could create even a suggestion of idolatry, or of idolatrous death cults. Therefore, they cannot even be present with a dead body other than with immediate family members; and may not engage in mourning practices which are imitative of pagan cults. As for their formation of covenant of marriage and family, they

[15] *Sefer HaMitzvot*, Negative Commandments, no. 63. *Mishneh Torah*, *Yesodei HaTorah* 5:10.

may not marry in a manner which might create even a distant suspicion of either impropriety or of their condoning impermissible marriages by others. The parallel to *Kohanim* constructed by the Sages as the third set of situations in which there is a special concern for *Chillul Hashem* is as to other persons who, while not *Kohanim*, are living models of righteous behavior, whose actions are therefore associated directly with the Divine will and the Divine nature. Therefore, if such a righteous person acts in a debased manner, it constitutes a repudiation of the nature of God, in a manner parallel to breach of the Covenant by engaging in idolatry.

4.1.3 Ravad's Use of *Chillul Hashem*

We can now return to the way in which Ravad used the law of *Chillul Hashem* as grounds for overcoming the law of Rava. According to Rava, as limited by later Sages, it was forbidden for a Jew to testify as a single witness against a fellow Jew in a non-Jewish *Magista* (corrupt) court. However, according to Ravad, in a situation where the failure to testify would result in *Chillul Hashem*, as would be the case if the Jewish defendant was known to the witness to be lying, and would then escape his just liability to the non-Jewish plaintiff – then the single Jewish witness was obligated to testify even in a *Magista* court, in order to attempt to avoid the *Chillul Hashem*. In all prior discussion of the law of *Chillul Hashem*, the law operated either to intensify a prohibition by adding the charge of *Chillul Hashem* to the already criminal behavior, or to prohibit an act which was otherwise permissible, on the grounds that while permissible its performance would result in a *Chillul Hashem* and therefore needed to be forbidden. By contrast, in Ravad's presentation, an act which was forbidden according to Jewish law would be made not only permissible, but mandatory, in consequence of the application of the law of *Chillul Hashem*. What precedent is there for this extreme power resulting from application of the law of *Chillul Hashem*?

I have been able to discover only a single instance in the literature of the Talmudic era in which this particular power of the principle of *Chillul Hashem* might be reflected.

The ninth chapter of the Book of Joshua describes the deceptive behavior of the Gibeonites, a tribe resident in the land of Canaan. The Gibeonites, fearing utter destruction at the hands of the Israelite army entering Canaan, disguised themselves as exhausted travelers, told Joshua and the Israelite Elders that they had heard of the wonders of the Israelite people and had traveled from a distant place to enter into a treaty with the Israelite people. Joshua and the tribal heads, taken in by the deception, publicly, by oath, entered into a treaty with the Gibeonites.[16] A few days later, when the deception was uncovered, and the local Gibeonite cities were discovered, the people demanded war against the local Gibeonites, but Joshua and the tribal leaders insisted on abiding by the treaty,[17] "The Israelites did not strike them, since the chieftains of the community had sworn to them by the Lord, the God of Israel."[18] In fact, when other local tribes heard of the betrayal of the Canaanite cause by the Gibeonites, they attacked Gibeon, and Joshua and the Israelite army rushed to their defense to uphold the treaty.[19]

This narrative is used by the *Talmud* to provide the supportive evidence for the position of Rabbi Judah, who maintains that any oath which is publicly made is not subject to annulment.[20] It is for that reason, according to Rabbi Judah, that Joshua and the Elders did not simply annul their vow, thereby annulling the treaty, freeing them to fulfill their Biblical duties to destroy the Gibeonite cities and kill the population (Deut. 20:12–18) or to drive them from the land (Ex. 23:29–33). It was, according to Rabbi Judah, the distinctive power of the public oath in the name of God that constrained Joshua and the Israelite people from executing what would otherwise have been their clear Biblical duties of war against and even extermination of the Gibeonites.[21]

By contrast, the position of the Sages was that even a publicly made oath was subject to annulment, particularly when the oath (and treaty) involved fraud in the inception, as in this case where the Gibeonites directly lied about an essential element of the facts – denying their local origins. That being the case, why did Joshua not simply declare the oath and the treaty to be null and void, and pursue his responsibilities to war against the Gibeonites? To which the Sages respond, "the reason the

16 Joshua 9:3–15.

17 Joshua 9:16–27.

18 Joshua 9:18.

19 Joshua 10:1–15.

20 *Gittin* 46a.

21 The Tosafists, *ad loc.*, s.v. *keivan d'amru*, resist the direct implication of the Talmudic discussion that according to Rabbi Judah the public oath itself has sufficient power to override the *DeOraita* obligations. They argue instead that the Biblical duties to war or drive them out would still have pertained because the oath itself would have been null in the face of its being contrary to these Divine commands. Their conclusion is that even according to Rabbi Judah, the real force which required Israelite violation of other Divine commandments was the operation of *Chillul Hashem*. The identical conclusion was arrived at by Rashba, Commentary to *Gittin* 46a, albeit via a different logical path.

Israelites did not slay them was (*M'shum Kedushat Hashem*,) because [this would have impaired] the sanctity of God's name." Thus, according to the Sages it was not the legal force of the oath in the Divine name which constrained the Israelites from the fulfillment of their Biblical duties, but rather the force of the *Chillul Hashem*, the desecration of the Divine name which would result from the appearance that the Israelite nation was in breach of its oath.[22]

We have before us, then, according to the majority and thus accepted position of the Sages, the following situation:

1. The Israelites have an affirmative duty to war against those Canaanite nations who do not accept the terms of a peace offer which would require them to accept the seven Noahite commandments and become fully subject to the political authority of the Israelite State and government.[23]
2. The Israelites have a duty to not allow residence in the land of Israel to non-Jews who have not accepted upon themselves the duty to adhere to the seven Noahite commandments.[24]
3. The Israelites were deceived into making an oath by the name of God, entering into a peace treaty with the Gibeonites which did not require the latter to adhere to the seven Noahite commandments, since they had represented themselves as a non-Canaanite nation which did not, and had no intention to, reside in the land of Canaan/Israel.
4. This oath and resultant treaty were not binding upon the Israelites due to the fraud in the inception of the agreement.
5. However, not adhering to the oath and the resultant treaty would result in violation of the Prohibition against *Chillul Hashem* – of profanation of the Divine name – since there was public knowledge of the oath and treaty, and the Israelites would be perceived as acting in breach of their oath by God's name.
6. But, honoring the oath and the treaty, which the Israelites are not obligated by law to do, would result in the failure to perform the Positive Divine Commandment of war against the Canaanite nations; and violation of the Negative Divine Commandment

[22] The language of Rambam, *Mishneh Torah*, *Hilchot Melachim* 6:5 is explicit that the reason for upholding the otherwise null oath was the concern with *Chillul Hashem*.

[23] Deut. 20:11–12. Rambam, *Sefer HaMitzvot*, Positive Commandments, no. 187. Rambam, *Mishneh Torah*, Laws of Kings 6:1.

[24] Exodus 23:33. Rambam *Sefer HaMitzvot*, Negative Commandments, no. 51. Rambam, *Mishneh Torah*, Laws of Idolatry 10:6.

of not allowing residence in the Land of Israel to non-Jews who have not formally accepted upon themselves the seven Noahite commandments.

7. In the face of these conflicting alternatives, the power of the prohibition against *Chillul Hashem* is, according to the Sages, of sufficient magnitude that it required the Israelites to honor their oath and treaty, despite the consequent non-performance of a positive duty; and violation of a prohibition.
8. That is, the avoidance of *Chillul Hashem* required the Jews in the time of Joshua to perform an otherwise prohibited act.

This is, I believe, the only Talmudic instance in which a prohibited act is made not only permissible/discretionary, but actually mandatory by the concern that failure to perform it will result in violation of the prohibition against *Chillul Hashem*. It is this precedent which could serve as the legal foundation for the position of Ravad. Of course, there are significant distinctions between the case of the Gibeonites and the case of testimony in non-Jewish courts. In the former case the concern with *Chillul Hashem* justifies direct overriding of *DeOraita* (revealed) laws, whereas in the testimony case the prohibition being overridden is of Rabbinic origin. On the other hand, in the Gibeonite case the laws overridden are violated through inaction, whereas in the testimony case the law is overridden by an affirmative act of testimony. Most confounding in comparing the two cases is that in the Gibeonite case the oath was actually made by the tribal leaders in a manner which implies that the nation as a whole is bound. Therefore, when the nation has a duty to prevent *Chillul Hashem*, it is the appearance of breach of a national oath which yields the duty resting on the nation as a whole to prevent the *Chillul Hashem*. By contrast, in the testimony case it is the Jewish defendant whose action would be causing the *Chillul Hashem*, while, according to Ravad, it is the witness upon whom the duty to prevent such a *Chillul Hashem* rests with a degree of gravity sufficient to cause him to violate a Rabbinic prohibition.

These distinctions appear less significant in the light of another Talmudic passage which treats a later event related to the Gibeonites. II Samuel, chapter 21 describes an extraordinary series of events in which King David consults with God about the cause of a famine in Israel. God informs David that the famine is national punishment "for Saul and for his bloody house, because he put to death the Gibeonites."[25] David

[25] II Samuel 21:1. Other aspects of this narrative were treated above in 3.2.1.3.

attempts to gain reconciliation with the Gibeonites, who demand that seven descendents of Saul be delivered to them to be killed by hanging, to which David consents. After the seven are killed by the Gibeonites, Rizpah, concubine of Saul, mother of two of the slaughtered men, did not allow the bodies of her two sons to be buried. Then David brought the bones of Saul and Jonathan to be buried together with the bodies of Saul's newly killed two sons and five grandsons, in the burial cave of Kish, the father of Saul, in the territory of the tribe of Benjamin. With this, the famine ended.[26]

The *Talmud*[27] raises two legal objections to the conduct described in this passage. Firstly, how could David have handed over the innocent sons and grandsons of Saul to be killed in the face of the explicit Divine command, "Parents shall not be executed for their children, nor shall children be executed for their parents, a person shall be executed for his own crime" (Deut. 24:16.)? The *Talmud* responds, "R. Hiyya b. Abba replied in the name of R. Johanan: It is better that one letter (law) be rooted out of the *Torah* than that the Divine name shall be publicly profaned." The clearest meaning of this teaching of Rabbi Jochanan is that if the breach of the national Jewish oath/treaty with the Gibeonites were not punished, it would constitute a desecration of the Divine name. The need to prevent such desecration would warrant overriding the Biblical law which forbad vicarious liability.

The second legal objection raised by this Talmudic passage is to the delay in burial of the sons of Rizpah, contrary to the explicit Biblical command, "Do not allow his body to remain hung on the tree overnight, rather you should bury him the same day, for the hung body is a disgrace to God." (Deut. 21:23). The *Talmud* offers a parallel response:

> R. Johanan replied in the name of R. Simeon b. Jehozadak: It is proper that one letter (law) be rooted out of the *Torah* so that thereby the heavenly name shall be publicly hallowed. For passers-by were enquiring, "What kind of men are these?" – "These are royal princes" – "And what have they done?" – "They laid their hands upon unattached strangers" – Then they exclaimed: "There is no nation in existence which one ought to join as much as this one. If [the punishment of] royal princes was so great. how much more that of common people; and if such [was the justice done for] unattached strangers, how much more so for Israelites"[28]

[26] II Samuel 21:2–14.

[27] *Yevamot* 79a.

[28] *Yevamot* 79a. The composite nature of this passage is self-evident. The later comment explains the teaching of Rabbi Jochanan in a manner which emphasizes the ethical

Again, the most direct understanding of this passage is that what the *Kiddush Hashem* achieved in the public display of the bodies of the princes of the House of Saul was to demonstrate that an oath taken, a treaty entered into, even with the lowest socio-economic class of persons in the nation, would be honored; and that the violation of such an oath and its resultant disgrace of God would be punished with the greatest severity.

The upshot of this passage is unequivocal – the duty to sanctify the Divine name, and its correlative, the duty to avoid the desecration of the Divine name, are of sufficient power to justify overriding express Biblical commandments, even ones as powerful as the ban against vicarious punishment and the duty of immediate burial. Therefore, despite the potential significance of the distinctions explored above, it appears that Ravad could in fact be relying on the power of the duty to prevent *Chillul Hashem*, as reflected in the case of the Gibeonites, as the basis for the shift from Rabbinically forbidden action to Rabbinically required action in the testimony case. This impression is intensified by the closing element in Ravad's presentation on this matter, where he says, "And most certainly in a court in which they would require him[29] to take an oath (the witness has a duty to testify), lest he come to make a false oath." The most logical reading of this sentence is that it has to do with an oath to be taken by the defendant – that in the face of the possibility that the defendant would actually lie even under oath, the witness has a special duty to prevent his fellow Jew from proceeding with his planned fraud. This would have special relevance for the duty to prevent *Chillul Hashem* since the critical Biblical text in which the general formulation of the crime of *Chillul Hashem* for intentional violation of law is found is the text related to false oaths (Lev. 19:12). By contrast, in regard to the witness the issue at stake is whether he ought to testify. There had been no consideration whatsoever of his testifying falsely, with or without an oath. The introduction of this element by Ravad is at least suggestive that he is building on the Biblical and Talmudic discussion of the Gibeonites as the basis for his contention that the duty of avoiding *Chillul Hashem* could result in the radical reordering of the legal duties for the witness.

It is worth noting that Ravad considers the behavior of the Jewish defendant to be a *Chillul Hashem* in the case he described, despite the

component of the treatment of unattached strangers, rather than the severity of the *Chillul Hashem* engendered by the breach of the oath specifically to the Gibeonites.

29 The question of who is the subject of "him," the defendant or the witness, was left open. See 4.1. at note 3.

fact that it is possible that the only other person besides the defendant and the witness who actually knew that a criminal fraud was taking place is the non-Jewish victim, that is the plaintiff himself. Nevertheless, for Ravad, that knowledge by a single non-Jew that a Jew is intentionally committing a wrong in violation of God's *Torah*, is sufficient to have this considered a *Chillul Hashem*. By contrast, while it is possible that greater notoriety as to the criminal behavior of the Jewish defendant might actually result from the testimony against him offered by the Jewish witness, he is viewed as duty bound to offer his testimony. The important implication is that support of Jewish criminal behavior is *Chillul Hashem*, a disgrace to God; but knowledge of Jewish efforts to produce justice against Jewish wrongdoers is *Kiddush Hashem*, a sanctification of God's name, even if in the process Jewish wrongdoing is revealed.

4.1.4 *Chillul Hashem* as a Factor for the *Rishonim* of Ashkenaz

The relevance of the issue of *Chillul Hashem* to the action of the potential witness himself was a matter addressed directly by the *Rishonim* of Ashkenaz. First to address the issue was Raavan, Rabbi Eliezer ben Natan of Mainz, c. 1090–1170, in his commentary to the Talmudic passage in *Bava Kamma* 113b-114a.[30] Raavan cites the legislation of Rava,[31] and when the passage asserts as the basis for excommunication the fact that the non-Jewish court will order payment by the defendant based on the testimony of a single witness, Raavan adds the precise words of Rashi, "with the result that he causes him loss not in accordance with the (Jewish) law."[32] Thus clearly for Raavan, the theory which underlies the restriction on the witness is that he would, through his testimony in the non-Jewish court, be causing indirect damages to the Jewish defendant which he would not have to suffer under the applicable Jewish law.

Raavan then adds the following:

1. It appears to me that in a location where the custom (in transactions) between a Jew and a non-Jew, is
2. that they appoint a Jew and a non-Jew to be the witnesses between them,
3. then it is permissible for the Jewish witness to testify,

[30] *Sefer Raavan*, Part 2, end of Tractate *Bava Kamma*, at p. 194b.
[31] With the expected omission of the words "*velo teva'o*."
[32] Rashi *Bava Kamma* 114a, s.v. *Apuma dechad*.

4. since from the outset they were accepted for that purpose.
5. For here it is said, "they only said this (restriction) in regard to a single witness
6. but in a case of two witnesses, they are not excommunicated";
7. and that is because the defendant is then found liable based on "complete testimony" (*edut gemurah*, that is, testimony by a full set of two witnesses).
8. Here too, since he is ordered to pay in accordance with the law –
9. we do not excommunicate (the Jewish witness).
10. Additionally, it would be a *Chillul Hashem*
11. if he (the designated Jewish witness) were not to testify,
12. since the non-Jewish party had relied on him –
13. he would say, "they are not trustworthy people!"
14. And even more, for it is the law of the land,
15. and "the law of the land is law."

In this striking passage, Raavan offers three separate reasons why a single Jewish witness, having been designated together with a non-Jewish witness at the inception of the transaction, would be permitted, or even obligated, to testify against a Jewish defendant in favor of a non-Jew in a non-Jewish court. The first reason, presented in lines 4 through 9 above, argues that the Jewish witness would be permitted to testify because, according to the Talmudic passage itself, such testimony would be permissible when there are two witnesses. Raavan uses the phrase *edut gemurah* (completely valid testimony) to describe this situation – despite the fact that he is specifically referring to a case in which only one of the witnesses is a Jew while the other is a non-Jew. Such a position might even have been taken by Rambam and the majority of *Rishonim* of Sefarad, according to whom the disqualification of non-Jewish witnesses is a matter of *DeOraita* law,[33] since Rambam nevertheless maintains that a party has the legal privilege to accept as a valid witness someone who is generally disqualified.[34] On the other hand, Raavan, emerging from the school of Rashi, apparently held like him and the majority of *Rishonim* of Ashkenaz, that non-Jews were eligible to serve as witnesses in Jewish courts by *DeOraita* law, but that they were disqualified by Rabbinic law.[35]

[33] Rambam, *Mishneh Torah*, Laws of Testimony (Evidence) 9:4. The source of this position of Rambam is challenged, *ad loc.*, by *Kesef Mishnah* and Radbaz, but more extensively by *Lechem Mishnah*.

[34] Rambam, *Mishneh Torah*, Laws of *Sanhedrin* 7:2. However, Rambam would require that the acceptance of that witness by the party would have had to have been done by a separate contractual act – with a *kinyan*.

[35] See Rashi to *Gittin* 88a.

This makes it simpler yet for him to assert that the initial designation of a non-Jew as a witness constitutes him as a fully valid witness, equivalent in Jewish law to any valid Jewish witness. We will return to the logic of this position in conjunction with the third justification for testimony, the binding nature of the law of the land. It is important to note that this rationale relieves the Jewish witness from the threat of excommunication and allows him to testify, but it generates no duty on his part to do so.

The middle, and indeed central element of the position of Raavan is that the failure of the designated Jewish witness to testify would constitute *Chillul Hashem*, a desecration of the Divine name, and the avoidance of that outcome necessitates the violation of the Rabbinic prohibition against testifying. As is the case for Ravad, so here for Raavan, the factor of *Chillul Hashem* has the capacity to shift prohibition to legal duty. But, by contrast to the position of Ravad where the threatened *Chillul Hashem* would be that of the false testimony of the defendant, that is, his violation of Jewish law; in the case of Raavan the threat of *Chillul Hashem* would be created by the witness himself in his observance of Jewish law's restriction against his testifying. Thus for Raavan, the witness is required to violate Rabbinic law in order to avoid the *Chillul Hashem*, which would be created by his own observance of the law.

There is a further significant contrast between the two positions. For Ravad the *Chillul Hashem* resides in the knowledge of the plaintiff that a Jew, an adherent of the Jewish Deity, is willing to lie for his own financial gain, implying that his Deity condones such action. In the case of Raavan the *Chillul Hashem*, more subtly, resides in the inaction of the witness, implying that his Deity does not require of him to act against the economic interest of a fellow Jew, in the greater interest of justice. This is the meaning of the sentence in the Raavan, "it would be a *Chillul Hashem* if he (the designated Jewish witness) were not to testify, since the non-Jewish party had relied on him – he would say, 'they are not trustworthy people!'" The inaction of the Jewish witness would constitute an apparently justifiable indication to the non-Jewish plaintiff that the Jewish Deity does not demand of His adherents that they act justly.

We must again take note of the fact that there is no suggestion in Raavan, as there had been none in Ravad, that the consequence of the testimony in bringing to light the illegal conduct of the Jewish defendant might itself constitute a wrongful act of *Chillul Hashem*. That could be explained in the following manner. If a non-Jewish plaintiff knows that the Jewish defendant is attempting to defraud him, and that a Jewish witness remains silent, thus enabling the commission of the fraud, then his reasonable conclusion might well be that "Jews and the Jewish Deity" condone criminal fraud – thus *Chillul Hashem*. On the other hand, if the plaintiff sees the witness, another Jew, join him in the attempt to prevent the execution of the fraud, then he cannot reasonably conclude that "Jews and the Jewish Deity" condone criminal fraud. Even if he loses the case, what the non-Jewish plaintiff would then hopefully conclude is that while one Jew attempted to defraud him, another Jew acted in a manner which represented the demand for justice taught by the Jewish Deity. Even if the latter *Kiddush Hashem*, the sanctification of the Divine name, is not achieved, at least the *Chillul Hashem* will have been avoided.

There are of course no guarantees as to exactly what the non-Jewish plaintiff will think, and beyond him, certainly no assurances as to what others in the society will know or think about the situation. Nevertheless, the duty to prevent even a possible desecration of the Divine name entailed in the conclusion by even a single non-Jewish person that the Jewish Deity condones crime or does not require acting on behalf of justice is of sufficient gravity not only to overcome the Rabbinic constraint on testimony in dishonest non-Jewish courts, but to actually require that such testimony be offered in an attempt to prevent the success of Jewish criminals. Loyalty to a fellow Jew is clearly set aside in favor of loyalty to God, and to His reputation in the broader world.

The Raaviah, Rabbi Eliezer ben Joel HaLevi (c. 1160–1235), grandson of Raavan, is cited by Rabbi Isaac ben Moses of Vienna (c. 1180–1250) in his *Or Zarua* as having preserved this particular element of Raavan's teaching in regard to the permissibility of testimony in *Magista* courts under such circumstances:

> If at the outset of the transaction he was designated as a witness, then it is *Chillul Hashem* (for him not to testify), and he can (*yachol*) testify on his (the non-Jew's) behalf, if there is no danger to (the) life (of the Jewish defendant).[36]

The closing note in this passage of the Raaviah is of great importance on both a theoretical and a practical level. As we have seen in our earlier discussion of the law of *Chillul Hashem* there are only three specific instances in which Jewish law imposes a duty to risk one's life rather than violate the law. In those three instances, putting oneself at risk is identified as acting *Al Kiddush Hashem*, in sanctification of the Divine name; while failure to accept the risk would constitute *Chillul Hashem*,

[36] Isaac ben Moses of Vienna, *Or Zarua*, *Piskei Bava Kamma*, ch. 10, sec. 450, s.v. *Katav Mori*.

the desecration of the Divine name. By contrast, in all other instances, one would have a duty to violate the law in order to avert the threat to life. This would include even the situation of false oaths, despite the fact that the *Torah* itself identified such conduct as desecration of the Divine name. Thus, in general, the avoidance of desecration of the Divine name, other than in the situations of idolatry, adultery and homicide, does not require that the individual put his life at risk. On the contrary, the duty created by Jewish law to protect one's own life would necessitate even the desecration of the Divine name in self-defense.

It is this proposition which underlies the closing comment of the Raaviah in the passage above. While the power of the duty to avoid *Chillul Hashem* is sufficiently strong to override the Rabbinic constraint on testimony as a single witness in a dishonest, non-Jewish court, if the consequence of such testimony would be a threat to the life of a Jewish litigant, then the *Chillul Hashem* would have to be tolerated in preference to the risk to life. The foundation of this position is found in the *Mishnah* in *Nedarim*:

> One may vow (falsely) to murderers, robbers and tax farmers
> That it (the produce which they demand) is *terumah*, even if it is not,
> Or that it belongs to the royal house, even if it does not.[37]

As explained by the *Gemara* in the following passage, this *Mishnah* allows a false oath to be made in defense of one's life or property, against a violent murderer or robber since the oath itself is viewed as coerced.[38] The case of the tax farmer is challenged by the *Gemara* on the grounds that he is acting legally as agent of the King and the law of the land is the law, as taught by Samuel. The response confirms that if the tax collector is acting within the authority of the King, then he is not a robber and a false oath to him would not be permitted – as it is forbidden to avoid tax obligations legally imposed by either Jewish or non-Jewish governments. The case of the *Mishnah* allowing the false oath refers solely to the situation of an unauthorized collector, or one who exploits his position by extorting funds beyond the authority granted to him by the ruler.[39] This proposition is repeatedly applied by Rambam in his Code[40] and in his responsa[41] in dealing with issues of false oaths made to threatening individuals who are violent robbers, acting outside the law.

37 *Mishnah, Nedarim* 3, at 27b.

38 *Nedarim* 28a.

39 *Nedarim* 28a. Rambam, Code, Laws of Robbery and Lost Property 5:10–14.

40 Rambam, *Hilchot Shavuot* 3:1–4.

41 Rambam, Responsa, ed. by Jehoshua Blau, vol. I, no. 210, at pp. 371–373. In another responsum, no. 299, at p. 687, Rambam seems to take an astonishingly broader view

Analytically what the Raaviah is suggesting is as follows. There exists a Rabbinic ban against testifying against a fellow Jew in favor of a non-Jew in a dishonest non-Jewish court. That ban would be overcome, and the testimony would be allowed, if the consequence of failure to testify would be *Chillul Hashem*. But, if the testimony by the Jewish witness could result in a threat to the life of the Jewish litigant, then *Chillul Hashem* itself would be overridden by the duty of defense of life. Thus, the initial constraint against testimony would be restored.

It is interesting that while Ravad explicitly indicates that the factor of *Chillul Hashem* creates a duty to testify,[42] and Raavan clearly implies the same,[43] Raaviah, while basing himself on his grandfather Raavan, restrains himself from using language of duty in regard to the testimony in a non-Jewish court even though the logic of his position would necessitate that conclusion.[44] On the one hand Raaviah says, as did Raavan, "then it is *Chillul Hashem* (for him not to testify)" suggesting that it is an affirmative duty for the witness to testify in order to avoid the *Chillul Hashem*. But then in the next phrase he chooses to say, "*veyachol leha'id lo*," "and he can testify on his (the non-Jew's) behalf," suggesting only the permissibility of testimony, not the existence of a duty to do so. Is this ambivalence in the Raaviah an indication of his sense of discomfort at directly expressing the existence of a duty to testify which prefers the economic well-being of the non-Jew over that of the witness's fellow Jew? As a matter of Jewish law it is unequivocally the case that the avoidance of *Chillul Hashem*, and thus the defense of the good reputation of God, does have priority over the enhancement of the economic well-being of fellow Jews. But, saying

that allows a false oath to be taken in a non-Jewish court to prevent his imprisonment. Blau, in his comments to that Responsum, note 5, reports the extensive literature of Gaonim and *Rishonim* in complete disagreement with Rambam's position. Rambam himself makes no reference to such an allowance in his Code. In his brief response, Rambam insists that the defendant making the false oath needs to have in mind the grounds on which he is in fact not liable to the plaintiff – parallel to Rambam's language and position in the context of false oaths made to individual violent murderers or robbers, *Hilchot Shavuot* 3:2. Since the plaintiff in this case is a Jew who brought the case to the non-Jewish court because Jewish law would not allow him to recover, it is possible that Rambam views the plaintiff in this case as an *Anas* – a violent person, against whom a false oath made with mental reservations is not a criminal offense.

42 Ravad to *Bava Kamma* 114a. "I say that this is a *Chillul Hashem*, and the witness has a legal duty (to testify) to prevent him from executing the crime."

43 Raavan cited in Moses of Vienna, *Or Zarua*, Piskei *Bava Kamma,* ch. 10, sec. 450. "Additionally, it would be a *Chillul Hashem* if he were not to testify, while the non-Jewish party had relied upon him – he would say, 'they are not trustworthy people.' "

44 Moses of Vienna, *Or Zarua*, *Piskei Bava Kamma*, ch. 10, sec. 450, s.v. *Katav Mori.*

so explicitly may have been felt by the Raaviah as a manifestation of disloyalty to fellow Jews which, while actually the law, should not be emphasized.

This ambivalence might explain why, on the one hand, the precise language of the Raaviah as cited by *Or Zarua* is quoted also by his student, Rabbi Meir ben Baruch of Rothenberg (c. 1215–1293).[45] But, on the other hand, in the paraphrase of the position of the Raaviah in the *Sefer HaAgudah* by Rabbi Alexander Suslin Hacohen (died c. 1349), he says, "And in *Sefer Raaviah*: where he (the Jewish witness) was designated, as it is customary to designate a Jew and a non-Jew, he is required to testify because of *Chillul Hashem*; but he should warn the Jew (beforehand) and tell him that he will testify."[46] *Sefer HaAgudah* clearly recognizes the legal force of the *Chillul Hashem* situation as not only allowing testimony, but requiring the Jewish witness to testify in order to avert the *Chillul Hashem*, despite the negative consequences to the Jewish litigant. The apparent disloyalty to his fellow Jew could at least, according to *Sefer HaAgudah*, be ameliorated by his novel suggestion that the witness should give prior notice to the Jewish litigant so that he can decide how he wants to proceed in the litigation.

The force of the *Chillul Hashem* argument introduced by Raavan and Ravad, requiring testimony against fellow Jews in non-Jewish courts, went unrefuted through the rest of the history of Jewish law. Not all authorities utilized the argument, and the tension evident in the Raaviah resulted in some wavering between indications of duty to testify in such situations, or just permissibility of testifying when an element of *Chillul Hashem* was present. But through the balance of the period of the *Rishonim* and the whole of the period of the *Acharonim*, this position is powerfully present in the hands of virtually all of the major authorities of Jewish law.

Thus, for Rosh,[47] Tur,[48] Bach[49] and eventually the *Aruch Hashulchan*,[50] the operation of *Chillul Hashem* always results in a duty to testify against a fellow Jew in a non-Jewish court. For *Shulchan Aruch*[51] and Chatam Sofer,[52] *Chillul Hasem* operates to make testimony only permissible, not mandatory.

[45] *Responsa of Maharam MiRottenberg*, vol. I, ed. Bloch, (Parma manuscript), no. 58; and vol. II, ed. Rabbinovicz (Levov edition) no. 58.

[46] *Sefer HaAgudah*, to *Bava Kamma*, sec. 137, edition of Elazar Brissel, Jerusalem, 1970.

[47] R. Asher ben Yechiel, Commentary of Rosh to *Bava Kamma*, ch. 10, sec. 14.

[48] Jacob ben Asher, Tur, *Choshen Mishpat*, 28.

[49] R. Joel Sirkis, Bayit Chadash to Tur, *Choshen Mishpat*, 28, note 2.

[50] R. Yechiel Michel Epstein, *Aruch Hashulchan*, *Choshen Mishpat*, 28:8.

[51] *Shulchan Aruch*, *Choshen Mishpat*, 28:3.

[52] R. Moshe Sofer, *Responsa Chatam Sofer* to *Choshen Mishpat*, No. 23.

Rabbi Meir ben Isaac (Rambi) of Carcassonne,[53] a student of Ravad, offers a fascinating minority stance on the impact of *Chillul Hashem*. While he clearly recognizes the force of the *Chillul Hashem* argument on the permissibility of testimony, he struggles to preserve some force for the legislation of Rava even as against the possibility of desecration of the Divine name. He offers the following novel interpretation of the original Talmudic passage. A single Jewish witness is not permitted to testify against a fellow Jew in a *Magista* court, a corrupt court, under threat of excommunication, and with the possibility of financial liability if the Jewish defendant later testifies in a Jewish court that the witness had lied in the non-Jewish court[54]. A single witness testifying against a fellow Jew in a *Dawar* court, an honest court, is not subject to excommunication, nor to monetary liability, but, says Rambi, "*Ein ruach Chachamim nocheh heimeno*," "the spirit of the Sages is not pleased with him."[55] While this additional moral constraint proposed by Rambi has no legal force or enforceability attached to it, it could well serve as a source of reluctance in competition with the desire for the achievement of justice which would otherwise move the single Jewish witness to testify. However, Rambi argues, in this latter situation, the presence of the motive of *Kiddush Hashem* would be sufficient to overcome the "displeasure of the Sages," to allow him to testify.[56]

According to Rambi, the force of the value of sanctification of the Divine name would be sufficient to allow, albeit not to require, testimony against a fellow Jew in a fundamentally honest non-Jewish court. By contrast, the power of the constraint against testimony in a corrupt court, with its accompanying threat of excommunication and financial liability for losses so caused to a fellow Jew, is of a magnitude which even exceeds the duty to prevent *Chillul Hashem* or to perform *Kiddush Hashem*. While Rambi offered no accompanying commentary as to how he weighed these competing factors to arrive at his conclusion, the outcome itself bespeaks a sense of abject horror at the very thought of a Jew, even just through his participation as a witness, collaborating in an essentially corrupt judicial

[53] Cited in Ashkenaze, *Shita Mekubetzet* to *Bava Kamma* 113b, s.v. *VehaRam za"l Misarkesta*.

[54] *Ibid.*: "And it is reasonable to say that he (the witness) is liable to pay (or *oh* – but preferably read *iy*) if this one (the defendant) swears in Jewish court that he (the witness) had sworn falsely against him."

[55] This is one of a broad set of Rabbinic terms intended to reflect extra legal guidance and persuasion in regard to actions which are discretionary – denominated as *Reshut*, or *Pattur U'Muttar* – according to the law itself.

[56] Rambi offers no parameters for the nature of the *Kiddush Hashem* which would motivate the witness to testify.

process. His position represents a powerful perception of testimony in an unjust court as a form of profound disloyalty to fellow Jews, as a form of illicit participation in causing the unjust outcome.

4.2 TO PREVENT A FELLOW JEW FROM PERPETRATING A CRIME (*CHIYUV LEHAFRISHO MIN HAISSUR*)

The Ravad's presentation of his contention that a single witness might be obligated to testify even in a corrupt non-Jewish court against a fellow Jew when the Jewish defendant's claim has no truth to it, is based on the legal proposition that "the witness has a legal duty (to testify in order) to prevent him (the defendant) from executing the crime."[57] This teaching of Ravad was cited by Meiri (Rabbi Menachem ben Shlomo L'beit Meir, c. 1249–1316) in the following manner:

> But (in a case in which) a (Jewish defendant) lacks a defense valid by Jewish Law – then he (the witness) should testify (*ve'tavo alav beracha*) and may Blessing be visited upon him. And this is the Law and what is fit, so that his friend may be prevented from executing his forbidden act.[58]

There are two distinct differences between the teachings of Ravad and Meiri on this matter. Firstly, Meiri completely omits the issue of *Chillul Hashem*, leaving the duty to testify as a responsibility of the witness, not to prevent the desecration of the Divine name, but simply to prevent a fellow Jew from executing the crime which he is intending to perform.[59] Secondly, Meiri avoids the explicit use of Ravad's word "*ve'tzarich*," "and he is required to," replacing it with the slightly softer "*ve'chen hadin ve'hara'ui*," "and this is the law and what is fit." Meiri leaves no doubt about the responsibility of the Jewish witness to testify in such a circumstance – but he eases the blow to the duty of loyalty to fellow Jews by implying a somewhat regretful tone to the language of the

[57] Ravad, Commentary to *Bava Kamma* 113b, in *Sefer Chiddushe HaRavad al Masechet Bava Kamma*.

[58] Menachem Meiri, Beit HaBechira to *Bava Kamma*, last comment to 113a, s.v. *Gedolei Hamepharshim*.

[59] It is difficult to know whether this variation in the quotation of Ravad by Meiri is because he had a different text of Ravad before him, that is one other than the British Museum manuscript utilized by Professor Atlas. This possibility is intensified by the fact that Rashba also quoted this position of Ravad with significant omissions from the text that is before us, including the reference to *Chillul Hashem*, but omitting the discussion of duty to prevent a fellow Jew from sinning.

requirement – as if it needed to be done by legal and moral coercion, not by free choice. Despite these differences, the underlying principle of Jewish law to which both Ravad and Meiri subscribe is that the Jewish witness would be duty bound to testify against a fellow Jew in order to prevent his fellow from executing the crime which he is apparently intent on performing. What precisely is the foundation for this position in Jewish law?

A distinctive element of Biblical legislation is the crime of enabling another to commit any violation of law. The source of this prohibition is the middle section of the verse Leviticus 19:14: "you shall not place a stumbling block before the blind." The Talmudic-era Sages denied that this passage refers to a literal act of causing injury to a blind person – since that would be covered by the normal law of tort liability. To what then does this refer? The *Midrash Halacha* responds: "Before a person who is blind in some matter, you should not give advice which is not appropriate for him."[60] The *Midrash* illustrates this by offering a case in which A encourages B to sell his property, without revealing to B that A himself intends to acquire the property because of its great hidden value. The *Talmud* offers two further illustrations of the violation of this law:

> Rabbi Nathan said: How do we know that a person should not extend a cup of wine to a *Nazir*, nor a limb torn from a living animal to a Noahite? We are so taught by "You shall not place a stumbling block before the blind."[61]

The continuation of that Talmudic passage as it appears before us insists that the prohibition pertains only in a situation in which the potential sinner would not otherwise have had easy access to the material necessary for the commission of his crime, for example if the *Nazir* was on the other side of a river where no wine was located, and you row the wine across to offer it to him.

Based on this and other Talmudic passages, the Tosafists define the elements necessary for the commission of this crime of "aiding" in the commission of a crime by reference to the three elements in the verse itself:

1. The "blind person" (the *iver*) is a Jew or non-Jew who is inclined and likely to violate a law by which he is bound.
2. The "stumbling block" (the *michshol*) is the material goods or emotional or psychological encouragement which the blind person lacks, thereby restraining him from committing the crime.

[60] *Sifra* to Leviticus 19:14. Cited by Rashi to that verse.
[61] *Avodah Zarah* 6a–b.

3. The "forbidden placing" (*lo titen*) is the act of delivering "the stumbling block" to the blind person when you know that he does not otherwise have access to it – thereby making probable his commission of the crime.[62]

Rambam differs from the Tosafists in one essential element. He makes no reference to the requirement that the "stumbling block" (*michshol*), the material or the counsel being offered to the potential criminal be otherwise out of his reach.[63] The significant impact of this omission is that, according to Rambam, even if the potential criminal has other easily accessible sources for the same goods or counsel, one is still forbidden to provide them. This is in contrast to the Tosafists for whom the violation of *Lifnei Iver* is restricted to the situation where there is a more direct causal connection between the act and the crime then committed (for example, by providing weapons to a terrorist or a criminal regime which does not have any other easy access to weapons). For Rambam, no matter whether the criminal does or does not have such easy access, providing him with a weapon makes you complicit in the subsequent crime under the law of *Lifnei Iver*.[64] Despite the causal connection being so attenuated, for Rambam there is strict liability for providing wrongful counsel or just the implicit encouragement or approval of his behavior by providing the potential sinner with the materials necessary for the commission of his crime. This is why Rambam can directly include as violation of *Lifnei Iver* situations in which the actor does not "make the crime possible," but does no more than "strengthen the hands of the sinner."[65]

Thus far, the Law of *Lifnei Iver* generates only a duty to refrain from behavior which would injure another party by contributing to the likelihood of his committing a sinful act. It does not, thus far, yield a duty to prevent the other from effectuating his sinful intent.[66] That is, *Lifnei*

[62] *Tosafot Avodah Zarah* 6b, s.v. *Minayin shelo yoshit*.

[63] Rambam, *Mishneh Torah*, Laws of Idolatry 9:8–9. Laws of Homicide and Guarding of Life 12:12–15.

[64] For extensive exposition of this position of Rambam, see Rabbi Nachum Rabinovitch in his commentary to Rambam's *Mishneh Torah*, Yad Peshutah, Jerusalem, Maaliyot Press, 1990, to Hilchot Avodah Zarah 9:8. Also in his article, "All Jews Are Responsible for One Another," in Jacob J. Schacter (ed.), *Jewish Tradition and the Non-Traditional Jew*, The Orthodox Forum series, Jason Northvale, NJ, Aronson, Inc., 1992, pp. 177–204, at pp. 179–180 and notes 6–7.

[65] Rambam uses the latter phrase twice in Laws of Homicide and Guarding of Life 12:14. See also Rambam, Laws of Robbery and Lost Property 5:1 in regard to the purchase of stolen property.

[66] The critical nature of this distinction for Jewish law is explored further below.

Iver criminalizes speech or action which makes a sin more probable, but it does not criminalize the inaction of failing to prevent the sinner from acting, nor does it make its correlative, the action of preventing the criminal from executing his sin, a legal duty. While the *Talmud* itself makes reference to the value of *L'afrushei me'issurah*, of preventing a person from committing a sin, it never explicitly connects that value to the law of *Lifnei Iver*.[67] The explicit connection between the two principles is made by the Tosafists who maintain that preventing a fellow Jew from sinning is a Rabbinically imposed duty, as an extension of the law of *Lifnei Iver*.[68]

Rambam clearly agrees that there exists a legal duty of preventing a person from committing a sin. Thus, for example, based on an explicit Talmudic source, he maintains that if one sees a person wearing a garment of *Shatnez* (consisting of wool and linen woven together), he is duty bound to tear the garment off the person, even if the consequence will be public embarrassment to the "sinner," indeed even if the "sinner" is his own teacher.[69] Rambam limits the application of this duty to situations in which a *DeOraita* law (revealed law) is being violated, since as to a Rabbinic law, the principle of *Kevod Habriyot*, defense of human dignity, would prevent the observer from stripping the garment off the sinner in public.[70] But Rambam in that passage does not indicate the source of the duty. Nor, in the passages in which he treats the Law of *Lifnei Iver*, does Rambam indicate the existence of a related duty to prevent the sinner from executing his sinful intent.[71] What then is the source of this duty according to Rambam and to which layer of the law does it pertain, revealed law or Rabbinic law?

It would appear to be the case that Rambam considers the duty to prevent a fellow Jew from committing a sin to be one element of the *DeOraita* law of rebuke. The following is his language in *Mishneh Torah*:[72]

It is a *mitzvah* for a person who sees that his fellow Jew has sinned or is following an improper path [to attempt] to correct his behavior and to inform him that he is causing himself a loss by his evil deeds as [Leviticus 19:17] states: "You shall

[67] See e.g. *Shabbat* 40b.

[68] *Tosafot* to *Shabbat* 3a, s.v. *Bava DeRaisha*.

[69] Rambam, *Mishneh Torah*, *Hilchot Kela'im* 10:29; based on *Berachot* 19b. Both Kesef Mishneh and Radbaz comment on that passage in Rambam and attempt with some difficulty to explain how he derives the law from that text in the *Talmud*.

[70] Rambam, *Mishneh Torah*, *Hilchot Kela'im* 10:29.

[71] See e.g. Rambam citations above in note 63.

[72] Rambam *Mishneh Torah*, *Hilchot Deot* 6:7, trans. by Rabbi Eliyahu Touger, Moznayim Press. Available online at www.chabad.org/library/article_cdo/aid/910346/jewish/Chapter-Six.htm.

surely admonish your colleague." A person who rebukes a colleague – whether because of a [wrong committed] against him or because of a matter between his colleague and God – should rebuke him privately. He should speak to him patiently and gently, informing him that he is only making these statements for his colleague's own welfare, to allow him to merit the life of the world to come. If he accepts [the rebuke], it is good; if not, he should rebuke him a second and third time. Indeed, one is obligated to rebuke a colleague who does wrong until the latter strikes him and tells him: "I will not listen." Whoever has the possibility of rebuking [sinners] and fails to do so is considered responsible for that sin, for he had the opportunity to rebuke the [sinners].

The primary Talmudic source from which Rambam draws the laws of rebuke refers only to words, speech, as the medium of fulfillment of this *Mitzvah*. "How do we know that one who sees in his friend some debased quality, that he is obligated to chastise him."[73] Following that approach, in his *Sefer Hamitzvot*, Rambam says specifically, "We are commanded to rebuke the sinner or one who intends to sin, and to prevent him from doing so with words of rebuke."[74] Yet when he records this law in *Mishneh Torah*, as we saw above, Rambam places primary emphasis on action and only secondary importance on speech, as he says:

It is a *mitzvah* for a person who sees that his fellow Jew has sinned or is following an improper path [to attempt] to correct his behavior and to inform him that he is causing himself a loss by his evil deeds as [Leviticus 19:17] states: "You shall surely admonish your colleague."

He thereby encompasses the action of attempting to correct the sinner within the revealed law of rebuke. That is, for Rambam, the very essence of the duty of rebuke is in reality the legal duty to prevent a fellow Jew from committing a sinful act. If that can be achieved through words alone, then that minimal speech is required, but if words will not suffice, then action to achieve the restraining purpose is mandated by the verse in the *Torah* itself.

The central source for the position of Rambam in encompassing action in the duty to prevent sinful conduct is the Talmudic passage in Shevuot where the Sages explore the question of Jewish covenantal mutual responsibility for one another. Says the *Talmud*:

As to all of the sins of the *Torah*, is there not communal responsibility (for the actions of individuals)? Does it not say (Leviticus 26:37) "they shall stumble over one another," meaning over the sins of their brothers – for all Jews are

[73] *Arakin* 16b.

[74] Rambam, *Sefer Hamitzvot*, Positive Commandments, no. 205.

responsible for one another!!? That is only when it was within their power to prevent (the sinful conduct) and they failed to do so.[75]

The *Talmud* here clearly assumes that there is mutual responsibility amongst Jews to prevent sinful conduct, without any limitation to just words as the medium of such prevention. Similar passages in both the Babylonian *Talmud*[76] and the Jerusalem *Talmud*[77] imply the lack of distinction between speech and action in regard to the duty to prevent fellow Jews from sinning. It is particularly in a passage in the Jerusalem *Talmud* that a more direct connection is made between the general duty to prevent another Jew from sinning and the *Torah* law of rebuke.[78] In that passage, the general rule of preventing sinful conduct is directly associated with the ruling that is a hallmark of the law of rebuke, that "as one is obligated to speak that which can be heard (by the sinner), so is one obligated to refrain from saying that which cannot be heard."

In sharp contrast to the position of Rambam, the Tosafists seem totally unpersuaded, based on the relevant passages in the Babylonian *Talmud*, that the Commandment of Rebuke contains elements other than speech. If then, the *Talmud* requires action to restrain a Jew from committing a sin, that requirement could not, for the Tosafists, be derived from the Commandment of Rebuke. Rather, as they in fact argue, it must constitute a Rabbinic extension of the law of *Lifnei Iver*. The law of *Lifnei Iver* indeed regulates not only speech, but behavior as well. However, the *DeOraita* law of *Lifnei Iver* is limited to being a causal party to the sinful act – that is, it forbids causing another to sin through your speech or action. It does not, on the *DeOraita* level, create a duty of rescue – it does not affirmatively mandate preventive behavior and criminalize the omission, the failure to prevent the other from committing the sin. According to the Tosafists it is precisely this second layer of duty of rescue which is by Rabbinic law added to the law of *Lifnei Iver*. That is why, according to the Tosafists, while it is clear that the *DeOraita* Law of *Lifnei Iver* prohibits causing either a Jew or a non-Jew to violate any law by which he or she is bound; this Rabbinical layer of *Lifnei Iver*, imposing a duty to rescue from sin, and criminalizing the failure to do so, pertains only to fellow Jews.

75 *Shavuot* 39a,b. Parallel in *Sanhedrin* 27b-28a.

76 See e.g. *Berachot* 20a, the case of Rabbi Adda bar Ahavah.

77 See e.g. J. *Sotah* 7:4. See also Rabbi Yehuda Amital, "Rebuking a Fellow Jew: Theory and Practice," in Schachter (ed.), *Jewish Tradition and the Non-Traditional Jew*, Northvale, NJ, Jason Aronson Inc., 1992, pp. 119–138 at note 64.

78 J. *Sotah* 8: 2.

This explains in turn an interesting discrepancy between the writings of Ashkenaz *Rishonim*, and the *Rishonim* of other schools. For the *Rishonim* of Sepharad and of Provence, as we have seen, the force of the duty to prevent a fellow Jew from executing his intended crime is of sufficient power to result in at least permissibility, if not the duty, to testify against the fellow Jew even in a dishonest non-Jewish Court. By contrast, this argument is rarely, if ever, raised by any Ashkenaz Rishon. For the former group of *Rishonim*, the duty to prevent performance of the crime is itself a *DeOraita* legal duty, an element of the law of rebuke, which clearly has the capacity to override the Rabbinic constraint against testimony in a corrupt non-Jewish court. By contrast, for the Ashkenazic heirs to the position of the Tosafists, the duty to prevent execution of a crime by another Jew is itself only a Rabbinic extension of the law of *Lifnei Iver*, and when it conflicts with another Rabbinic law which constrains testimony, there is no inherent reason to grant priority to the latter over the former.

If we look now at the underlying competing values, we can gain another level of understanding of the nature of this debate. The Rabbinic prohibition against testimony against a fellow Jew in a corrupt non-Jewish court was motivated by the loyalty responsibility a Jew was duty bound to express for the economic well-being of fellow Jews. It is this loyalty responsibility which led Rashi and the vast majority of early and late Rabbinic scholars to assert that the underlying basis of the excommunication to which a violator of this law would be subjected was that he would have caused economic liability, i.e. economic injury, to a fellow Jew that was not warranted according to Jewish law. It is only because such injury was indirect that Jewish law could not simply hold the perpetrator liable for the injury, but instead had to use excommunication either as the threatened punishment or as the instrument of generating economic compensation to the victim.

The struggle we have been observing thus far in the writings of the Gaonim and *Rishonim* is this: what happens when this loyalty responsibility comes into direct conflict with another area of loyalty responsibility imposed by Jewish law? In the Gaonic literature, the competing loyalty responsibility was the loyalty to principles of justice in the relationship between litigants – whether the litigants were both Jews, or even if one was a non-Jew. In the first approach of Ravad, the competing loyalty was the loyalty to the reputation of God Himself – the avoidance of *Chillul Hashem*. In this third set, dealing with the duty of *lehafrisho min ha'issur*, the competing loyalties both relate to duties of the witness toward the

Jewish litigant. The first duty is to protect the economic well-being of the fellow Jew – loyalty to his economic security. But, in this instance, the second, competing duty is to the spiritual condition of the very same fellow Jew – generated by the legal duty to actively prevent him from committing a sin, by which the sinner would injure both the intended victim of his crime, and himself through a breach of his covenant with God. What happens then when the competing loyalty responsibilities both inhere in the protection of one person; one duty mandating the protection of his economic well-being, the other mandating the protection of his spiritual well-being?

For Rambam and apparently Ravad, and with them the *Rishonim* of both Sepharad and Provence, the answer to this question is crystal clear. The *DeOraita* duty of rebuke mandates granting priority to the spiritual well-being of the perpetrator, rather than granting priority to his economic well-being in regard to an indirect injury which is itself only granted protection by Rabbinic law. Therefore, for Rambam and his school of thought, the witness would be obligated to testify against his fellow Jew in a corrupt non-Jewish court despite the resultant risk of indirect economic injury to the fellow Jew, in order to achieve the higher magnitude loyalty to the spiritual well-being of the Jewish defendant. A parallel application of this same principle is evident in the assertion by R. Yosef Karo that while an outstanding scholar would be exempt from the obligation to testify in an inferior (possibly untrustworthy) Jewish court, he would be obligated to testify if there were an element present of *leafrushei meissura*, of an opportunity to prevent the defendant from actually achieving the execution of his criminal intent.[79]

By contrast, for the Tosafists, the Jewish legal duty to engage in action which would deter a fellow Jew from committing a sin is itself only a Rabbinic extension of the law of *Lifnei Iver*, in which case, it is not simple to compute its capacity to override another Rabbinic duty – to protect a fellow Jew from indirect economic injury which might result from a testimony against him in a corrupt non-Jewish court. The competing loyalties in this instance, for the Tosafists, produce a standoff in which it is not possible to declare that the witness has a legal duty to prevent the Jewish defendant from executing his sin, at the expense of his actively risking economic injury, albeit indirectly, to his fellow Jew. That is, his Rabbinically imposed duty to protect a fellow Jew from indirect economic injury is not obviously overridden by his Rabbinically imposed

[79] *Shulchan Aruch*, *Choshen Mishpat*, 28:5.

duty to protect the spiritual well-being of his fellow Jew. The outcome, therefore, according to the Tosafists is simply: first, do no harm – the prevention of wrongdoing is not, by itself, sufficient grounds to warrant the indirect injury which could result from testimony. Of course, as we have seen for Raavan, and will see according to other *Rishonim* of Ashkenaz, the absence of this particular ground for justifying or mandating testimony against a fellow Jew, even in a corrupt non-Jewish court, did not prevent the identical conclusion from being arrived at based on other legal principles.

4.3 WHEN REQUIRED TO TESTIFY BY NON-JEWISH LAW: BEING SUBJECT TO TWO MASTERS

We have already seen the introduction by Raavan of the notion that when the non-Jewish legal system requires a Jew to testify, he is bound to do so under Jewish law. Thus, in the case in which at the outset of a transaction between a Jew and a non-Jew, each of the parties had designated a co-religionist as his witness for the transaction, then Raavan contends, aside from other reasons why the Jewish witness might be bound to testify, there is also the element of the Jewish law principle: the law of the land is the law, *Dina de Malchuta Dina*. The relevant passage reads as follows:[80]

> It appears to me that in a location where the custom (in transactions) between a Jew and a non-Jew, is that they appoint a Jew and a non-Jew to be the witnesses between them, then it is permissible for the Jewish witness to testify, since from the outset they were accepted for that purpose ... since he is ordered to pay in accordance with the law – we do not excommunicate (the Jewish witness.) Additionally, it would be a *Chillul Hashem* if he (the designated Jewish witness) were not to testify, since the non-Jewish party had relied on him – he would say, "they are not trustworthy people!" And even more, for it is the law of the land, and "the law of the land is law."

Like others, Raavan equivocates in his terminology, speaking at the outset only about the permissibility of testimony by the Jewish witness, but then introducing two grounds which could serve as a basis for a legal duty to testify – *Chillul Hashem* and *Dina de Malchuta Dina* – without so denominating them.

A fascinating utilization of the same principle, without even using the legal terminology of *Dina de Malchuta Dina*, is to be found in the writings of Rambam. Rambam codifies the state of Jewish law in regard to

[80] *Sefer Raavan*, Part 2, end of Tractate *Bava Kamma* at note 156.

the use of non-Jewish courts, on the basis of the Talmudic and Gaonic teachings, as follows:

> Any person who adjudicates through gentile judges and their courts, even if their laws are the same as the Jewish laws, is considered a Rasha (a wicked person.). It is as if he disgraced, blasphemed, and lifted up his hand against the *Torah* of Moses our teacher. As the *Torah* says, (Exodus 21:1): "These are the judgments that you shall place before them"; (and the Rabbis taught) "Before them" and not before gentiles, "before them" and not before inexpert people.
>
> If the gentiles have greater power, and the opposing litigant is a powerful person from whom one cannot recover property through the Jewish judicial system; one should summon him before the Jewish judges first. If he did not desire to come, one may receive authorization from the court and rescue one's property from the litigant by litigating in a gentile court.[81]

Rambam is clearly, in this passage, dealing with a situation in which two Jewish litigants are involved, parallel to the Talmudic passage on which his position is based.[82]

Elsewhere in his Code, Rambam deals with the situation of litigation in a Jewish court between a Jew and a non-Jew.[83] According to the Talmudic passage on which Rambam is based,[84] such litigation in a Jewish court raises complex questions of conflicts of law. Should Jewish law apply, as it is the law of the Jewish party; or ought Noahite law be applied, since that is the law which Jewish society views as appropriately pertaining to gentiles? Rambam understands the *Talmud* to resolve the question based on the distinction between the treatment of idolatrous (*Aku'm*) versus non-idolatrous (*Ger Toshav*) non-Jews. The category which Rambam calls *Ger Toshav* encompasses two groups of persons. First, the non-Jewish legally confirmed resident alien in the land of Israel who has accepted upon himself the civic responsibilities of the Seven Noahite Commandments as the law regulating his conduct. In its technical form, this category existed only during the period of the First Temple, until its destruction in 586 B.C.E., when the institution of the Jubilee Year was discontinued.[85] The second group is a broader one which is applicable at all times and in all places, referring to all non-idolatrous non-Jews who adhere to the Seven Noahite commandments.[86]

[81] Rambam, *Mishneh Torah*, Laws of *Sanhedrin* 26:7, trans. by Eliyahu Touger, modified for greater clarity.

[82] *Gittin* 88b.

[83] Rambam, Laws of Kings 10:12.

[84] *Bava Kamma* 113a-b.

[85] Rambam, Laws of Idolatry, end of 10:6.

[86] Rambam, Laws of Idolatry 10:2. Also see comments of Ravad and of *Kesef Mishneh* to Rambam, Laws of Idolatry, at end of 10:6.

The relationship to the *Ger Toshav*, Rambam contends, is to be conducted, "with graciousness and kindness, as one would with a fellow Jew. For we are commanded to rescue him, as it says (Deut. 14:21) 'unto the stranger in your gates you shall give it to be eaten.' "

One additional factor needs to be introduced here. According to Rambam, the mutual relationship between fellow Jews is always governed by their common state of being bound by Jewish law.[87] But the relationship of Jews to non-Jews is primarily governed by their common state of being bound by Noahite law.[88] There are instances in which Jewish law elevates the duties incumbent upon Jews toward non-Jews beyond the reciprocal duties embedded in Noahite law. We have seen precisely such an instance in the application of the Biblical law of *Lifnei Iver* to create a duty upon Jews to not cause a non-Jew to violate the Noahite laws by which he is bound, despite the absence of reciprocity of that duty within the Noahite laws themselves. However, the norms which generally govern the relationships between Jews and non-Jews are the Noahite laws. Therefore, in litigation between a Jew and a *Ger Toshav* non-Jew in a Jewish court, the court is bound to apply the legal system which is the common basis of the relationship between the parties, that is Noahite law.

What, however, is the basis of the governance of the relationship between a Jew and an idolatrous non-Jew? By definition, the idolatrous non-Jew is not an adherent of the Noahite laws, and therefore there cannot be reciprocity between the parties which would be recognized by the application of Noahite law to their litigation. The choice of law which then confronts the court is either the application of the Jewish legal system which binds the Jewish litigant, or the Noahite law which also binds the Jewish litigant in his general relationship to non-Jews, despite the fact that this particular non-Jew is not a consenting party to the binding authority of Noahite law. That is, either choice would be based on the binding authority of that particular legal system of just one of the litigants – the Jewish party. One further factor then enters.

As to an idolator, in sharp contrast to the *Ger Toshav*, the *Torah* commands (Deut. 7:2), "*Lo techanem,*" "you shall not be gracious unto them." The *Talmud* understands this to mean that a Jew is not to grant any economic advantage to idolators.[89] The result according to the *Talmud*,[90]

87 We will see further explication of this shortly in regard to the testimony issue.

88 Dov Frimer, "Israel, the Noahide Laws and Maimonides: Jewish-Gentile Legal Relations in Maimonidean Thought," *Jewish Law Association Studies*, 2, 1986, pp. 89–102.

89 *Avodah Zarah* 20a.

90 *Bava Kamma* 113b.

and as codified by Rambam,[91] is that in litigation between a Jew and an idolator in a Jewish court, since either the application of Jewish law or the application of Noahite law would be based on the fact that the Jewish party is committed to both of them, the court ought to resolve its conflicts of laws problem in the manner which is most advantageous to the Jewish party. Thus, like an act of jurisdiction shopping by the court itself, that legal system should be applied that would result in the most advantageous outcome to the Jewish party.

Thus, while Rambam's treatment of civil law issues in the *Mishneh Torah* deals primarily with the way in which the relationship between two Jews would be litigated in a Jewish court, he has dealt also in his Code with the situation of two Jews litigating in a non-Jewish court, and with the situation of a Jew and a non-Jew litigating in a Jewish court. Strikingly, in the entire *Mishneh Torah*, Rambam does not deal with the issue of litigation between a Jew and a non-Jew in a non-Jewish court. Of course, given what we have seen earlier in the *Tosefta*,[92] this omission by Rambam is simply further confirmation of the Talmudic position that there was no objection to litigation between a Jew and a non-Jew in a non-Jewish court. This was why early and late authorities, struggling with the question of the rationale of the Law of Rava restricting testimony against a fellow Jew in his litigation with a non-Jew in non-Jewish courts, rejected the possibility that that Rabbinic legislation was an extension of the *DeOraita* ban on litigation between Jews in non-Jewish courts.[93] How could the law of *Lifneihem* ban testimony in cases in which it permitted the litigation itself?!

Where then in his Code would Rambam record the legislation of Rava? Certainly not in the Laws of *Sanhedrin* where he codifies the prohibition against litigating with a fellow Jew in a non-Jewish court. Perhaps it would make sense to record this law in the Laws of Testimony, which deal with issues of testimony in Jewish courts. In a surprising move, the only place where Rambam refers to the legislation of Rava is in *Sefer Madda*, in the Laws of the Study of the *Torah*.[94] There, in Chapter 6, Rambam performs one of his masterful consolidations by bringing together all twenty-four instances in which the *Talmud* had specifically recorded that someone would be subject to the penalty of excommunication.[95] It would

[91] Laws of Kings 10:12.

[92] See above 3.1.2.3.

[93] See above 3.1.

[94] Rambam, Laws of Study of the *Torah* 6:14(9).

[95] Leibson, "Determining Factors in Herem and Nidui," vol. II, pp. 292–342. At the start and at the end of the article, Leibson argues persuasively that the number twenty-four in

appear that the location of the laws of excommunication in Laws of Study of the *Torah*, rather than in one of the sections of the Code devoted to criminal law or the penal system is due to the fact that the grant of authority for excommunication was not to the judiciary alone, but to any recognized community scholar. Since the Law of Study of the *Torah* encompasses the duties of respect of scholars and the authorities which devolve upon them in consequence, it serves as the appropriate location in which to codify the circumstances under which scholars as well as courts are entitled to issue discretionary writs of excommunication.

Rambam there codifies the legislation of Rava as the ninth instance in which excommunication can be ordered, in the following manner:

> One who testifies against a Jew in the courts (*Arkaot*) of idolators,
> and through his testimony caused monetary loss to him (the Jewish litigant),
> not in accordance with Jewish Law, is to be excommunicated until he pays.[96]

This is a very bizarre codification of the legislation of Rava. The problems are numerous.

1. Rambam does not even mention that Rava's case in the *Gemara* relates specifically to a situation in which the other litigant, in whose favor the Jewish witness testifies, is a non-Jew. In Rambam's version, the other litigant might well be another Jew, and the penalty of excommunication would still apply.
2. Rambam does not record the permissibility of such testimony when there are two witnesses. Is that also forbidden according to him?
3. Nor does Rambam record the critical distinction between the *Magista* court, where, according to the *Gemara*, even a single witness may testify, as opposed to the *Dawar* court where testimony by a single witness could result in excommunication. Rambam uses the generic term *Arkaot*, which by his time was a commonly used term to describe all non-Jewish courts. Is the distinction between honest and corrupt courts of no significance to Rambam?
4. Rambam makes no reference to the procedural similarities between the Jewish court and the *Dawar* court in requiring an oath when

the original Talmudic passage was a round number, not a closed list, despite Rambam's insistence on counting exactly twenty-four such instances, see pp. 293–298 and particularly the reference to Shraga Abramson at p. 296, in footnote 19.

[96] Leibson, *ibid.*, at p. 324 inexplicably asserts that the legislation of Rava is quoted in the *Talmud* as an anonymous statement and is associated with Rava because it appears in a sequence of teachings by Rava. While the latter point is correct, there is no printed or manuscript version of this passage in *Bava Kamma* 113b in which the attribution to Rava is not present.

there is only a single witness. But doesn't that serve as a fair predictor of a common outcome, or at least, of procedural fairness in the non-Jewish court?

5. Rambam adds an element which is completely absent in the Talmudic text of the legislation of Rava, that the excommunication would be terminated upon payment by the witness to the Jewish litigant of the sum that the latter had been required to pay in consequence of the testimony. Does this represent a shift in the purpose of the excommunication from penalty for wrongdoing to coercive measure for requiring compensation for loss?

In all, what exactly is the intent of Rambam in this passage? Why does his treatment of the legislation of Rava differ so radically from the treatment of this law in any of the preceding Gaonic literature, or for that matter, from its treatment by any of the other *Rishonim*?

Rambam's position becomes clarified through an understanding of his stance on a number of related matters. First, Rambam systematically distinguishes between the duties of a Jew toward fellow Jews under Jewish law and the duties that same Jew might have under non-Jewish law which could be binding under the principle of *Dina de Malchuta Dina*, the law of the land is the law. Shmuel Shilo has established that the position of Rambam in regard to *Dina de Malchuta Dina* is very extensive.[97] Shilo calls particular attention to the breadth of the language of Rambam, as he declares, "where the law of the State is an established law, … we follow the law of the State because in all monetary matters we abide by the law of the State."[98] While Rambam requires that the government be strong and authoritative in its jurisdiction;[99] and that it apply laws equally to all residents of the State[100] as preconditions of Jewish legal recognition of the authority of its laws, he clearly views the government's authority as extending to all forms of economic, civil matters, to the exclusion of religious or ritual observances.[101]

Second, Rambam would be quite justified in pointing out that the language of the legislation of Rava does not assert, nor does it create, an *ab initio* prohibition against testimony of any sort in non-Jewish courts. As

[97] Shmuel Shilo, "Maimonides on Dina de Malchuta Dina (The Law of the State is Law)," *Jewish Law Annual*, I, 1982, pp. 146–167. See particularly pp. 150–154, and note 25 on p. 151.

[98] Rambam, *Hilchot Zechiya Umattanah* 1:15; cited by Shilo, *ibid.*, at pp. 150 and 151.

[99] Shilo, *ibid.*, at p. 148, based on Rambam, *Hilchot Gezelah* 5:18.

[100] *Ibid.*, at 150, based on Rambam, *Hilchot Gezelah* 5:14.

[101] *Ibid.*, based on Rambam, *Hilchot Zechiya Umattanah* 1:15.

we have noted above, no such proscription existed before the legislation of Rava, and according to Rambam, no such proscription exists in consequence of the legislation of Rava. After all, the Talmudic Sages knew how to declare behavior to be proscribed. They had many terms to describe the varying degrees of prohibition, those that they uncovered in their interpretations of prior Biblical or Rabbinic texts, and those which they created anew in their own legislation. But Rava does not declare that testimony is forbidden. What Rava does decree is that if in consequence of a Jew testifying against a fellow Jew in a non-Jewish court, the Jewish litigant suffers loss not in accordance with Jewish law, that there is potential liability of the witness to the injured litigant which can be pursued in a Jewish court. The act of testifying itself remains, even according to Rava, as understood by Rambam, a discretionary act within the framework of Jewish law. If the Jewish witness prefers to testify, or understands his responsibility to be to testify, or if it be the case that the Law of the Land requires him to testify, he is not barred by Jewish law from doing so.

However, the legal responsibility which the Jewish witness has to his fellow Jew, to avoid any form of economic injury to him, is determined not by the law of the land, nor by his own preference or conscience, but by Jewish law. Therefore, whatever decision the Jewish witness makes in regard to the discretionary activity of testifying against a fellow Jew in a non-Jewish court, he cannot relieve himself of the responsibility that he bears to that fellow Jew within the framework of Jewish law. Until the time of Rava, whatever choice the witness made, he could not be subject to any negative consequences since his conduct would never be the direct cause of injury to the Jewish party to the litigation in the non-Jewish court. While the primary level of legal duty which each Jew bears toward the economic well-being of all persons is to do no harm, the definition of liability for harm extends only to the direct consequences of the behavior. Any indirect consequences would be classified by Jewish law as *Gerama* – indirectly caused injury – for which there would be no monetary liability.[102] In the case of testimony in a non-Jewish court, the decision of the court itself is the instrument of potential harm to a litigant; the testimony of the witness is an element for deliberation by the judges, but does not rise to the level of direct cause of the injurious outcome.

Thus for Rambam, the entire purpose of the legislation of Rava was to create the potential for accountability of the Jewish witness for any harm

[102] See Zevin, *Encyclopedia Talmudit*, entry *Gerama b'Nezikin*, vol. VI, columns 461–497, at 485–497.

which he might cause to the Jewish party in litigation in a non-Jewish court. For Rambam, one of the underlying purposes of excommunication is precisely the creation of such a level of accountability in situations in which no actual crime or tort was committed, but injury might be sustained by an innocent party. Thus, for example, later on the same Talmudic page as the legislation of Rava, the *Talmud* reports the following parallel situation. If an owner of land sells his property to a violent person, thus creating risk to his neighboring Jewish property owner, then the Jewish vendor can be ordered into excommunication until he undertakes liability for any damages that might in the future be incurred by his neighbor.[103] The Jewish vendor has committed no crime, and were his neighbor to eventually suffer some loss by damage caused by the new violent property owner, the vendor would bear no legal liability since he would not have been the direct cause of the damages. The role then of the legislation which threatens the vendor with excommunication is clearly an equitable remedy designed to assure that he does undertake responsibility for the security of his neighbor in a manner that goes beyond the initial requirement of the law. The remedy is not to make him monetarily liable, but to threaten excommunication if he fails to make good the damage to his neighbor which he set in motion.

For Rambam, the case of the Jewish witness in the non-Jewish court is perfectly parallel to the case of the vendor to a violent purchaser. The legislation of Rava did not create a new crime, nor did it generate a new layer of financial liability in cases of indirect injury. It created a new equitable remedy for a Jewish litigant who claims to have suffered monetary loss in consequence of testimony against him by a fellow Jew in a non-Jewish court. The remedy is, essentially, a hearing before a Jewish court in which the Jewish court would have the discretionary authority to order the witness to be excommunicated until he compensated the Jewish litigant for the loss he caused but for which he could not be held directly liable under Jewish law due to its being a form of *Gerama* – of indirect injury. Of the essence in this situation is the recognition that excommunication, by its very nature, is a discretionary power which a court or an individual scholar in a community could exercise in the greater interest of safeguarding Jewish communal values. A plaintiff is not "entitled" to the remedy of excommunication, and a court is never duty bound to order anyone to be excommunicated, as a court would be duty bound to find in favor of one or another party to a civil litigation in the presence of two eye-witnesses who testify to criminal or to tortuous behavior.

[103] *Bava Kamma* 114a.

Given this analysis, it would appear that in fact according to Rambam there is, even after the legislation of Rava, no a priori criminality, no violation of a Rabbinic prohibition, in testifying against a fellow Jew in a non-Jewish court, even when the other party is a non-Jew, even when the witness is the sole witness, and even if the court is dishonest. This is why Rambam omits all of those factors from his codification of the law of Rava. All the law of Rava did was to vest in Jewish courts the authority to conduct a secondary, post facto, hearing in the relationship between the Jewish witness and a Jewish party who claims that the former had caused him unconscionable injury through his testimony in a non-Jewish court. The Jewish court would then have the discretion, if it concluded that the Jewish litigant in fact suffered an unjust loss, to threaten the Jewish witness with excommunication unless he compensates the litigant for the loss he has suffered.[104] It is striking though that Rambam provides no indication whatsoever as to what criteria the Jewish court is to use in this situation other than the broad guideline of the litigant having been caused to suffer "loss not in accordance with Jewish law."[105]

This analysis of the position of Rambam would leave the potential witness in a conflicted position. On the one hand, he is free to exercise his discretion as to whether to testify – Jewish law will not instruct him to refrain and might even indicate that he is duty bound to testify if the non-Jewish civil law requires him to do so. On the other hand, his testimony might subject him to a subsequent lawsuit by the Jewish litigant, in a Jewish court, in which he might be subject to excommunication for the consequences which he had brought about through his testimony, unless he agrees to compensate the Jewish litigant. On top of which, the liability to which he might be subject in the Jewish court is extremely unpredictable since it is a matter of equitable discretion on the part of the judges, based partially on the unknown outcome of the litigation in the non-Jewish court, and not subject to the usually knowable standards of financial liability within Jewish law.

It may very well be the case that this conflicted position, according to Rambam, is the unavoidable consequence of exilic Jewish life in which the Jew is the subject of two masters, the Jewish law as administered by

104 Leibson, "Determining Factors in Herem and Nidui," vol. II, at p. 342.

105 Leibson, *ibid.*, does not explicate the criteria for the exercise of this discretionary authority.

Jewish courts to govern the relationship between fellow Jews, and the law of the land that regulates the conduct of the Jew in his interaction with the non-Jewish legal system administered by non-Jewish courts in all civil matters in which they claim jurisdiction. Rather than attempting to reconcile the two systems in all matters that affect Jews, Rambam is willing to allow the tension to stand, as if emphasizing the ambivalence, the uncertainty and insecurity of exilic Jewish life. What remains certain according to Rambam is that if the law of the land mandates testimony in the non-Jewish court, even against a fellow Jew in favor of a non-Jew, even as a single witness in a dishonest court, the Jew is bound to testify. But it is equally certain according to Rambam that the legal governance of the relationship between the Jewish witness and the injured Jewish litigant is not exhausted by their interaction in the non-Jewish court, but that equitable remedies are available through Jewish courts, which have the final word on their legal and moral responsibilities toward each other.

Rambam, having raised the possibility that the witness might be monetarily liable to the Jewish litigant, set off an 800-year-long debate that is still not fully resolved.

4.4 TO AVOID MONETARY OR BODILY PENALTY FOR REFUSAL TO TESTIFY

The legislation of Rava had created the possibility that a potential witness against a fellow Jew in a non-Jewish court, whose testimony would be in benefit of a non-Jewish litigant, might be subject to excommunication if his testimony might result in monetary loss to the Jewish party not in accordance with Jewish law. As we have seen, according to some authorities, that witness might even be required to make monetary compensation to the Jewish party to whom he had indirectly caused such loss.

But what if, on the other hand, the potential witness himself could be punished by the non-Jewish authorities, either by monetary fine or even by imprisonment, for his failure to testify? Would his duty to defend himself against such penalty justify his testimony against the interest of his fellow Jew?

In order to understand the deliberation of the *Rishonim* around this next issue, it is necessary for us to return to the latter part of the *Gemara*

Bava Kamma 114a, to the teaching of Rav Ashi which follows upon the teaching of the legislation of Rava, as cited above:[106]

11. R. Ashi said,
12. When we were at R. Huna's academy, we raised this question:
13. A prominent man (*Adam Chashuv*) upon whom they would rely as two (witnesses),
14. since they will determine monetary liability on the basis of his testimony (alone), ought he not to testify –
15. or perhaps, since he is a prominent man
16. he cannot escape, and may testify?
17. The question remained undecided (*Teiku.*)

In our previous exploration of the earlier part of this text, lines 1–10,[107] we had noted the distinction between what was apparently the original legislation of Rava and what was later Amoraic or Saboraic addition of explanation and limitation of the new law.[108] A similar scan of the latter part of the passage, lines 11–17, yields important information that will help us understand the Talmudic teaching of Rav Ashi.

Three indications lead us to a literary division of our passage into an initial statement by Rav Ashi and a subsequent explanatory addition to it. Firstly, many scholars have noted that questions raised in the academy in the form of *Ibayah*, "we raised this question," as in our text on line 12, were uniformly brief texts consisting only of a question and an answer, to which later generations added extensive explanatory comments such as the logical or textual argument for each side of the question.[109] Secondly, most manuscripts insert the word *mahu*, or *mai*, meaning "what is the law" after the first two words of line 13 – thus reading *Adam Chashuv mahu*?[110] ("what is the law related to an *Adam Chashuv*?") These words, *mahu* and *mai* are classical Amoraic forms of closing a question,[111] to be followed solely by the answer.[112]

The outcome we are led to is that the initial question reported by Rav Ashi had to do with only one specific element of the law of Rava,

[106] See above 2.1, lines 11–17 of the quoted text, and footnotes there.

[107] See above 2.1.

[108] See above 2.1.5.

[109] DeVries, *Mechkarim BeSafrut HaTalmud*, pp. 188–193; Albeck, *Mavo LaTalmudim*, pp. 508–511. Weiss, *Mechkarim BeTalmud*, pp. 231–237.

[110] Rabbinovicz, *Dikdukei Soferim* to *Bava Kamma*, 114a.

[111] For another instance of *mahu* followed by an explanatory addition see H. Klein, "*Gemara* and Sebara," *J.Q.R.*, 38, 1947–48, at p. 73.

[112] For instances of *mahu* followed by *teiku*, as in our passage, see J. Fraenkel, *Rashi's Methodology in His Exegesis of the Babylonian Talmud* (Heb.), Jerusalem, 1975, at p. 195.

namely, the identity of the Jewish witness: "If he is a prominent man, (*Adam Chashuv*) what is the law?" It is to this question that the initial Talmudic response is *Teiku* – the question remained undecided. We need to explore who this *Adam Chashuv* was, and why Rav Ashi and his colleagues thought that the Law of Rava might not apply to him.

I have elsewhere dealt extensively with the term *Adam Chashuv*, and the following passages are excerpted or summarized from that longer treatment in order to serve the needs of this particular application of the term.[113] The term itself, *Adam Chashuv*, does not appear in *Tannaitic* literature.[114] However, the idea that a person's "importance" could impact on the way in which specific laws apply to him, is found expressly once in *Mishnah*,[115] and three times in *Tosefta*.[116] In each case, an otherwise legally permissible activity was prohibited to a person described as a *mitchashev*, a "prominent person."[117] While these specific cases provide no special clue as to the identity of the prominent person, and indeed were only of minor impact in the Amoraic discussions,[118] they may have provided the ideational seed out of which the later usage of *Adam Chashuv* developed.

The term *Adam Chashuv* appears in thirty distinct sugyot in the Babylonian *Gemara*[119] and not at all in the Palestinian *Gemara*.[120] In sixteen of those instances the *Gemara* resolves a conflict between the stated law and the contrary behavior of an individual scholar by asserting that a distinctive standard of behavior is expected of an *Adam Chashuv*.[121] In eight instances,

113 Berman, "Adam Hashub," Dinei Israel, vols. 13–14, pp. 123–154.

114 The word *Chashuv* does appear once in relation to persons, in *Mechilta*, Bo, sec. 1 (Horowitz Rabin edition p. 1, line 16), in an initial attempt to establish that the Biblical order of listing of the forefathers is an indication also of their relative importance. The *Midrash* then rejects the suggestion.

115 *Mishnah Sheviit* 8:11.

116 Once in *Tosefta Avodah Zarah* 1:2, and twice in *Tosefta Avodah Zarah* 2:7. It is odd that the article on *Adam Chashuv* in Zevin, *Encyclopedia Talmudit*, vol. I, pp. 175–180, omits this Tosefta material altogether.

117 In *Mishnah Sheviit* 8:11 the prominent person is prohibited from bathing in a public bath which was heated with inedible vegetation produced in the Sabbatical year. In *Tosefta* A.Z. 1:2 he is prohibited from greeting an idolator on the day of his pagan festival. In *Tosefta* A.Z. 2:7 he is prohibited from attending a pagan theater or stadium.

118 *Mishnah Sheviit* 8:11 and *Tosefta* A.Z. 1:2 are never cited in the Babylonian *Gemara*. The text of *Tosefta* A.Z. 2:7 is quoted in the Babylonian *Gemara*, but due to an orthographic change was understood in a manner which made it irrelevant to our concerns. See Berman, "Adam Hashub," footnote 119.

119 Kasowski, *Thesaurus Talmudis*, vol. I, pp. 207–208.

120 Dov Revel, "*Adam Chashuv*" (Heb.), *Ner Maaravi*, 1, 1924, pp. 7–21, at pp. 12–13.

121 *Berachot* 19a; *Shabbat* 12b, 51a, 142b; *Megillah* 22b; *Moed Kattan* 11b, 12a, 12b (twice); *Ketuboth* 52b, 86a; *Bava Metzia* 73a; *Avodah Zarah* 8b, 28a, 48b; *Hullin* 134b.

the conflict between two legal teachings is resolved by the assertion that one of them reflects the distinctive standard of the *Adam Chashuv*.[122]

In the remaining six cases, the *Gemara* simply asserts the existence of a distinctive standard of conduct applicable to an *Adam Chashuv*.[123] In five additional instances, an Aramaic parallel term is used in place of *Adam Chashuv*, namely, *gavra dechashiv*, or simply, *dechashiv*.[124]

In this total of thirty-five passages, there are nineteen *Amoraim* who are identified as the *Adam Chashuv*, or the *gavra dechashiv*. Strikingly, seventeen of them lived in the first four generations of *Amoraim*, in the period between 220 and 375 C.E., and every one of them was the Head of an Academy.[125] Similarly, the Palestinian scholars referred to as *Adam Chashuv* in the Babylonian *Gemara*, were also Heads of Academies in Israel in that same period of time.[126]

The conclusion that is inescapable is that the term *Adam Chashuv* was not simply an honorific description related to persons who were bearers of particular personality traits, or who had achieved some distinctive spiritual stature, but that for approximately a century and a half, from 220 till 375 C.E., in Babylon/Persia it was the technical term which served as the title of the Head of a Babylonian or Palestinian Rabbinic Academy.[127] The Talmudic texts which deal with the *Adam Chashuv* thus portray for us the distinctive status of the Head of the Academy as someone who occupied a position of special religious leadership, who exercised a significant role in communal governance, and who had a special relationship to the non-Jewish authorities.[128]

We are now in a position to return to the question that motivates our current analysis of the term *Adam Chashuv*. In our passage of *Bava Kamma* 114a, Rav Ashi reported a question raised in the academy of his teacher R. Kahana[129] as to the applicability to an *Adam Chashuv* of

[122] *Berachot* 53a; *Pesachim* 110a; *Ketuboth* 75a; *Kiddushin* 7a; *Bava Batra* 9a; *Avodah Zarah* 29a; *Hullin* 107b; *Arakhin* 19a.

[123] *Shabbat* 21b, 151a; *Taanit* 14b; *Moed Kattan* 28a; *Bava Kamma* 114a; *Bava Metzia* 9b.

[124] *Berachot* 18b; *Megillah* 22a; *Moed Kattan* 17a; *Gittin* 59b; *Bava Batra* 10b. See Kasowski, *Thesaurus Talmudis*, vol. XIV, pp. 771–772. Also see Berman, "Adam Hashub," footnote 126.

[125] See Berman, "Adam Hashub," text and related footnotes 128–140.

[126] *Ibid.*, text and related footnotes 144–151.

[127] Note the possibly related usage in Codex Theodosian, XVI, 8, 15, of the term *spectabilis*, "the respectable," in reference to the Patriarch. Cited by Hugo Mantel, *Studies in the History of the Sanhedrin*, Cambridge, MA, Harvard University Press, 1961, at p. 239.

[128] See Berman, "Adam Hashub," text and related footnotes 174 and 183.

[129] All of the manuscripts and many of the *Rishonim* read here "R. Kahana," in place of "R. Huna." Rabbinovicz, *Dikdukei Soferim*, *Bava Kamma*, at p. 281, note 20. This

Rava's legislation restricting testimony by a Jew, against a fellow Jew, in a non-Jewish court. Rav Kahana, who died before 375 C.E.,[130] was clearly using the term in its exclusive sense of Head of an Academy. Therefore, in our continuing analysis of the question reported by Rav Ashi we have to assume that his original intent was that it is the distinctive religious, social and political role of the Head of an Academy which would make it impossible for him to evade his responsibility to testify in a non-Jewish court. To this straightforward question the *Talmud* declares, *Teiku*, "the matter remains unresolved."

This simple exchange became more complicated with the advent of the second stage in the presentation of the Law of Rava. As indicated previously, the original broad general restriction against a Jew testifying against a fellow Jew in favor of a non-Jew, in a non-Jewish court, was limited by the contention that such restriction applied only when the Jewish witness was the sole witness in a *Magista* court – which would issue judgment based on that testimony alone. By contrast, were the testimony to be offered by two witnesses, even in a *Magista* court, it would be permissible for the Jew to testify. Or, even if there was only a single witness, were the testimony to be offered in a *Dawar* court, such testimony would be permissible since the *Dawar* court, like a Jewish court, does not rely solely on the evidence of a single witness, but would then require the defendant to take an oath. Thus limiting the original Law of Rava, in the position of this second stage of the law, even a single Jewish witness would be permitted to testify against a fellow Jew, in favor of a non-Jewish plaintiff, in a *Dawar* court.

This development in the Law of Rava required some modification of the understanding of the question of Rav Ashi. Now, the particular identity or status of the Jewish witness should be irrelevant since any single witness, even an *Adam Chashuv*, is permitted to testify in a *Dawar* (fundamentally honest) court, as any single Jewish witness would be forbidden to testify in a *Magista* (fundamentally corrupt) court. Why then should Rav Ashi be raising the question of the status of the Jewish witness – which should be irrelevant to the ruling of Rava as understood in the second stage? The *Adam Chashuv*, like any other Jew would be permitted to testify in a *Dawar* court, and forbidden to make an appearance as a witness in a *Magista* court.

reading seems most reasonable since Rav Ashi was in fact a student of R. Kahana and often reported on discussions which took place at his academy in Pum Nahara. See Hyman, *Toldot Tannaim VeAmoraim*, vol. III, p. 847 for a listing of such instances.

[130] Hyman, *Toldot Tannaim VeAmoraim*, vol. I, p. 247.

It is at this point that a new rationale for the problem of Rav Ashi was introduced into our text, consisting of mid-line 13 through line 16. The new rationale suggests that the problem is that if an *Adam Chashuv* testifies as a single witness, even in a *Dawar* court, his social and religious status is such that the court will assign credibility to his testimony beyond what it would assign to the testimony of any other single witness, and would issue judgment in favor of the non-Jewish plaintiff based purely on the sole testimony of the *Adam Chashuv*. The *Talmud* then spells out a new dilemma which arises under these circumstances. If the *Adam Chashuv* then proceeds to testify in the *Dawar* court as a single witness, would he be subject to excommunication because he would have caused a loss to a fellow Jew not in accordance with Jewish law, violating the protective intent of the Law of Rava? Or should he be exempt from such punishment due to the fact that as an *Adam Chashuv*, as a public figure of such stature, he would not have the capacity to avoid testifying? To this newly reconfigured question of Rav Ashi the *Talmud* still appends the original response, *Teiku* – the matter remained legally unresolved.

But the new understanding of the question of Rav Ashi raises one essential problem which did not exist in the original form of his question. The distinctive position of the *Adam Chashuv* which, in this newly configured question, is asserted to be the grounds which might justify his exemption from the penalty under the Law of Rava, resides in the fact that *lo matzi mishtamit lehu*, "he cannot escape." The implication of the contrast between the *Adam Chashuv* and any other Jewish witness is that an average person would be justifiably punished by excommunication for his testimony as a single witness against a fellow Jew in a *Magista* (corrupt) court, because he would have had the capacity to evade any duty to testify. It is therefore the voluntary nature of his testimony, his willingness to betray the covenantal duty of loyalty that he has, to protect the material well-being of a fellow Jew from the unjust action of a corrupt court, that is then the legal basis for the penalty of excommunication.

It is for that reason that there might be an essential difference between the average person and the exceptional *Adam Chashuv*. The latter, precisely because of his distinctive status in the eyes of the non-Jewish as well as of the Jewish community, simply cannot avoid offering the testimony which he has in a *Dawar* court. Thus the question Rav Ashi is now understood to be raising is, should the *Adam Chashuv* be immune from penalty under the Law of Rava because his testimony is not truly voluntary – his position demands that it be offered despite his presumed reluctance to monetarily injure the Jewish defendant. Or should even the

Adam Chashuv be fully subject to excommunication under the Law of Rava because, whether voluntary or not, in the final event he is causing harm to a fellow Jew beyond what is just according to Jewish law?

The early *Rishonim* of Ashkenaz uniformly held that the circumstances of the *Adam Chashuv* constituted a basis for exemption from excommunication due to his inability to evade the responsibility to testify, and that the same principle would then be applicable to any single Jewish witness who was unable to avoid offering testimony. Thus, for example, Raavan (Rabbi Eliezer ben Natan of Mainz, c. 1090–1170) concludes that in the face of the Talmudic *teiku*, the lack of resolution of the question, there would be no excommunication of an *Adam Chashuv* were he to testify.[131] His rationale is that the failure to testify "would constitute a desecration of the name of God; that they (the gentiles) should not say 'The best of them is as a brier'(*Micah* 7:4)."[132] His use of the *Chillul Hashem* argument as the basis for permissibility of testifying is, however, not a distinctive element applicable to the *Adam Chashuv*. Raavan himself, as we had seen, specifically maintains that for any Jew, the presence of *Chillul Hashem* would justify testimony even as a single witness in a *Magista* court.[133]

Similarly, Rabbenu Tam (c. 1110–1171), as cited by Mordechai ben Hillel (1240–1298), maintained explicitly that the inability to avoid testifying, *lo matzi le'ishtamuti*, served as a basis for exemption from excommunication for any single Jewish witness even in a *Magista* court.[134] The intent of Rabbenu Tam in this matter is even more clearly expressed in the version of his teaching reported in the *Hagahot Mordechai* of Samuel ben Aaron of Schlettstadt, where the penalty of excommunication is explicitly applicable "only to a single witness who was able to avoid" testifying, but did not do so.[135]

Scholars of both Provence and Spain also subscribed to this significant limitation on the applicability of the Law of Rava, on the strength of the exemption universally recognized as having been granted to the *Adam Chashuv* who was unable to avoid testifying. Thus, Rabbi Isaac ben Abba Mari of Marseilles (c. 1120–1190), in *Sefer HaIttur*, seamlessly integrated the law of the *Adam Chashuv* with that of any single witness

[131] *Sefer Raavan*, vol. II, end of Tractate *Bava Kamma*, at pp. 194–195.

[132] *Ibid.*

[133] See above, 4.1.4.

[134] Mordechai to *Bava Kamma*, at sec. 157.

[135] *Hagahot Mordechai*to *Bava Kamma*, at sec. 212.

in a non-Jewish court, and asserts that "if he can avoid testifying, he should avoid it, but if he cannot, then it is permissible."[136]

Likewise RaMaH, Rabbi Meir Halevy Abulafia (1170–1244, Toledo), supports the exemption from excommunication when avoiding testimony is not possible. He, however, introduces a significantly different condition which makes the testimony unavoidable. He says:

> Even as to excommunication, that is only when he ought to have avoided testifying, but did so (testified). But where he could not have avoided testifying, for example if they (the non-Jewish court) would obligate him to take an oath that he did not know any evidence, and if he refused to take the oath they would compel him either bodily or monetarily, then he may go and testify and we do not excommunicate him.[137]

In this passage it is self-evident to RaMaH that it would not be permissible for the Jewish witness to take a false oath in order to avoid testifying against his fellow Jew. The only question is whether his loyalty duty to protect the economic well-being of his fellow Jew would require him to personally submit to physical torture or to economic loss[138] in consequence of his attempt to protect the Jewish litigant by refusing to testify and being unwilling to make a false oath. Abulafia's answer to that question is unequivocal – he should not suffer either bodily injury or economic loss in order to avoid offering truthful testimony despite its negative impact on his fellow Jew.

Further conformity with this position is evidenced in *Piskei Ri'az* of Rabbenu Isaiah ben Elijah of Trani (Rabbenu Isaiah Acharon, 1235–1300), who spells out what the alternative might be if the *Adam Chashuv* were legally constrained from testifying. In that situation, says Riaz, "if he were not permitted to testify, he would have to save himself by expenditure of his own money so as not to have to go and testify."[139] He does not inform us whether he has in mind the need to bribe the court to

[136] *Sefer HaIttur*, end of section on Kabbalat Ha'edut, Warsaw edition, p. 62b. Note should be taken however of the imprecision of his language in this passage in his failure to make explicit that he is referring to testimony in *Magista* courts as opposed to *Dawar* courts where by the Talmudic passage itself there is no objection to testimony of a single Jewish witness.

[137] Cited in Ashkenaze, *Shita Mekubetzet* to *Bava Kamma*, 113b-114a, s.v. *Aval HaRamah zal.*

[138] This association between monetary loss and bodily injury is powerfully made in the Talmudic insistence that the Biblical mandate, to return lost property, "and you shall return it unto him" (Deut. 22:2), also serves as an independent foundation for the duty of rescue of life or prevention of bodily injury. *Bava Kamma* 81b and *Sanhedrin* 73a.

[139] *Piskei Ri'az*, to *Bava Kamma*, ch. 10, Law 2, para. 19, at p. 189.

relieve him of the duty to testify, or to simply pay the plaintiff the value of his claim against the Jewish defendant, out of his own funds. In either case, R. Isaiah maintains that the witness would not stand under any such duty, but would be permitted to testify.

However, Riaz has now enabled us to reformulate the question raised by the modification of the initial question of Rav Ashi. Given the duty of loyalty which a Jew has to protect the property of a fellow Jew, which led to the Law of Rava, threatening excommunication if a Jew does testify in a non-Jewish court against his fellow Jew in the benefit of a non-Jew – is a potential Jewish witness obligated to suffer personal financial loss in order to fulfill his loyalty obligation? Further yet, would his failure to act in that manner constitute an impermissible instance of his being a *Matzil atzmo be'mamon chavero*, that is, engaging in "the rescue of his personal property at the expense of the property of his fellow Jew"?!

Certainly, by operation of the usual laws of personal injury, the witness could not be held liable for the untoward consequences suffered by the Jewish defendant as a result of the testimony of the Jewish witness. As we had previously seen, the effect of the testimony on the Jewish defendant depends upon the independent action of the non-Jewish court and is therefore not the direct cause of the loss to the Jewish party. That was the entire reason that the special legislation of Rava was necessary to begin with. Such is the case even in the extreme instance of the law of *Moser*, where one who is coerced to reveal the whereabouts of the property of a fellow Jew in order to protect his own property is still not liable for the loss to his "victim," so long as he does not actually physically deliver the property into the hands of the oppressor.[140] This is why, even though the *Moser* benefits from having revealed the property of the "victim" to the oppressor, he is not liable to pay for the loss since he is subject to the general exemption from liability of a coerced party, *Ones, Rachmana patrei*.[141] It is only when a person acts directly, personally, to hand over

[140] Rambam, *Mishneh Torah, Hilchot Chovel U'Mazzik* 8:2. And see above text and footnotes at 3.2.3.2 See also Zevin, *Encyclopedia Talmudit*, vol. VI, s.v. *Gerama B'nezikin: Garmi*, at columns 495–497.

[141] See Zevin, *Encyclopedia Talmudit*, vol. II, s.v. *Ones*, p. 162. For the particular application of this principle to coercion through monetary matters, as opposed to through threat of death, see *ibid.* at p. 166. A fascinating application of this principle is reflected in an earlyAshkenazic *Takanah* related to a person who had been defamed (informed upon) and thereby risked punishment by the ruler. He in turn defended himself, in the course of which he caused loss to another innocent fellow Jew. The *Takanah* holds him not liable, and asserts that only the original informer is subject to penalty. Responsa of Maharam of Rothenberg, Prague edition, Sec. 1022, para. No. 81, cited in Zevin,

a property to an oppressor which the latter would otherwise not have access to, that he could be held liable even though he acted to defend himself or his own property. Thus, Rambam maintains that a person being pursued, fearful of being killed, who protects himself by directly damaging the property of an innocent, uninvolved, third party, would be held liable for the damage caused, since he has directly damaged the property of another person.[142]

The distinctive issue raised by Rav Ashi clearly presumed the awareness of the general exemption of a party who caused indirect injury. The question that had been raised in the academy of Rav Kahane was whether the special penalty introduced by Rava that went beyond the parameters of the regular law, to impose excommunication upon a person causing indirect injury through testimony in a non-Jewish court, would also be inapplicable in the face of the element of coercion. It is that question which the *Talmud* refuses to resolve, and leaves standing with the response of *Teiku*. And it is to this issue which the *Rishonim* had been responding as they consistently maintained that not only the *Adam Chashuv*, but any Jew who was effectively coerced to testify by threat of personal injury or injury to his property, would not be subject to excommunication under the legislation of Rava.

Rabbenu Asher ben Yechiel (c. 1250–1327) cut through the entire discussion of the special case of the *Adam Chashuv* by proposing that the unresolved question, the *Teiku*, was to be viewed as leaving the case outside the applicable range of the legislation of Rava, and that, therefore, Rosh said, "*azil u'mas'hid*," the *Adam Chashuv* "may proceed and testify."[143] This equated the *Adam Chashuv* to any other single Jewish potential witness who would be permitted to testify in a *Dawar* court.[144]

This eliding of the *Adam Chashuv* case was followed by Rabbi Jacob ben Asher and by Rabbi Joseph Karo to the point that the *Adam Chashuv* exception warranted no mention whatsoever in their respective codes,

Encyclopedia Talmudit, supplement to article s.v. Cherem deRabbenu Gershom, at p. 772.

142 Rambam, *Mishneh Torah, Hilchot Chovel Umazzik* 8:13. It is only a third party rescuer who would not be held liable for such damages to an innocent bystander, *ibid.* 8:14, as special Rabbinic legislation enacted in order not to deter rescue of life by third parties.

143 Rosh, *Commentary to Bava Kamma*, ch. 10, sec. 14.

144 Rabbi Joseph Karo, in *Beit Yosef* to Tur, *Choshen Mishpat*, ch. 28, s.v. *bameh devarim amurim*, suggests that the technical reasoning of Rosh was that the unresolved Talmudic question was to be viewed as a matter of doubt in regard to a monetary matter (*Teiku d'mamon*), which is to be determined leniently.

but in both instances their silence was understood to be in confirmation of the position of Rosh that, for any Jewish single witness, the inability to avoid testifying would exempt him from liability to excommunication under the legislation of Rava.[145] (Further comments made by Rabbenu Asher on this matter in this very same passage will be dealt with in the following chapter.)

4.5 IF REFUSAL OR FAILURE TO TESTIFY WOULD THREATEN THE SECURITY OR THE ECONOMIC WELL-BEING OF THE JEWISH COMMUNITY

Rabbenu Asher offers a detailed examination of the implications of the text of the legislation of Rava. He reports the conclusion of the *Gemara* that even a single Jewish witness may testify in a *Dawar* court, but that in a *Magista* court, while two may testify, a single Jewish witness may not testify.[146] He then goes on to identify other circumstances not explicitly indicated in the Talmudic discussion in which testimony by a Jew against a fellow Jew, in favor of a non-Jew, in a non-Jewish court, would not run foul of the legislation of Rava. He reports three situations in which even a single witness may or must testify in a *Magista* court, and one situation in which two may testify despite the fact that it could result in an outcome of liability for the Jewish party which he would not have to suffer in a Jewish court. He says as follows:[147]

> (1) But if a Jew is suing a non-Jew for payment, and (the latter) claims that he had paid, or that he had never owed the money – then he (the Jewish witness) may testify (in the *Magista* court). For, even in a Jewish court the defendant could relieve himself of obligation by his claim that he paid the debt. And since in a Jewish court the non-Jewish defendant could so

[145] Sirkis, to Tur, *Choshen Mishpat*, ch. 28; and see also Sirkis, *Bayit Chadash*, s.v. *Bameh devarim amurim*. Also see *Shulchan Aruch, Choshen Mishpat*, 28:3 where reference to *Adam Chashuv* would have been expected, but is absent. See Karo's explanation of his position, based on his understanding of the Tur, in his *Beit Yosef* to Tur, *Choshen Mishpat*, 28, at s.v. *Bameh devarim amurim*.

[146] Strikingly, our printed editions of the text of Rabbenu Asher to *Bava Kamma*, ch. 10, sec. 14, contain the additional words *velo teva'o*, "and he had not been subpoenaed." This would suggest the permissibility of a single witness testifying in a *Magista* court purely on the grounds of his having been summoned to do so. However, as Rabbinovicz reports in *Dikdukei Soferim* to *Bava Kamma* 113b, manuscripts of this text of Rabbenu Asher do not include the phrase, and it was apparently added to his quotation of the *Gemara* by a later copyist only after the text of the *Gemara* itself had been amended in this manner.

[147] Rabbenu Asher to *Bava Kamma*, ch. 10, sec. 14.

relieve himself of liability, the Jewish witness may testify, since it is analogous to testimony by two witnesses who are permitted to testify (even in a *Magista* court.)

(2) This restriction applies only to a single witness (in a *Magista* court) not to two. Albeit, even in a situation of two witnesses, it is also possible for the Jewish defendant to deny liability based on *Hafka'at Halva'ato* (in a manner which would result in his not being liable in a Jewish court, but would be held liable in the non-Jewish court based on the testimony of the two witnesses) nevertheless (the witnesses may testify) since they are not actually causing him any loss of his own property.

(3) And all of this pertains when the non-Jewish party had not at the outset designated him as a witness. But, if from the outset (of the transaction between himself and the Jewish defendant), the non-Jewish party had designated this Jew to serve as witness, then it would be a desecration of the Divine name (*Chillul Hashem*) if he were not to testify.

(4) And certainly this is so at a time when the (non-Jewish) statute provides, in regard to Jewish litigants, that a non-Jewish witness is not granted full credibility in testimony against a Jew unless there is a Jewish witness with him. (Under these circumstances) if Jews would withhold their testimony (i.e. refuse to testify against fellow Jews), they will revoke this statute and grant full credibility to the testimony of non-Jewish witnesses against Jewish litigants.

The first of these exemptions from applicability of the legislation of Rava was already well established by Rabbenu Jacob Tam in his contention that testimony by a Jewish witness in favor of a non-Jewish defendant who was sued by a Jewish plaintiff in a non-Jewish court was perfectly permissible, since it simply left the status quo intact, and could not cause the Jewish party to now have to expend money or transfer property which was currently in his possession.[148]

In similar manner the second case of Rabbenu Asher was well established in the writings of the Tosafists.[149] On the one hand, they recognized that the claim of *Hafka'at Halva'ato* in Jewish law resulted in the Jewish borrower of the funds having a better claim than any other living person to the money which had been lent to him by the now deceased non-Jewish lender, since he had full legal possession of the funds and no living person had legal ownership. However, they were clearly loath to confirm that the Jewish borrower had a sufficiently just claim to title as to result in his having a cause of action in Jewish law against a fellow Jew who, through testimony in a non-Jewish court, caused him to have

[148] As reported by Mordechai to *Bava Kamma*, ch. 10, sec. 212.

[149] *Tosafot Bava Kamma* 114a, s.v. *Apumah dechad.*

to return the funds to those who were the legal heirs of the lender under the non-Jewish law.[150]

The third case reported by Rosh, where a Jewish witness had been designated at the outset of the transaction between the parties, is based on the prior teaching of Rabbi Eliezer ben Nathan of Mainz (Raavan, c. 1090–1170.)[151] Raavan had offered three reasons for the permissibility of testimony by a Jew designated at the outset of the transaction to serve as a witness together with a non-Jew. First he argued that such a pair of witnesses were a perfectly valid set of witnesses according to Jewish law by virtue of their acceptance by the Jewish party. Secondly, he argued for the existence of a duty to testify in such instances due to the factor of *Chillul Hashem*. Thirdly he argued for the duty to testify on the grounds of the binding nature of the law of the land. Yet, when Raavan was quoted by his grandson, R. Eliezer ben Yoel HaLevy of Bonn (Raviyah, 1140–1225), he is reported to have cited only the rationale of *Chillul Hashem*.[152]

Likewise, Rosh, in our passage, omits the first and third arguments in support of permissibility of the Jewish witness testifying together with a non-Jew and refers only to the argument of *Chillul Hashem*. His omission of the first claim might be explained by a slight variation in his presentation of the facts of the case. In Raavan it is possible to argue that the Jewish party to the transaction had himself originally participated in the designation of the pair of witnesses, one Jewish and one non-Jewish, in which case the claim that they together constituted a valid pair of witnesses even according to Jewish law is very strong. In fact, Rosh himself not only agrees that prior acceptance of an invalid witness makes his testimony fully admissible, but he goes further than Rambam in this regard in not requiring that any formal *kinyan* – contractual act – be done by the party.[153] But in contrast to Raavan, when Rosh describes this case, he

150 This may be one of a number of instances in which an original Rabbinic theological or ideological teaching was assigned broad legal force as a legal fiction, but was then limited in its applicability due to the perceived unjust consequences of giving it full legal effect. Compare, for example, the principle of *Ger shenitgayer kekatan shenolad dami* ("a convert to Judaism is like a newborn child"), Yevamot 22a; or *Goy sheshavat chayav mita* ("a Gentile who observes the Sabbath is capitally liable"), Sanhedrin 58b; or the equation of Sabbath violation and idolatry, Eruvin 69b. It is striking that so many of these instances, as in our case, relate to boundaries between Jews and non-Jews.

151 Cited and quoted above at 4.1.4.

152 Thus, Isaac ben Moses of Vienna (c. 1180–1250) in *Or Zarua* to *Bava Kamma*, sec. 450; and R. Meir ben Baruch of Rothenberg (c. 1215–1293) in Responsa Maharam of Rothenberg, Bloch edition, based on Parma manuscript, vol. I, no. 58.

153 Rosh to *Sanhedrin* 24a, at ch. 3, secs. 4–5. So clearly in Jacob ben Asher, *Kitzur Piskei HaRosh* to *Sanhedrin*, ch. 3, law 4.

speaks only of the designation of the Jewish witness by "the non-Jewish party."[154] If in fact the Jewish party to the transaction had not so designated the witnesses, then indeed it would not be possible to argue that the subsequent testimony of the two witnesses together would constitute completely valid testimony according to Jewish law. Of course, this modification by Rosh also served to eliminate the only rationale under which the testimony by the Jewish witness would be permissible, but not mandatory. By contrast, the latter two justifications of testimony introduced by Raavan, the need to avoid *Chillul Hashem* and the duty of obedience to the law of the land, would both result in the presence of a Jewish law legal duty to testify against a fellow Jew, in the benefit of a non-Jew, in a non-Jewish court. This makes for a more powerful contrast to the initial Law of Rava asserting that such testimony would warrant the Jewish law penalty of excommunication.

The fourth case presented by Rosh introduces a factor which further justifies not merely permissibility, but legal duty to testify. Again, the fourth case is as follows:

> (4) And certainly this is so at a time when the (non-Jewish) statute provides, in regard to Jewish litigants, that a non-Jewish witness is not granted full credibility in testimony against a Jew unless there is a Jewish witness with him. (Under these circumstances) if Jews would withhold their testimony (i.e. refuse to testify against fellow Jews), they will revoke this statute and grant full credibility to the testimony of non-Jewish witnesses against Jewish litigants.[155]

Strikingly, Rabbenu Asher in this case makes no reference to the legal basis for the resultant obligation on the part of the Jewish witness to testify. In the first case, he explicitly indicated that the basis for permissibility was the analogy to two witnesses. In the second case, he explicitly indicates that the basis for permissibility was the fact that there would actually be no monetary harm caused to the Jewish defendant. In the third case, the legal duty to testify was based on the element of *Chillul Hashem*, desecration of the Divine name that would result from a refusal to testify. Yet in this fourth case, Rabbenu Asher seems to make an argument for the duty to testify based on the threat of revocation of the beneficial law which would result in injury to the economic well-being of the local Jewish community. How exactly does that amount to a legal

[154] See above, case (3).
[155] Rabbenu Asher to *Bava Kamma*, ch. 10, sec. 14.

foundation for even permissibility to testify, let alone for a Jewish law duty to testify?

It is of course possible that Rabbenu Asher viewed this legal conclusion as simply self evident in the light of the nature of the constraint and of the competing interest. When all is said and done, the legislation of Rava was designed to discourage testimony in non-Jewish courts in situations which could not result in legal liability for the witness because of the indirect nature of the causal connection between his testimony and the negative economic effect on the Jewish defendant. Rava used the mechanism of excommunication as an effective way of discouraging such activity which would be viewed as a manifestation of failure of loyalty to the economic well-being of a fellow Jew. What then of a situation in which the choice to defend the Jewish party, to express loyalty to him by refusing to testify against him, was counterbalanced by the factor of loyalty to the broader Jewish community who would all be put at economic risk resulting from the possible revocation of the favorable law regulating testimony in non-Jewish courts in transactions between Jews and non-Jews? It is possible that for Rabbenu Asher this weighing of competing loyalties would result in an obviously necessary conclusion – that testimony by the Jewish witness is mandatory as a manifestation of loyalty to the entire Jewish community.

It is also possible, however, that such utilitarian reasoning alone would not have been sufficient as a basis for Rabbenu Asher's position. It is noteworthy that Rabbenu Asher opens his description of the fourth case with the words, *vechol she'ken*, meaning, "and certainly," or which could be translated as "by *a fortiori* (reasoning)." He might then just be building on the rationale of the previous case in which the non-Jewish party had designated the Jewish witness at the outset of the transaction, where the refusal of that Jew to testify in later litigation would certainly be a *Chillul Hashem*, as noted previously by Raavan and those who followed him, in consequence of which he would certainly have a Jewish law duty to testify despite the negative outcome to his fellow Jew. Rosh may then simply be adding that the element of *Chillul Hashem* in refusal to testify would "certainly," or "by *a fortiori* reasoning" be present where it was not simply the non-Jewish party who had designated the Jewish witness, but where the designation of a Jewish witness in such a transaction was actually mandated by non-Jewish law as a means of protecting the Jewish parties. In such a case the *Chillul Hashem* is not only itself a factor which would require testimony by the designated Jewish witness, but that the *Chillul Hashem* itself would have an even further detrimental impact – beyond the disgrace of God's (honest) name – in that it could result in the revocation of the non-Jewish law protecting Jewish parties engaged in commercial enterprises with non-Jews. The technical legal justification then for the existence of a Jewish law duty to testify would remain based entirely on the law of *Chillul Hashem*.

A further possibility is that Rabbenu Asher might have been aware of Raavan's third rationale for what became Rabbenu Asher's third case, of the binding nature of the law of the land. Rosh might not have seen the relevance of its application to that case, in which, by his description of the facts, it was exclusively the non-Jewish party who himself had designated the Jewish witness, independent of any legal requirement that he do so. But Rosh might certainly have seen that legal factor as an additional element that would make for a Jewish law duty to testify in his own fourth case in which the designation of the Jewish witness was in fact required by the non-Jewish law. While Rabbenu Asher makes no explicit reference to the applicability of this principle to the immediate case, there is no doubt that the tradition of applicability of *Dina de Malchuta Dina*, as we have previously documented, would be fully applicable in the fourth case Rosh described.[156]

One further speculation in regard to the position of Rabbenu Asher is that the law of the land and its attendant threat of deprivation of that protection being unequivocally to the detriment of the Jewish community results in a particular legal presumption as to the intent of the Jewish party to the original transaction. That is, that in the face of his awareness of that threat, Jewish law would presume that a Jewish person who entered into a transaction with a non-Jew in which both a Jewish and a non-Jewish witness were designated, would have fully accepted the validity of that pair of witnesses, and could therefore later not be heard to object to testimony on the part of the Jewish witness. Such acceptance, even without explicit *kinyan*, contractual act manifesting his intent, would, according to Rabbenu Asher, be sufficient to establish the permissibility of testimony by that witness, and when co-joined with the factor of *Chillul Hashem*, would make the testimony doubly a matter of legal duty according to Jewish law.[157]

The reason that I have entered into these speculative explanations of the rationale of Rabbenu Asher is because of the way in which his son, Rabbi

[156] See above, 4.3.

[157] Rosh to *Sanhedrin* 24a, ch. 3, secs. 4–5. Also Jacob ben Asher, *Kitzur Piskei HaRosh*, ch. 3, law 4; and more fully in Tur, *Choshen Mishpat*, ch. 22.

Jacob ben Asher, later explicated the position of his father. In his summation of his father's practical legal decisions, extracted from his father's extensive running commentary to the *Talmud*, Rabbi Jacob says:[158]

> Nowadays, a Jew who knows evidence in the benefit of a non-Jew, to the detriment of a fellow Jew, must testify on his (the non-Jew's) behalf, before non-Jewish judges, if the non-Jew summoned him.

This appears to be a condensation and summation of the latter two cases discussed by Rabbenu Asher, the case of designation of the Jewish witness by the non-Jewish party, and the case of the protective statute which requires the presence of one Jewish witness in transactions between a Jew and a non-Jew. In both of these cases Rabbenu Asher had asserted the presence of a Jewish law duty for the Jewish witness to testify in the non-Jewish court. The grounds for that duty were, primarily, the concern with *Chillul Hashem*; but possibly also because of the consent of the Jewish party to the otherwise constrained witness, and further due to the possible application of the principle of the law of the land as binding. Rabbi Jacob ben Asher seems here to avoid committing himself on the legal foundation for the existence of a duty to testify against a fellow Jew in a non-Jewish court, while expanding the application of the duty to any situation in which the non-Jewish party had summoned the Jewish witness to testify.

It is indeed striking that in this short passage Rabbi Jacob ben Asher is making it clear that the summons to testify is not even being issued by the court, but rather by the non-Jewish party. It is the singular "non-Jew," meaning the non-Jewish party; not the plural "non-Jewish judges," whose summons generates the duty to testify. This is consistent with the position of Jewish law itself in regard to the general legal duty to testify. Rambam already insists that the Biblical duty to testify in consonance with one's knowledge of the facts of a case pertain "when he is summoned to testify in a monetary matter."[159] Likewise, Rabbi Jacob ben Asher himself reports that it was the position of his father Rabbenu Asher that the onset of the Jewish law duty to testify in a Jewish court is initiated by summons either by the party or by the court. Thus he says,

> They (witnesses) are not obligated (to testify) unless they are summoned to testify on his (the party's) behalf, even (if the summons is issued) outside (independently) of the court.[160]

[158] Jacob ben Asher, *Kitzur Piskei HaRosh*, *Bava Kamma*, ch. 10, law 14.

[159] Rambam, *Mishneh Torah*, Laws of Testimony 1:1.

[160] Jacob ben Asher, *Kitzur Piskei HaRosh* to *Shavuot*, ch. 4, law 15.

The effect of this teaching of Rabbi Jacob ben Asher is quite radical, it would create a new and extremely broad exception to the legislation of Rava. The kind of court, honest or dishonest, would no longer matter; the number of witnesses would no longer matter; the judicial procedure of the non-Jewish court would not be relevant; whether the outcome of the judicial process would actually result in liability of the Jewish party not in accordance with Jewish Law would also not matter – there would be no constraint on a Jew testifying against a fellow Jew, in favor of the non-Jewish party, in a non-Jewish court, no threat of excommunication – so long as the Jewish witness had been summoned to testify either by the non-Jewish party or by the court itself. According to this position, what exactly is it that has overcome the duty of loyalty to the material well-being of one's fellow Jew? It could certainly not be simply a duty to respond affirmatively to the request for aid from the non-Jewish party. Why should such a claim have standing against the covenantal duty to fellow Jews? Is Jacob ben Asher proposing a legal presumption that in every instance in which a non-Jew requests testimony of a Jew in a non-Jewish court, the refusal of the Jew to participate would result in disgrace to the Divine name? Why should such a response be irrebuttably presumed rather than simply having its presence evaluated on a case-by-case basis?

Indeed, it appears to be the case that Rabbi Jacob ben Asher himself backed off from the extreme nature of his own interpretation of the position of his father.[161] In his code of Jewish law known as the Arba Turim, Rabbi Jacob ben Asher abandons the very broad language which he so strikingly used in *Kitzur Piskei HaRosh*. Instead, he reverts to the language of Rabbenu Asher himself, but only omits the second case, that of the permissibility to testify against the Jew who falsely claims that he had either never borrowed, or already repaid a loan from a deceased non-Jewish lender (the case of *Hafka'at Halva'ato*.)[162] Instead of merging the latter two cases of Rabbenu Asher into a single vast exemption, in the Tur, Rabbi Jacob preserves the original language of his father, reporting the duty to testify when the witness had been designated at the outset of the transaction – due to *Chillul Hashem*; and the duty to testify when the result of a refusal might be the revocation of a beneficial statute requiring the inclusion of a Jewish witness to transactions between Jews and non-Jews.

[161] Jacob ben Asher, Tur, *Choshen Mishpat*, ch. 28.

[162] *Ibid.* He may have felt secure doing so because of his prior insistence that the basis for the restriction was the financial loss caused to the Jewish party, whereas in this instance, as the Tosafists had pointed out, there was no actual loss.

But, his concluding comment in this section is, "And he is not obligated to testify until he is summoned to testify on his behalf."[163] This might well be understood to be a last-ditch attempt to regain the broad exemption he had previously formulated in the *Kitzur Piskei HaRosh*. Otherwise, why does he leave this reference to subpoena to the very end of the passage rather than introducing it at the outset of the chapter when he posits the very existence of a duty to testify for a fellow Jew in a Jewish court, which, already according to Rambam, is dependent upon the witness being summoned to testify?[164] Locating this comment after the three instances in which his father had allowed for exemptions, requiring the testimony against a fellow Jew in a non-Jewish court, could lead us to think that Jacob ben Asher, here in the Tur was now positing a fourth exemption, of great breadth – that testimony would always be mandatory when a subpoena had been issued, on the grounds of some very broad concern for the combination of *Chillul Hashem* and the threat to the economic well-being of the community that could result from the resistance to a subpoena. The argument might be made that while even in the three instances in which he, following his father Rosh, had asserted that there would be a duty to testify, the duty is contingent on his being summoned by the affected party to testify; it could still be the case that summons alone would be a sufficient condition to overcome the constraint against testimony propounded in the legislation of Rava. This in fact is the way in which Tur is understood by Rabbi Joel Sirkis (Bach) (1561–1640).[165]

It might very well be that it was precisely to avoid this interpretation of the Tur that Rabbi Joseph Karo, in his commentary to this passage in the Tur, insists that the closing phrase is not an independent justification for requiring testimony against a fellow Jew in a non-Jewish court, but is a supplemental condition applicable to all of the prior situations of duty to testify, including the opening indication of the existence of a Jewish law duty for a Jew to testify in litigation between fellow Jews in Jewish courts.[166] To secure that understanding of the position of Jewish law, Karo, in his *Shulchan Aruch*, moves the reference to being summoned from its location at the end of the passage, to the very beginning, immediately after indicating the existence of the legal duty to testify in Jewish courts.[167]

[163] *Ibid.*

[164] Rambam, *Mishneh Torah*, Laws of Testimony 1:1.

[165] R. Joel Sirkis, Bach to Tur, *Choshen Mishpat*, ch. 28, s.v. *Umah sekatav HaRosh*.

[166] Karo, *Beit Yosef to* Tur *Choshen Mishpat*, ch. 28, s.v. *V'eino chayav*.

[167] *Shulchan Aruch, Choshen Mishpat*, 28:1. This was where the statement was originally located also in Rambam's codification of this law, *Mishneh Torah*, Laws of Testimony 1:1.

We are now in a better position to return to an issue raised early in our deliberation on the Talmudic text record of the legislation of Rava. We had noted the appearance of the phrase *ve'lo teva'o*, "and he was not summoned," as an interpolation into the text in a manner which would have indicated that in any situation in which the Jewish witness had been subpoenaed to testify he would not be subject to the threat of excommunication.[168] That phrase does not appear in manuscripts of the *Talmud*, and first appears in the edition of *Bava Kamma* printed in Basel in 1578. We had noted the suggestion of Rabbinovicz in his *Dikdukei Soferim* that this interpolation may have been done in the censoring of the *Talmud* by Cardinal Marco Marini, in an attempt to legitimize and promote Jewish participation in the process of litigation in non-Jewish courts.[169]

We may now consider an alternative approach to the question of how this phrase made its way into the printed text. Early manuscripts of the commentary of Rabbenu Asher still did not include this phrase in its quotation of the Talmudic text of the legislation of Rava. However, as we have seen, Rabbi Jacob ben Asher had proposed this idea in his *Piskei HaRosh* as a consolidation of the multiple cases in which his father had maintained that testimony by a Jewish witness in a non-Jewish court would actually be mandatory. We could consider the possibility of a two-step textual migration of the phrase, firstly from *Kitzur Piskei HaRosh* into the text of Rosh himself through the thought of a learned copyist of Rosh adding to the text of the latter based on the writing of his son. (After all, who would better know the intent of Rosh than his own son recording the *Halachic* conclusions of his father?!) This would explain the appearance of the phrase *ve'lo teva'o* only in later manuscripts and then in printed editions of Rosh.[170] The *Talmud* commentary of Rabbenu Asher had replaced the study of the Digest of the *Talmud*, the *Sefer Halachot*, authorized by his antecedent Rabbi Isaac Alfasi (1013–1103). Given its popularity, it is worth considering the possibility that by 1578, with both the Rosh and the *Kitzur Piskei HaRosh* having already been published,[171] a learned Jew, preparing text for a non-Jewish typesetter for a new printing of the *Talmud*, might well have "corrected" the version

[168] See above 2.2.3 and related footnotes.

[169] See above 2.1.3 and note 29.

[170] See 2.1.3, note 25.

[171] The Rosh was printed in the editio princeps of the Bomberg *Talmud* in 1520–23. Marvin J. Heller, "Earliest Printings of the Talmud," in Sharon Lieberman Mintz (ed.), *Printing the Talmud: From Bomberg To Schottenstein*, Yeshiva University Museum, 2006, pp. 61–78, at p. 74. *Kitzur Piskei HaRosh* of Jacob ben Asher was published in Constantinople in 1575. Jewish Encyclopedia, 1906, article entitled Jacob ben Asher.

of the Talmudic text before him, in consonance with the version which appeared in the commentary of Rabbenu Asher.

We return now to the fourth case of Rabbenu Asher which mandates testimony by the Jewish witness in a situation in which his failure to testify would threaten revocation of a beneficial law, and thereby put the Jewish community at risk. Despite the absence of explicit legal justification for this motive overriding the legislation of Rava, and despite its tenuous connection to the concern with *Chillul Hashem*, the permissibility to testify in such instances was upheld, and read broadly. An interesting example of this application of the position of Rabbenu Asher is found in the Yam Shel Shlomo of Rabbi Shlomo ben Yehiel Luria (Maharshal, Poland, c. 1510–1574.) He initially argues that in this case of Rabbenu Asher, the Jewish witness need not even have been designated at the outset of the transaction, but that,

> where the non-Jewish judges knew that the Jew had been present at the transaction; and that therefore he probably knew (what had transpired); and that his not testifying they would sense is due to our *Torah* instructing that he not testify in their (the non-Jews') benefit; and there is then a danger of the revocation of the (beneficial) statute – in such a circumstance it is permissible (to testify.) Likewise in the time of my troubles I heard of an actual case of this sort. A Jew did not want to testify and the matter came before the nobleman ("*hegmon*"), who sensed the matter (why the Jew did not want to testify). He said to that Jew, "You yourselves are causing the nullification of the King's statute authorizing your survival here."[172]

Both in this paragraph and in his opening paragraph summarizing his legal conclusions, Maharshal softens the conclusion of Rabbenu Asher by asserting that under such circumstances it is "permissible (to testify)," while Rabbenu Asher himself clearly indicated that in such a case it is obligatory to testify as it would be in the prior case where failure to testify would constitute desecration of the Divine name. Despite this softening, the underlying assumption that the public interest of the community would override the duty of loyalty to the material well-being of the individual Jewish litigant, is unequivocally upheld.

[172] Shlomo ben Yehiel Luria, *Yam Shel Shlomo*, to *Bava Kamma*, ch. 10, sec. 23, last column.

5

The Tension Between Responsa and Codification – Maharam Mintz, Rabbi Joseph Karo and Rabbi Moshe Isserlis

The competing interests reflected in the literature of Jewish law through the centuries in regard to testimony against fellow Jews in non-Jewish courts were not easily resolved. On the one hand the sheer power of the concept of *Arevut*, of mutual responsibility in the relationship between fellow Jews, embodied in multiple Jewish laws, which required the assumption of very high standards of responsibility for the well-being of fellow Jews, could not be easily overridden. On the other hand, as we have seen, these competing interests – such as the achievement of justice, the avoidance of *Chillul Hashem*, the duty to prevent fellow Jews from committing crimes, the responsibility to uphold the law of the land, defense of one's own physical and monetary well-being, and the protection of the security of the community – were also of great import, not easily dismissed. The tension between these competing interests played itself out differently in two divergent fields of Jewish jurisprudential endeavor, in the realm of legal responsa, and in the realm of codification of Jewish law, particularly in the fifteenth and sixteenth centuries.

5.1 MAHARAM MINTZ

Rabbi Moses ben Isaac ha-Levi Mintz (Maharam Mintz) (c.1420–1475), serving various communities in Germany, was queried about the following situation.[1] Isaac was the creditor of a non-Jew whom he sued in a non-Jewish court for collection of the debt which he alleged was still

[1] Responsa, Maharam Mintz, *Teshuvot Maharam Mintz*, first printed in Cracow, 1617, Number 44.

owed to him. The non-Jewish defendant asserted that the debt had been fully paid, and presented in his defense the deposition of a witness, a Jew named Moshe, who testified that he had been authorized by Isaac to collect the debt from the defendant, and that he had done so, and had attempted to deliver the funds to Isaac, but that Isaac had refused to accept the funds but intended to initiate a lawsuit against the non-Jewish debtor in a non-Jewish court. On the basis of Moshe's written testimony, the non-Jewish court found in favor of the defendant. Thereafter, Isaac initiated a law suit against Moshe in a Rabbinic court claiming that he had never authorized Moshe to collect that debt for him, that Moshe's deposition was totally false, and that he had suffered financial loss in consequence of Moshe's having testified falsely in the non-Jewish court. Isaac sued Moshe for payment of the amount of his denied claim against the non-Jewish debtor, as well as for further financial damages that he would now suffer in consequence of his loss of credibility in the non-Jewish court and community resulting from Moshe's testimony against him in the non-Jewish court. Moshe's defense was that he was fully permitted to testify in the non-Jewish court in this case since the Jewish party was the plaintiff, not the defendant and that, therefore, he did not cause the non-Jewish court to order any liability on the part of Isaac. Arguing further, in the alternative, Moshe claimed that even if he were forbidden to testify, he could not be held monetarily liable for any damage suffered by Isaac since he, Moshe, had presented only fully truthful testimony.

Maharam Mintz deals exhaustively with the claims of Moshe. Firstly, it is true that Rabbi Jacob ben Asher, in the Tur, quotes his father Rosh to the effect that:

> If a Jew sues a non-Jew who denies liability, and the non-Jew has a single (Jewish) witness – he is permitted to testify, for even according to Jewish Law a single witness in defense would relieve of liability.[2]

However, Maharam Mintz argues that this permissibility of testimony pertains only when the defendant's claim is that he has directly paid the creditor, for then, even in Jewish law, a single witness would be sufficient to prevent recovery by the plaintiff. Maharam Mintz maintains, in the case at hand, that the defendant does not claim payment directly to the creditor, but asserts payment to a third party without witnesses or documentary evidence to indicate that the creditor had authorized such payment through a third party. Therefore, in Jewish law the testimony of

[2] Jacob ben Asher, Tur, *Choshen Mishpat*, ch. 28.

the intermediary that he had received payment would not be sufficient to relieve the debtor of his liability to the creditor. Therefore, Maharam Mintz contends, Moshe was in fact in a situation in which he caused direct financial loss to Isaac through his testimony as a single witness in a non-Jewish court, upon whose testimony the court relied to find the defendant not liable. Strikingly, Maharam Mintz does not even introduce the question of the general honesty of the court as a means of distinguishing between the *Magista* versus the *Dawar* type of court, but uses solely the question of whether the procedural rule of the court is to issue judgment on the basis of a single witness under circumstances in which a Jewish court would not do so. Or, in other terms, the sole test of liability of the single witness is whether the actual outcome of the non-Jewish proceeding resulted in a loss to a fellow Jew that he would not have suffered under adjudication in a Jewish court. This imposes a severe limitation on the ruling of Rosh, which had greatly expanded the range of circumstances under which testimony would be permissible despite the actual negative economic impact on the Jewish litigant.

Maharam Mintz then moves on to the second element in Moshe's defense. He acknowledges the legitimacy of the position of Mordechai ben Hillel, which was regularly affirmed in the mainstream of legal decisions of Ashkenaz scholars, that even when a single Jewish witness is subject to excommunication under the legislation of Rava, there is no monetary liability to the Jewish party who suffers loss as a result of the testimony, so long as the testimony itself was fully truthful, since the injury is indirect. However, Maharam Mintz argues that the defense of truthful testimony is operative only when the witness was a person who qualified as a valid witness under Jewish law, and could therefore have permissibly testified on the matter in a Jewish court. If on the other hand the witness would have been disqualified from testimony in a Jewish court, then his testimony in a non-Jewish court would in fact result in a loss which would not be present in a Jewish court and he would therefore not be exempt from liability for the injury he caused. Such is the situation in the case at hand, Maharam Mintz contends, since Moshe would have been disqualified as a witness on this matter in a Jewish court, as a person who is affected by the outcome of the litigation, a *Noge'a b'davar.*[3] The reasoning on this is not made explicit by Maharam

[3] This very same position is asserted by Aryeh Leib Hacohen Heller (1745–1812) in *K'Tzot Hachoshen* to S.A. Ch.M. as a novel position without precedent. He was apparently unaware of the responsum of Maharam Mintz.

Mintz, but apparently what he has in mind is that if the debtor were to have been found liable to pay the creditor, then he would have sued Moshe for the return of the money which he had given to Moshe as payment of the debt to Isaac. Thus Moshe was an interested party whose testimony would certainly have been excluded by a Jewish court, and could therefore be held monetarily liable for the loss he caused to Isaac through his testimony in the non-Jewish court. Here again, while Mordechai ben Hillel had eased the consequences on a witness even when his testimony was not permissible, Maharam Mintz heightened the penalty to the witness so as to impose financial liability even beyond the excommunication he would suffer.

As factual evidence that Moshe acted in his own economic interest rather than out of conviction that his testimony was actually permissible according to Jewish law, Maharam Mintz points out that Moshe did not ask for permission to testify from the Rabbi and leaders of the community. Indeed, he goes further to argue that had Moshe done so, he might even have been able to avoid testifying altogether because the leaders of the Jewish community might have helped him make a case before the non-Jewish court that his testimony would be inappropriate due to his personal interest in the outcome of the case.[4] Interestingly, Maharam here speaks somewhat positively of the non-Jewish court in Rothenberg, as a court that is "not a *magista* court, nor a court of amateur jurists (*hedyotot*)."[5] Yet he does not choose to refer to the court in affirmative terms, as a *Dawar* court, apparently because that would force him to contend with the explicit indication of the Talmudic text that allows the testimony of a single witness against a fellow Jew in a *Dawar* court. The consequence of this approach is that Moshe is asserted to be acting in a manner that "rescues his own funds at the expense of his fellow Jew," for which he is to be held financially liable. This then is the third instance in this responsum in which Maharam Mintz uses novel and creative interpretative devices to avoid what are otherwise clear legal justifications for the permissibility of the testimony by Moshe.

At the close of this paragraph, Maharam Mintz raises and dismisses the most significant foundation for the permissibility of Moshe's testimony, the language of Rabbi Jacob ben Asher in *Kitzur Piskei HaRosh*:[6]

4 *Teshuvot Maharam Mintz*, at 42a, column 1, s.v. *vechen.*

5 *Ibid.*

6 Jacob ben Asher, *Kitzur Piskei HaRosh*, *Bava Kamma*, ch. 10, law 14. See above, 4.5. The source in the printed text of Maharam Mintz, in an obvious scribal error, is "as is found in SeMaK."

Nowadays, a Jew who knows evidence in the benefit of a non-Jew, to the detriment of a fellow Jew, must testify on his (the non-Jew's) behalf, before non-Jewish judges, if the non-Jew summoned him.

But Mintz then adds:

This is no justification for Moshe, for that only applies when
the witness cannot avoid testifying at all,
and probably only if he had consulted with the leaders of the community,[7]
and also he would needed to have warned the Jew,[8]
and also this is not applicable to a *noge'a b'davar* (an interested and therefore disqualified witness.)

In piling on these four restrictive elements to the position of R. Jacob ben Asher, Maharam Mintz has essentially emasculated the position which was intended to, and was understood as, creating a requirement to testify in the non-Jewish court when the witness had been subpoenaed. Particularly in the first element, allowing the testimony even when under subpoena, but only if the witness had no possible way of avoiding testimony, radically alters the distinctive position of R. Jacob ben Asher by, in effect, only allowing testimony under continued restrictive circumstances. The second and third elements, while having precedent in earlier Rabbinic discussion,[9] had never previously been attached to the position of Jacob ben Asher. And so, once again, Maharam Mintz propounded novel and unprecedented limitations on testimony within the context of positions which had otherwise been understood as yielding at least permissive results, if not actually mandating such testimony.

As his fourth point, Maharam Mintz argues that even were it permissible for Moshe to testify in this case, he need not have testified as fully as he did. He might, for example, have said that while he had collected the money on behalf of Isaac, he had not yet actually delivered it to him but had sent him a letter informing him that the collection had been made – but that perhaps the letter had gotten lost in the mail. Such testimony might have rescued Isaac from any danger or loss in the non-Jewish court, leaving the matter to be worked out between Moshe and Isaac. Instead, through his actual testimony, Moshe had endangered Isaac "financially and bodily."[10] This unevidenced assertion of the magnitude of the threat to Isaac resulting from the testimony of Moshe serves as justification

[7] Later in this responsum, Mintz drops the hesitancy and actually requires such consultation.

[8] Later in this responsum, *ibid.* at p.42b, column 2, s.v. *Gam*, Mintz bases this duty upon the principle of duty of rescue of life as in Lev. 19:16.

[9] See above, 3.1.

[10] *Teshuvot Maharam Mintz*, at p. 42a, columns 1–2, s.v. *Lachen*.

for Maharam Mintz to now assert that Moshe, "through his excessive testimony, had handed over (*masar*) Isaac into the hands of the non-Jews."[11] While he later in the responsum insists that Moshe is not literally a *Moser*, as we shall see, his introduction of the language of *Mesirah* at this point provides us with some insight into why Maharam Mintz had in the three prior sections deflected so significantly from what ought to have been seen as legal justifications for the testimony by Moshe.

Indeed, as Maharam Mintz proceeds in this lengthy responsum, his animus toward Moshe becomes increasingly evident. He believes that Moshe has lied about his actions and about his intentions, as well as about the conduct of Isaac, and has attempted to circumvent the law and demeaned the Rabbis and the community leaders, all for his own personal security and benefit, without any concern for the impact upon another Jew, and:

> Therefore, it is fit to fine him and to punish him sevenfold for his sins, including liability for damages. And, (this should be done) even if he had testified truthfully, since he testified excessively in violation of the law, as I have explained; and certainly so if he testified falsely.[12]

Mintz is clearly not going to allow Moshe to escape liability for his debased conduct, even if he cannot quite prove that Moshe is lying, and even if in order to hold him liable he will need to severely restrict the principles of Jewish law, which Moshe is exploiting in his own defense. Mintz has one other serious problem in holding Moshe financially liable for the injury to Isaac. Having denominated Moshe as an informer, a *Moser*, Mintz needs to acknowledge that the established law is that a *Moser* can only be held financially liable after the fact if he had acted with evil intent; but, if he had acted in self-defense, or even just in defense of his own property, he is not liable.[13] Mintz therefore softens his language, and then repeatedly refers to Moshe as "someone debased, like a *Moser*."[14] This allows him to impose financial liability on other legal grounds, as someone who rescued his own property at the expense of the property of his neighbor. It also allows him later on to argue that the Jewish court can impose an oath upon Moshe to test the truthfulness of his claims, and

[11] *Ibid.* This assertion that Isaac was at substantial threat of financial and bodily harm is apparently the theory under which Maharam Mintz considered it possible that Moshe might have been permitted to testify incompletely or even falsely, in Isaac's defense.

[12] *Ibid.* There are many more comments to this effect throughout the rest of the responsum.

[13] *Ibid.* Thus, Mintz citing Mordechai ben Hillel to *Bava Kamma* 117a, and Agudah quoting R. Eliezer MiTulla, at *Bava Kamma* sec. 155.

[14] *Ibid.*, at 42b and 43b.

that Moshe is not disqualified from taking such an oath by virtue of his being an informer, because he is only like an informer.[15] This sidestepping of the law of informer, was accompanied by his assertion that there was to be no excommunication applied in this instance as would apparently have been necessary in application of the legislation of Rava, because that too would have precluded a Jewish court from imposing financial liability. Maharam Mintz proposes rather that given the criminal conduct of Moshe the court should impose the penalty of lashes unless he pays an amount to be determined by the court.[16] Thus, in the final event, there would be only a single judicially imposed penalty, payment of damages to Isaac, which is definitely Mintz's desired outcome, and which he clearly assumes Moshe will choose in preference to receiving lashes.

This striking responsum by Rabbi Moses ben Isaac Mintz is a powerful illustration of the creative capacity of a Jewish jurist to achieve what he considers to be a truly just outcome in a case in which the law appears to be on the side of an evil-doer. But while justice might have been served in this case, the old adage of "hard cases make bad law"[17] requires us to ask whether Mintz's radical steps limiting the permissibility of testimony in non-Jewish courts and his repeated characterization of impermissible testimony as "like *Mesirah*" seriously influenced subsequent codifications and later responsa. To explore those questions we will now turn to an examination of the commentaries and codification by Rabbi Joseph Karo, and the commentaries, codificatory notes and responsa of Rabbi Moshe Isserlis.

5.2 RABBI JOSEPH BEN EPHRAIM KARO

Rabbi Joseph Karo in his *Shulchan Aruch*, addresses the issue of testimony against a fellow Jew, in favor of a non-Jew, in a non-Jewish court, in two separate locations. His fullest codification of this matter appears in a series of paragraphs in *Shulchan Aruch*, *Choshen Mishpat*, in Laws of Testimony, chapter 28, directly in paragraphs 3 and 4, as follows:[18]

[15] *Ibid.*, at 43b, column 1, s.v. *Vegira'on*.

[16] *Ibid.*, at 43b, s.v. *Achen*.

[17] For the origin of this adage, see, www.phrases.org.uk/meanings/hard-cases-make-bad-law.html

[18] Rabbi Joseph Karo, *Shulchan Aruch*, *Choshen Mishpat*, New York, Otzar Halacha Inc., 1960, ch. 28, paras. 3–4. Para. 5 also contains essential information, albeit addressed only obliquely. I will deal with that paragraph later on. I will incorporate here the comments, the *Hagahot*, of Rabbi Moshe Isserlis (RaMA), in italics, but I will deal with them later on in the text.

28:3. If a non-Jew sues a Jew, and there is a Jew who has testimony in favor of the non-Jew, in opposition to the Jew, and he is the sole witness, and the non-Jew subpoenas him to testify on his behalf – in a place where the non-Jewish law is to hold a defendant monetarily liable on the basis of testimony of a single witness, it forbidden for him to testify for him [the non-Jew], and if he did testify, he is to be excommunicated.

Hagah: But he is not liable to pay since he can claim, "I testified truthfully." But if it is possible to demonstrate that he testified falsely, then he is liable to pay. And if the other (Jewish) party admits that he had testified truthfully, he is not to be excommunicated.

And if from the outset (of the transaction) the non-Jew had designated this Jew to be a witness, then there would be a descration of God's name (Chillul Hashem) if he fails to testify on his behalf, and he must testify for him.[19]

28:4. If a Jew sues a non-Jew, and the defendant denies any liability, and the non-Jew has a single (Jewish) witness, he is permitted to testify on his (the non-Jew's) behalf if he had subpoenaed him.

Hagah. And a fortiori that two witnesses are permitted to testify since even according to Jewish Law the party would be held liable based on their testimony. And likewise in a place where they do not hold a party liable based on the testimony of a single witness, they are permitted to testify. Two relatives are considered as a single witness, since in our Law we do not hold a party monetarily liable based on the testimony of a single witness.

For Rabbi Joseph Karo, as had been the case in Jewish law since late Talmudic times, the critical issue to be addressed was that appropriate loyalty to a fellow Jew required the maintenance of core standards of justice as they are determined by Jewish law. But, as we had seen from the time of the earliest Amoraic limitations on the legislation of Rava, the determination of justice was not based so much on identical outcomes as on similarity of standards of procedural justice, particularly of evidentiary rules. Of course, common evidentiary rules do not guarantee identical outcomes since the substantive law is likely to vary. Nevertheless, the most consistent reading of the Jewish law standard for permissibility of testimony against a fellow Jew in a non-Jewish court remained a negative formulation of the two-witness requirement, that is, that the court would not consider the testimony of a single witness as dispositive; supplemented by the allowance of the use of a single witness to impose an oath on the defendant, or even to serve as an effective defense in cases of full denial of indebtedness by the defendant. The clarity of this proposition for Karo is embedded in the opening section of chapter 28, paragraph 3, above, and

[19] See Shabbatai ben Meir HaKohen (1621–1662), Siftei Cohen (ShaKh) to Sh. A., Ch. M. 28, note 8, referring to Responsa of Rama, no. 269.

the opening sentence of the following paragraph, 28: 4 above. In both of these texts, drawn directly from the text of the Tur, albeit with slight literary modification, the singular criterion determining the permissibility of testimony is the evidentiary rules of the non-Jewish court. In fact Karo explicitly deemphasizes the monetary outcome by omitting from paragraph 3 a critical phrase found in the Tur explaining why such testimony would not be permissible, "because he causes him loss not in accordance with the (Jewish) Law."[20] This deemphasis of the monetary loss to the Jewish defendant also serves Karo's interest since he, in agreement with Mordechai ben Hillel, maintains that the penalty of excommunication is punishment for the offensive insolence (*bishvil dechatzif*), but results in no monetary liability to the party indirectly injured by the testimony.[21]

A second factor which allows or requires testimony according to Karo is the presence of a risk of *Chillul Hashem*, desecration of God's name. Quoting the text of the Tur, the source of which was the teaching of Rosh, Karo confirms the assertion which ran through the entire fabric of Ashkenaz and Provencal Jewish law, that the risk of desecration of the Divine name was of such magnitude as to yield a duty to testify even against a fellow Jew, in favor of a non-Jew, even in a corrupt non-Jewish court – i.e. in a court that did not uphold the Jewish law evidentiary standard of non-reliance on a single witness.[22] The case cited by Tur and Karo was that of the Raavan, Rabbi Eliezer ben Nathan of Mainz (c. 1090–1170), who had originally proposed that if a Jew and a non-Jew had jointly designated a Jew as witness to their transaction, that Jew would be required to testify, even against his fellow Jew, if he were eventually called upon to do so. We have previously noted that Raavan himself had asserted three reasons for this duty to testify, but that his grandson, Raviyah, as well as Rosh, Tur and now Karo, all cite only the singular rationale of *Chillul Hashem*.[23] Karo describes the facts of the case in the same manner as his predecessors, but in contrast to Raavan, as involving not joint designation of the witness by both parties, but rather sole designation of the witness by the non-Jewish party.

It is striking, however, that Karo omits the Tur's final case cited in the name of the Rosh:

> And certainly this is so, nowadays when the (non-Jewish) statute provides, in regard to Jewish litigants, that a non-Jewish witness is not granted full credibility

[20] Tur, *Choshen Mishpat*, ch. 28. See text above for fuller treatment of the position of Tur and the contrast with elements of Karo at 4.5.

[21] Karo, *Beit Yosef to* Tur, *Choshen Mishpat*, ch. 28, at s.v. *Bameh devarim amurim*.

[22] See above 4.1.

[23] See above 4.5.

in testimony against a Jew unless there is a Jewish witness with him. (Under these circumstances) if Jews would withhold their testimony (i.e. refuse to testify against fellow Jews), they will revoke this statute and grant full credibility to the testimony of non-Jewish witnesses against Jewish litigants.[24]

It may simply be the case that such legislation was unknown to Karo and therefore appeared to be irrelevant. Or it is possible that Karo eliminated this case precisely in order to avoid the conclusion which was later arrived at by Rabbi Joel Sirkis in Bayit Chadash (BaCH), his commentary to the Tur, that a much broader exemption from the restrictive legislation of Rava resided within this case. Sirkis had argued, as I alluded to earlier, that according to the Tur, as according to Jacob ben Asher in *Kitzur Piskei HaRosh*, there was a general requirement for Jews to testify in non-Jewish courts in any situation in which they had been subpoenaed to testify.[25] In his comment, Sirkis clearly adopts as determined law the position of Tur and Rosh as he understood them – that in any situation in which the non-Jewish court or the non-Jewish party had subpoenaed a Jew to testify, he was obligated to testify, whether or not he had been designated as a witness at the outset of the transaction, and even if he was a single witness and the court was a *Magista* court that would issue judgment against the Jewish party on the basis of his testimony alone. He goes even further in suggesting that the Jewish witness ought not even attempt to escape his responsibility to testify.[26] He does, however, add a note of caution as a reflection of customary practice:

Nevertheless it is customary in most communities that no Jew would testify in favor of a non-Jew, against a fellow Jew, unless he had first made an inquiry of a Rabbinic court, and he would then act in accordance with their instructions, deviating neither to right or left. And if he had testified without so inquiring of a Jewish court, he could be punished, even though he had not violated *Torah* Law.[27]

This is a not uncommon position for decisors of Jewish law to take when confronted by a persuasive permissible position and a more restrictive position to which some adhere – to argue that while the law itself is in fact permissive, in those communities in which the more restrictive position is adhered to it has the force of custom and must be complied with.[28]

[24] See above, beginning of 4.5.

[25] See above 4.5. Jacob ben Asher, *Kitzur Piskei Harosh, Bava Kamma*, Ch. 10, Law 14.

[26] Sirkis, *Bayit Chadash* to Tur, *Choshen Mishpat*, ch. 28, at s.v. *U'mah shekatav HaRosh*.

[27] *Ibid.*

[28] For an identical instance in BaCH, see Sirkis' comments to Tur, *Even HaEzer*, ch. 115, s.v. *Umah shekatav vedavka* in regard to whether married women are required to cover their heads in a courtyard or the interior of their homes.

By contrast, Karo explicitly rejects the possibility of the exempting force of a subpoena by his language in *Shulchan Aruch*, *Choshen Mishpat* 28:3, where he specifies that the impermissibility of testimony by a single witness in a court which would issue judgement based entirely on that testimony would pertain even in a situation in which the witness had been subpoenaed. It is only in the situation described at the end of that paragraph, where the witness had been so designated at the outset of the transaction, that he would be required to testify; and then, only due to the reason of *Chillul Hashem*, not simply because he was summoned.

We need, however, to consider yet a third possibility for Karo's omission from his code, of the final case of Rosh. He may have felt that this case is redundant since the basis on which testimony by the Jewish witness would be permitted in this case would still be the principle of the duty to avoid *Chillul Hashem*, rather than an independent rationale related to the economic security of the community. This position is in fact directly argued by R. Joel Sirkis who maintains that even without his novel contention that Rosh and Tur intended to introduce a broad exception for the subpoenaed witness, this case would not have needed to be mentioned at all since in the immediately prior case Rosh and Tur had already confirmed that in any situation in which there is *Chillul Hashem* there is a requirement of testimony by the Jewish witness.[29] Presumably then, according to BaCH, the motive of permissibility to testify in the fourth case is not just the economic security of the community, as is implied but not stated explicitly by either Rosh or Tur. Rather, it is because the non-Jewish government, observing that Jews refuse to testify against fellow Jews, would be convinced that the Jewish religion, that is the God of the Jews, allows for dishonesty and theft, and would be motivated to revoke the law requiring a Jewish witness since that would not contribute to a just outcome in litigation. The critical issue according to BaCH is not the economic impact on Jews, but the disgrace to God in the failure of Jews to support justice, that is, *Chillul Hashem*. Could this be also the position of R. Joseph Karo?

Some credence to this possibility might emerge from analysis of the first part of a subsequent paragraph in *Shulchan Aruch*, *Choshen Mishpat*, chapter 28, paragraph 5:

> A scholar who knows evidence in benefit of a Jew, and was summoned to testify in a Jewish court (whose judges were) of lesser standing than himself, then

[29] Sirkis, *Bayit Chadash* to Tur, *Choshen Mishpat*, ch. 28, s.v. *Umah shekatav HaRosh*.

if it was testimony related to a monetary matter, he is not obligated to go to testify *Hagah: rather they should send (a representative) to him and he should testify.* But if (in the litigation) there is some element of prevention of wrongdoing (*Afrushei me'Issurah*), then he is obligated to go and to testify.

The Talmudic passage upon which this position of Karo is based makes it clear that the initial teaching, that the scholar need not testify, is based on the principle of the duty to honor the *Torah*, which is embodied in the person of the scholar.[30] That value, the *Gemara* insists, is of greater import than the value of the duty to testify. However, the *Gemara* continues, if the outcome of the litigation could eventually result in the commission of a crime, (for example by erroniously declaring a married woman free to remarry due to the lack of testimony that her husband is still alive)[31] then he must testify, for it is written "'There is no wisdom nor understanding nor counsel against the Lord' (Proverbs 21:30), wherever there is a disgrace of the Divine name, the honor of a scholar is not upheld." For R. Moshe Isserlis in his Hagah to this paragraph in *Shulchan Aruch*, the competing values are the honor of the greater scholar versus the honor of the lesser Rabbinic court, in which the former has priority. There is no way in which the testimony itself could be withheld from the court, all that is allowed in the greater valuing of the honor of the greater scholar is that he does not have to appear in person before the lesser court. But, if in consequence of even that lessened effect of the personal testimony there might be an erroneous judgment resulting, for example, allowing an illicit marriage, then the prevention of the disgrace of God's name would obviously have priority over the honor of the human scholar.

Whether one reads this passage in consonance with Karo or in consonance with R. Isserlis, the underlying teaching is the same, that knowingly acting in a manner which might allow a crime to result constitutes a desecration of the Divine name, a *Chillul Hashem* – which one is duty-bound to prevent. We previously established that according to Raavan, Ravad and Meiri there could be a legal duty to testify in favor of a non-Jew, against a fellow Jew, in a non-Jewish court, indeed even in an unjust non-Jewish court, when such testimony would serve the purpose of preventing the commission of a crime, such as the Jewish defendant actually successfully executing his fraud against the non-Jewish plaintiff.[32] That conclusion was based on the reasoning that such prevention of wrongdoing was

[30] Rashi, *Shevuot* 30b.

[31] Rashi, *Shevuot* 30b, s.v. *aval belssurah.*

[32] See above 4.2.

a legal duty derived either from the affirmative commandment of chastizement, or from the negative precept of not enabling crimes, that is not placing a stumbling block before the blind. But here, the Talmudic passage itself, and certainly its exposition by both Tur and R. Joseph Karo, provide us with yet another perspective on the duty to prevent wrongdoing by fellow Jews. Explicitly for the Talmudic passage and for Karo, the duty to prevent Jews from committing crimes, even inadvertently, also derives from the fact that Jewish wrongdoing is a desecration of the Divine name and that we are bound to prevent such *Chillul Hashem*.

This approach suggests a two-fold consequence. Firstly, it aligns the *Shulchan Aruch* fully with the *Rishonim* of Ashkenaz for whom the prevention of Jewish wrongdoing would itself generate a legal duty to testify against a fellow Jew in a non-Jewish court. This much is unequivocal in the language of Karo himself, which we saw just above in *Shulchan Aruch, Choshen Mishpat* 28:5. But beyond that, it suggests that the breadth of understanding of the notion of *Chillul Hashem* by Karo could certainly also encompass, as it did for the BaCH, the perception by a non-Jewish government that Jewish refusal to cooperate in the national striving for justice, as evidenced by their refusing to testify against fellow Jews in fundamentally honest courts which even attempted to protect Jews precisely by requiring the pairing of a Jewish with a non-Jewish witness – was also a *Chillul Hashem*, which would then yield at least the permissibility of such testimony, possibly even a duty to testify.

At this point it is vital to note a further significant omission from the *Shulchan Aruch*. In this codification of the legislation of Rava, the latter part of the Talmudic passage, related to the *Adam Chashuv*,[33] the prominent person, is totally absent. To refresh our memories, the *Adam Chashuv* passage raised the following question. While under the legislation of Rava it was not permissible for a single witness to testify in a *Magista* court, it was permissible for him to testify in a *Dawar* court where his single testimony would not be fully relied upon for issuance of judgment against the defendant. What if, asks the *Gemara*, the witness is a prominent person whose testimony might in fact be relied upon fully even by a *Dawar* court – suggesting that he should not testify- but, on the other hand, as a prominent person he cannot escape from the view of the court, and his refusal to testify would have severe reprecussions for him – could he therefore testify? The *Talmud* had left this as an open, unresolved question, declaring "*Teiku*."

[33] *Bava Kamma* 114a.

In our earlier treatment of this text,[34] we noted that Rosh had maintained that in the face of the lack of resolution of this question, it is to be viewed as permissible for the prominent person to testify under those circumstances.[35] The entire discussion of *Adam Chashuv* is then omitted by Jacob ben Asher in his Tur.

But Karo actually explains the omission in his commentary to the Tur.[36] He argues that according to Rosh, the unresolved question as to the *Adam Chashuv* is treated like any other unresolved financial matter, namely leniently in the benefit of a defendant. Thus, the prominent person, who might be sued by a Jewish party for loss he had suffered as a result of the prominent person's testimony against him as a single witness in a non-Jewish court, would be a defendant in such a lawsuit, and since his liability had not been confirmed by the law of the *Talmud*, but had been left as an unresolved question, a court could not hold him liable. In this regard, Karo points out that the *Adam Chashuv* is in the same situation as any other Jewish witness, it being permissible for him to testify as a single witness in a *Dawar* court. But in his case, it is on account of his being unable to avoid testifying without serious injury to himself, without our being told whether that injury is purely financial, or bodily or reputational. In consequence, says Karo, the actual law which applies to the prominent person is identical to the law applicable to any other person. For this reason, he concludes, the Tur was able to completely omit any reference in his code to the distinction between a regular person and the prominent person – for no distinction exists. Karo then concludes by linking to this reasoning the position of Mordechai ben Hillel,[37] that pursuant to this position, if any Jew were to testify as a single witness against a fellow Jew even in a *Magista* court – one which would issue judgment against the Jewish defendant on the basis of that testimony – there could be no monetary liability. Why not? Impliedly, because his testimony must have been motivated by his desire to avoid the negative consequences that would result to him if he failed to testify, and based on the equation of the prominent person with any other Jew, such action could not result in any financial liability to the witness. In fact, as we saw earlier, the combination of the indirect nature of the injury through testimony, and the perception by the witness that he was being coerced to

34 Above, at the beginning of 4.4.

35 Rosh to *Bava Kamma*, ch. 10, sec. 14

36 *Beit Yosef* to Tur, *Choshen Mishpat*, ch. 28, at s.v. *Bameh devarim amurim*.

37 Mordechai to *Bava Kamma* at sec. 157, and *Hagahot Mordechai* to *Bava Kamma* at sec. 212.

testify, was sufficient for almost all *Rishonim* to establish the exemption of the witness from penalty under the legislation of Rava.[38]

The significance of this passage in the *Beit Yosef* is that Karo proceeded himself to completely omit from the *Shulchan Aruch* any reference to the *Adam Chashuv*. He thereby aligned himself completely with the position of Rosh, Rabbenu Tam, Mordechai and Tur before him, that the prominent person could testify as a single witness in a *Dawar* court despite the fact that they might rely on him as the equivalent of two witnesses. And, by like token, any other Jew could testify as a single witness in a *Magista* court despite the fact that the court would issue judgment against a Jewish defendant based solely on his testimony – in both cases because of the presence of some form of economic or other experienced coercion which *o matzui le'ishtamuti*, "he could not escape."

This brings us to one final element in the position of Rabbi Joseph Karo. There is another passage in the *Shulchan Aruch* in which he does deal with the issue of testimony against fellow Jews in non-Jewish courts. The Tur in *Yoreh Deah* chapter 334 had incorporated the entire text of Rambam, *Mishneh Torah* in which were listed the twenty-four instances in which excommunication could be ordered.[39] That list was preserved in its entirety by Karo in the *Shulchan Aruch*, *Yoreh Deah*, chapter 334, paragraph 43. The ninth instance in that list is:

> One who testifies against a Jew in the courts (*Arkaot*) of violent (*anasin*) idolators, and through his testimony caused monetary loss to him (the Jewish litigant), not in accordance with Jewish Law, is to be excommunicated until he pays.

The most striking disparity between this passage in *Shulchan Aruch Yoreh Deah* and the passage we had been studying previously, *Shulchan Aruch Choshen Mishpat* 28: 3–5, is that in the latter, as we have just seen, Karo had excluded any financial liability, even in situations in which excommunication could be imposed. By contrast, in the passage he quotes from

[38] See above, 4.4. For the Tur, *Choshen Mishpat*, ch. 28, it appears that there is neither monetary liability nor excommunication. Karo himself in *Beit Yosef* at s.v. *Bameh devarim amurim* cites Mordechai as excluding financial liability but not the possibility of excommunication. In *Shulchan Aruch*, *Choshen Mishpat* 28:3, Karo explicitly preserves the possibility of excommunication in such situations while he is silent as to any possible monetary liability, thereby indicating its absence.

[39] Rambam, *Mishneh Torah*, *Hilchot Talmud Torah* 6:14. See above 4.3. The only difference between this text and that which appears in the Rambam is the inclusion of the word *anasin*, "violent" persons. The word, however, appears to be a late addition to the text since the Cracow edition of 1578 does not include that word.

Rambam, it is clear that the excommunication itself is simply an instrument through which the court can coerce the payment of damages.

This apparent contradiction was already noted by Rabbi Joshua Falk (1555–1614) in his commentary to the Tur,[40] and in his commentary to the *Shulchan Aruch*.[41] In both instances, Rabbi Falk appears to be responding to the *Shulchan Aruch* as a unitary text in which the positions of Rabbi Joseph Karo and those of Rabbi Moshe Isserlis are to be presumed to be perfectly consonant with each other and therefore he has one possible resolution through distinguishing on the facts, based on a distinction made by Rabbi Moshe Isserlis suggesting that there is in fact no financial liability when the witness is known to have testified truthfully, while there could be financial liability when it is possible to demonstrate that the witness had testified falsely. Recognizing the weakness of this resolution as not being reflected in the texts, he considers another possibility, that there is never financial liability, but in a situation when the witness is subject to the usual period of 30 days of excommunication, if he wants to end that period early, he can pay the person against whom he had testified and be immediately released from the excommunication. But Rabbi Falk recognizes also the weakness of this resolution as not being reflected in the actual language of the texts.

An alternative approach might recognize the distinctive nature of this composite list of twenty-four persons who are subject to excommunication, created by Rambam, and the attitude toward it taken by Rabbi Joseph Karo. In *Kesef Mishneh*, Karo's commentary to the *Mishneh Torah*, Karo twice points out problems which would have led us to think that the list should have been modified in his own recording of it. In number 6, Rambam says, "One who had not accepted upon himself the judgment of a court, is to be excommunicated until he pays." Karo points out that this is not consonant with the Talmudic source which ends the period of excommunication with the party's verbal acceptance of his duty to comply.[42] In fact, Karo points out, Rambam himself so records the law later on in *Mishneh Torah*.[43] Karo then suggests that Rambam did not feel the need to be precise in this listing since the essential location of this ruling was to be found later in his code. We might then have expected that when Karo himself

[40] Falk, Drisha to Tur, *Choshen Mishpat*, ch. 28, at note 13.

[41] Falk, *Sefer Meirat Einayim*, to *Shulchan Aruch*, *Choshen Mishpat*, 28: 3, at note 21.

[42] *Bava Kamma* 112b-113a. *Kesef Mishneh* to Rambam, *Hilchot Talmud Torah* 6:14:6 s.v. *Mi Shelo Kibbel*.

[43] Rambam, *Mishneh Torah*, *Hilchot Sanhedrin* 25:8

recorded this list in *Shulchan Aruch*, he ought to have corrected the text, but he did not.[44] Similarly, as number 20 in the list, Rambam includes, "a ritual slaughterer who fails to examine his knife in the presence of the (local) scholar." To which Karo comments[45] that Tur already indicated that this rule is no longer applied nowadays.[46] Again we might have expected Karo to have omitted this instance from the listing which he provided in the *Shulchan Aruch* of persons who may be excommunicated, but he did not do so.[47] It is odd, however, that Karo did not even make reference to the inexactness of Rambam's record of number 9, our text above, which refers to monetary liability not mentioned in the *Gemara*, but is impliedly justified by Rambam by his reversing the Talmudic order of numbers 8 and 9, since number 8 does in the *Talmud* specify the use of excommunication as a means of enforcing financial liability.

It is then possible that Karo had decided to keep Rambam's list fully intact despite its inexact elements, and that he would simply correct those problems at their appropriate places in his code. Indeed, in the appropriate places in the *Shulchan Aruch*, he reports number 6 in consonance with the Talmudic statement,[48] he omits the law related to the ritual slaughterer[49] and he omits any reference to financial liability for wrongful testimony in a non-Jewish court.[50] Why would he allow for this inexact text, particularly in the laws of Niddui and Cherem? Perhaps because he understood that rather than positing legal liabilities, the twenty-four instances of excommunication listed by Rambam are fully discretionary in the hands of the Rabbinic courts, and that in regard to number 9, our text, such discretion allows also for the imposition of a monetary fine despite the technical absence of any basis in law for liability for having indirectly caused loss to the Jewish defendant in a proceeding in a non-Jewish court. With that, Karo may also be accepting the Rambam's understanding that an individual who is bound by the non-Jewish law of the land to testify against a fellow Jew in a non-Jewish court may choose to comply with that requirement, but that he remains subject to the authority of a Jewish court, which

[44] *Shulchan Aruch*, *Yoreh Deah*, ch. 334, para. 43, no. 6.
[45] *Kesef Mishneh* to Rambam, at no. 20.
[46] Tur *Yoreh Deah*, ch. 18.
[47] *Shulchan Aruch*, *Yoreh Deah*, ch. 334, para. 43, no. 20.
[48] *Shulchan Aruch*, *Choshen Mishpat*, 11:4.
[49] It does not appear as expected in *Shulchan Aruch*, *Yoreh Deah*, ch. 18.
[50] *Shulchan Aruch*, *Choshen Mishpat*, 28:3–5.

could potentially impose upon him a monetary fine for the compensation of the person who suffered financial loss in consequence of his choice.[51]

In sum then, the position of Rabbi Joseph Karo in the *Shulchan Aruch* and in his commentaries to Tur and Rambam's *Mishneh Torah* reflect fully the consensus of the *Rishonim* whose positions we had previously examined in detail. He clearly understood and indicated that the legislation of Rava did not create a new basis for financial liability, but that it did manifest the Rabbinic desire that potential witnesses in non-Jewish courts should take seriously their duty of loyalty to their fellow Jews so that, for example, the mere fact that one had been subpoenaed to testify would not in and of itself justify participation in a proceeding within a fundamentally unjust court. On the other hand, a variety of other interests and values could well override the value of loyalty to the material well-being of fellow Jews, such as the achievement of justice; the avoidance of *Chillul Hashem* both in terms of the individual's actions and in terms of the impact of the disgrace of God's name on the economic and physical security of the community; responsibility for the spiritual well-being of fellow Jews reflected in the duty to prevent them from committing crimes; the defense of one's own physical and monetary well-being; and possibly even keeping open as a possibility simply the responsibility to uphold the law of the land.

Strikingly, virtually none of the constraints to testimony insisted upon in the responsa of Rabbi Moshe Mintz is so much as raised as possibilities in the text of *Shulchan Aruch* of Rabbi Joseph Karo. In 28:3, Karo does not indicate the possibility of monetary liability based on whether the witness was eligible to testify according to Jewish law. In 28:4, he does not limit the permissibility to testify depending upon the precise nature of the claim by the Jewish plaintiff. Not having accepted the position of Jacob ben Asher, who allowed testimony in any situation of subpoena, he did not need to introduce limitations on that rule related to ability to avoid testimony. Nor does he require advance consultation, or warning of the Jewish defendant in any situation in which testimony would be permissible, as does Maharam Mintz. Finally, Karo does not require any form of limitation on testimony when it is permissible, not does he at any point denominate such a witness as being "like a *Moser*."

[51] See above, 4.3. Karo so indicates at the conclusion of his comment in *Kesef Mishneh* to Rambam, *Talmud Torah* 6:14:6 s.v. *Mi Shelo Kibbel*.

5.3 RABBI MOSHE ISSERLIS (RAMA)

The contrast between the deeply restrictive approach of Maharam Mintz in his responsa, and the broadly permissive approach of Rabbi Joseph Karo in his Code and commentaries, begs further exploration through the writings of Rabbi Moshe Isserlis, who wrote in all three genres of Jewish legal literature, responsa as well as code and commentaries.

The notations (*hagahot*) of RaMA to the two paragraphs of the *Shulchan Aruch* on which we have been focused seem to tend toward even more explicit leniency than that indicated by R. Joseph Karo. In *Shulchan Aruch, Choshen Mishpat* 28:3, Karo had omitted any reference to the possibility of monetary liability, even when a single witness had testified in a *Magista* court and was therefore liable to excommunication. As we saw just above, the apparent contradiction between that omission and Karo's explicit preservation of the language of Rambam in *Shulchan Aruch, Yoreh Deah* 334:43 (20), referring to the witness being subject to "excommunication until he pays," led to alternative understandings as to whether Karo in fact held that monetary liability was never present, or whether there would be circumstances when monetary liability could be present. RaMA appeared to be intent on leaving no doubt as to the position of Ashkenaz on this matter. He therefore adds, "Hagah: But he is not liable to pay since he can claim, 'I testified truthfully.' But if it is possible to demonstrate that he testified falsely, then he is liable to pay." This language, drawn directly from the position of Mordechai ben Hillel, leaves only a single situation in which financial liability for damages to the Jewish defendant would be possible, that is, if it is proven that the witness had lied in his testimony in the non-Jewish court.[52] The emphasis placed by RaMA on the claim of truthfulness of the testimony as the basis for the witness not being financially liable also means that he does not require that the witness simultaneously needs to plead that he could not avoid testifying. While even purely voluntary testimony as a single witness could subject the witness to excommunication, it could still not leave him liable to financial payment to the Jewish defendant so long as the witness testified truthfully.

RaMA then adds yet another leniency to his treatment of the testimony of a single Jewish witness against a Jewish defendant, in favor of the non-Jewish plaintiff in a non-Jewish court. He adds at the conclusion of that

[52] Mordechai to *Bava Kamma*, ch. 10, para. 157; and see *Hagahot Mordechai* to *Bava Kamma*, ch. HaGozel Kamma, para. 212.

section, "And if the other (Jewish) party admits that he had testified truthfully, he is not to be excommunicated." This position of RaMA conforms with the teaching of the Tosafists that even if by operation of Jewish law the defendant would not be held liable, but in reality the money was due to the non-Jewish plaintiff, as in the case of *Hafka'at Halva'ato*, the Jewish witness could not be punished for his truthful testimony that resulted in the failure of the position of the Jewish party.[53] The position similarly echoes the position of Ravad who maintained that excommunication could not be imposed on a Jewish witness in a case where the Jewish witness had in fact produced a "just" result, even if that were not the result that would have been achieved in a Jewish court, and even if it was achieved via his testimony in a fundamentally corrupt court.[54] Of further interest in this formulation by RaMA is the implication that while a Jewish party might have pursued a false claim against a non-Jew in a non-Jewish court, after he lost that case due to the testimony of a fellow Jew, he would not subsequently bring that false claim to a Jewish court in order to recover his "loss" caused by the Jewish witness, but would rather confirm that the Jewish witness had testified truthfully. The justice of the outcome would preclude the penalty of excommunication from being imposed on the witness.

The closing element of *Shulchan Aruch, Choshen Mishpat* 28:3 is the teaching of Karo that if the Jewish witness had been designated at the outset by the non-Jewish party to the transaction, to serve in that capacity, then the failure of the Jew to testify would constitute a *Chillul Hashem*. To which the RaMA then simply adds *ve'ya'id lo*, which I have translated as "and he must testify for him." The language of Karo in and of itself clearly indicates that due to the element of desecration of the Divine name it would be permissible for the Jewish witness to testify in such a case, and that he would clearly not be subject to excommunication for doing so. What then is added by the declarative statement of RaMA, *ve'ya'id lo*? Rabbi Isserlis seems here to be indicating to us that the presence of *Chillul Hashem* not only permits the testimony, but requires that the testimony be offered, thus clearly aligning him with the position of Ravad and others who unequivocally maintain that the avoidance of *Chillul Hashem* requires a Jew to testify against a fellow Jew, even in favor of a non-Jew, even in a non-Jewish court, indeed even in a corrupt non-Jewish court.[55] While it is possible, indeed likely, that

[53] *Tosafot, Bava Kamma* 114a, s.v. *Velo amaran.*
[54] See Ravad to *Bava Kamma* 114a, and our treatment of his position above at 4.1.
[55] *Ibid.*

this is also the position of Karo, since the avoidance of *Chillul Hashem* is clearly a revealed law duty, while the constraint against testimony in a non-Jewish court is a Rabbinic law, it appears that again RaMA is attempting to be unequivocal in his indication of the duty to testify under such circumstances.

In *Shulchan Aruch, Choshen Mishpat* 28:4, Rabbi Joseph Karo continues the discussion of the law regulating the conduct of a Jew who is a single witness in favor of a non-Jew, against the financial interest of the Jewish litigant, but in a situation in which it is the Jew who is the plaintiff and the non-Jew is the defendant. As we have seen, Karo rules, based on the prior teaching of Mordechai, that such testimony is permissible even in a court that issues judgment based on a single witness (a *Magista* court), since even by Jewish law, the burden of proof remains on the plaintiff and the sole role of the single witness would be to relieve the defendant of an oath.[56]

RaMA then offers the following addendum:

> 28:4 *Hagah*.(a) And afortiori that two witnesses are permitted to testify since even according to Jewish Law the party would be held liable based on their testimony. (b) And likewise in a place where they do not hold a party liable based on the testimony of a single witness, they are permitted to testify. (c)Two relatives are considered as a single witness, since in our Law we do not hold a party monetarily liable based on the testimony of a single witness.[57]

It is clear that this notation by RaMA is not intended only as a response to paragraph 28:4, since it relates not only to the situation in which the Jew is the plaintiff, but also to the prior paragraph, 28:3, where the non-Jew is the plaintiff. RaMA recognized that Karo had only addressed the question of testimony by a single witness and distinguished only as to when such testimony would be permissible and when it would result in the penalty of excommunication. RaMA had previously broadened the deliberation to indicate the general absence of monetary liability, but also the one situation when monetary liability could be present, as well as the situation of testimony by a single witness that would not even result in excommunication. But Karo had altogether not addressed the two distinctions expressly drawn in the Talmudic passage describing the legislation of Rava, namely the permissibility of testimony by two witnesses under all circumstances, and the permissibility of testimony by a

[56] Mordechai to *Bava Kamma*, ch. 10, para. 157.

[57] The division of this paragraph into clauses (a), (b) and (c), is mine, for the convenience of the following discussion.

single Jewish witness in a *Dawar* court, which does not issue judgment based exclusively on the testimony of a single witness.[58] It is those omissions, both related to situations of permissible testimony, which RaMA now attempts to remedy. In clause (a), he affirms the permissibility of two witnesses testifying against a fellow Jew in a non-Jewish court. He needs to specifically confirm permissibility because one might argue, as some had in regard to the position of Karo, that while *Shulchan Aruch* provides no penalty of excommunication for two witnesses, that it might remain an impermissible act, just bearing no penalty since there was no injury beyond that which the defendant would have suffered had the trial been conducted in a Jewish court. Or, one might argue that, according to Karo, the act of testimony even by two witnesses is not forbidden, but is morally offensive as a disloyal action undertaken against a fellow Jew. Or one might argue that, according to Karo, given his general references to the witnesses having been subpoenaed, he might maintain that such testimony even by two witnesses would be permissible only when the pair of witnesses had been subpoenaed to testify in the non-Jewish court. All of these possible positions seem to be dismissed by RaMA in his simple and straightforward declaration in 28:4, clause (a): "And afortiori that two witnesses are permitted to testify since even according to Jewish Law the party would be held liable based on their testimony." There is neither impermissibility, nor moral objection, nor limited conditions, just permission to testify.

Further clarification of when testimony against a fellow Jew in a non-Jewish court is perfectly permissible, is intended by RaMA in his comment in clause (b): "And likewise in a place where they do not hold a party liable based on the testimony of a single witness, they are permitted to testify." Karo at the beginning of 28:3 had indicated when a single witness would be excommunicated, and at the end of that paragraph he indicated when a single witness might be obligated to testify, at least according to RaMA's understanding of that clause. What is absent is again the explicit teaching of the *Talmud* that even according to the legislation of Rava the single Jewish witness would be permitted to testify if the non-Jewish court observed the rule of procedural justice honored in Jewish courts – not to establish liability of the defendant based exclusively on the testimony of a single witness (referred to in shorthand as testimony in a *Dawar* court).

[58] *Bava Kamma* 113b-114a. It is for this reason that Vilna Gaon *in Biur HaGra*, to *Shulchan Aruch, Choshen Mishpat*, 28:4, at his notes 27 and 28, related to clauses (a) and (b) of the paragraph, refers solely and directly to the text of the *Gemara Bava Kamma* 113b–114a.

However, RaMA does not make explicit at this point whether the permissibility is dependent solely upon the non-Jewish court's compliance with this specific procedural requirement,[59] or whether it is contingent upon the outcome being consistent with the outcome that would have been achieved had the case been tried in a Jewish court.[60] However, as RaMA moves into clause (c) of this comment, limiting the permissibility of testimony by two witnesses to exclude testimony by two relatives, (based on Mordechai's citation of the position of Rabbenu Tam),[61] on the grounds that Jewish law views them as not eligible to constitute a "pair" of witnesses, the implication is that in fact it is the consonance of procedural rules of evidence that determines permissibility rather than the outcome. Otherwise, Isserlis could have simply indicated that any substantive difference in rules of law applied by the non-Jewish court would result in a different outcome and thus should constrain a witness from testifying. In fact this approach makes much more sense in the attempt to prescribe standards by which a potential witness could determine in advance whether his testimony would be permissible, since the evidentiary rules, such as the existence of a two-witness standard, or the eligibility of relatives to testify together, could easily be established in advance, while the substantive rules that might be applied by the court in any given case would be much more indeterminate and therefore would not serve as a reasonable basis for the evaluation by a potential witness as to whether his testimony would be permissible or not.

How do these clear and unequivocal rulings of RaMA in his codification hold up in his application of them in the actual cases which came before him for decision and on which he wrote responsa? While he also, like Karo, did not introduce any of the limitations on testimony emphasized by Maharam Mintz in his responsa, did RaMA sustain that approach in his own responsa?

Three responsa written by Rabbi Moshe Isserlis reflect significantly on our issues.[62] Responsum number 52 deals only tangentially with the issue of testimony. Its primary focus is on upholding the excommunication of Joseph, a Jewish physician who settled in a community without

[59] As had been implied in the Gaonic Responsum of Hai and Sherira Gaon, see above, 2.2.3, where this procedural requirement was viewed as indicative of the general integrity of the particular non-Jewish court.

[60] As in the explicit language of Rashi to *Bava Kamma* 114a, s.v. *Apumah de'chad.*

[61] Mordechai to *Bava Kamma*.

[62] The responsa of Isserlis are here numbered in accordance with their appearance in Responsa of RaMA, ed. by Dr. Asher Siev, Jerusalem, Israel, 1970.

permission of the Jewish authorities and then insisted on litigating the question of their right to restrict his residing there, in a non-Jewish court. Apparently, one possible basis for arguing against the imposition of excommunication was that, according to the legislation of Rava, that penalty was to be imposed only when the witness had caused loss not in accordance with Jewish law. In the current case, Isserlis considers whether that could be used in defense of the physician, since he had apparently not caused such actual loss. Isserlis responds by sharply distinguishing between testimony and litigation. He argues that:

> while it is permissible to testify in a case where the outcome is consonant with the (Jewish) Law, nevertheless, you cannot derive rules concerning litigation from those regulating testimony, for the *Torah* itself was distinctively opposed to litigation (in non-Jewish courts), as it says (Ex. 21:1) "And these are the ordinances which you place before them," and not before non-Jews.[63] In addition, it appears that when a Jew is in litigation with a non-Jew, then testimony is permissible, but when a Jew litigates against a fellow Jew (in a non-Jewish court), it is indeed forbidden to testify even if the outcome is consonant with the (Jewish) Law, for he is then engaged in aiding a sinner.[64]

The fact that Isserlis, in this short passage, makes repeated reference to the similarity of outcome rather than to the common procedural requirement of non-reliance on a single witness, in sharp contrast to his Hagahah to *Shulchan Aruch*, *Choshen Mishpat* 28:3 section (b), seems to be a shift in emphasis in his evaluation of how one would determine permissibility of testimony in the situation of litigation between a Jew and a non-Jew in a non-Jewish court.

The sharp opposition of Isserlis to litigation in non-Jewish courts, and his unequivocal affirmation of the use of excommunication as the appropriate penalty for such conduct, elicited a fascinating footnote added by the publisher of the Warsaw edition of the Responsa of RaMA, published in 1710.[65] He noted:

> It is known that in the past few centuries' Jewish judges were granted authority to adjudicate between fellow Jews in accordance with Jewish Law, and that the decision issued by that Jewish court had full authority and force under the law of the country. Therefore it appeared to be wrongful if one Jew would coerce his fellow to adjudicate in non-Jewish courts. Such is not the case in our times, and in particular in our country, since the statutes of the nation include also Jews, and all persons adjudicate in the non-Jewish courts in accordance with the national

[63] As in the teaching of Rabbi Tarfon, *Gittin* 88b.

[64] Responsa of RaMA, responsum no. 52, at p. 260, col. 1.

[65] Recorded in Siev's edition of Responsa of RaMA, at p. 259, footnote 39.

statutes; and Jewish judges have no authority whatsoever to adjudicate in monetary matters, wherefore, there is no relevance to all that has been said about this. Also, all matters concerning varied forms of excommunication, all this is forbidden in our times under the law of the land, and the law of the land is the law. (The publisher.)[66]

But Isserlis himself clearly drew a sharp distinction between the fundamental permissibility of testimony in a non-Jewish court, even against a fellow Jew in the benefit of a non-Jew, with impermissibility being present by Rabbinic Law only under limited circumstances, as opposed to litigation in a non-Jewish court against a fellow Jew which was always presumptively impermissible according to *Torah* Law, albeit there were limited circumstances of permissibility. Clearly, according to Isserlis, in a situation in which both litigants are Jewish, but the case is allowed under Jewish Law to be litigated in a non-Jewish court, a Jewish witness would be permitted to testify, since the underlying theory of the Rabbinic restriction in that case would be that the witness is engaged in aiding a sinner.[67]

RaMA's responsum number 86 also deals only tangentially, but significantly, with our issue. One of the parties to the case brought before him claimed that another person should be deemed not credible as a witness since he had testified against the interests of the Jewish community in a non-Jewish court and was therefore subject to excommunication. Isserlis responds that even if the person was subject to excommunication, it had been the position of Mordechai ben Hillel that there would be no accompanying monetary liability since the witness could claim that he had testified truthfully. "Then certainly he should not be disqualified (for such testimony) if it were truthful, and no evidence had been introduced that his testimony had been untruthful."[68] This simple and unequivocal upholding of the position of Mordechai that there is no monetary liability for damage resulting to the Jewish litigant, even in a situation in which the witness could be subject to excommunication is perfectly consistent with Isserlis' position in his *Hagahah* to *Shulchan Aruch*, *Choshen Mishpat* 28:3. He also deals at some length with whether a Jew who initiated a legal action against a fellow Jew in a non-Jewish court, aside violation of

[66] See the discussion of this matter by Dr. Siev, in the Introduction, Responsa of RaMA, pp. 27–29, and particularly the evidence that such was not the actual conduct of Polish communities, at p. 29, note 49.

[67] This position conforms precisely with what we had noted very early in our study of this issue, in the Gaonic responsum of Hai Gaon and Sherirah Gaon. See above, 2.2.3.

[68] Siev, Responsa of RaMA, Responsum no. 86, pp. 354–377, at p. 375.

the prohibition mentioned above as the teaching of Rabbi Tarfon, is also considered a *Moser*, or like a *Moser*.[69] We will return to this matter shortly.

However, in Responsum no. 88,[70] RaMA seems to radically diverge from his positions in his *Hagahot* to *Shulchan Aruch*. The case was complicated and some of the facts were uncertain.[71] There had been a conflict between Reuven and Shimon in the presence of the elders and judges of the Jewish community, which took place in the courtyard of the Synagogue and was protracted into the night. Then, the light in the courtyard went out. In the resulting darkness, Shimon cried out that he had been struck violently by Reuven and had suffered bruises. The next day, Shimon submitted the matter (*masar hadavar*) to the city judge who had him write out charges of assault against Reuven. Shimon also showed the judge the wounds and bruises which he said had been inflicted upon him by Reuven. The matter was then held over until the arrival of the lord of the city, to whom Shimon then publicly submitted the matter and claimed that Reuven should be required to pay the lord of the city a specific sum of money, equivalent to the number of tiles on the roof of the Synagogue itself, for such was the law, to fine a person who struck another in the Synagogue. Reuven denied that he had struck Shimon. The lord of the city asked the Jewish judges if the claim of Shimon was true and they testified as to the facts above. The lord ordered, in accordance with their laws, that Shimon should take an oath as to the truth of his claim, and the lord would then rule on the matter. As Shimon prepared to take the oath, Reuven warned him publicly that he should not hand him over to the gentiles (*al yimsero bi'yedei Kusim*), by swearing and causing the lord to impose a fine. Rather, Reuven said, he would submit to a Jewish adjudication of the matter and he would do whatever the Jewish judges ordered. Additionally, Reuven said, he would like to convince the lord of the city to hand the matter over to Jewish judges, as the City Judge had already ordered that the matter be mediated by them. Shimon stubbornly turned his back and refused to hear of this and said that he did not want to go before Jewish judges, but, "I will go before the lord of the city unless Reuven does exactly what I want." RaMA then concludes the presentation of the facts with the precise questions that were posed to him in regard to this matter:

Behold all these matters are evident and clear as to the facts of the case. Your questions are: What is the law regarding Shimon, does he have the status of a

[69] *Ibid.*, at page 367.

[70] Siev, Responsa of RaMA, Responsum no. 88, pp. 378–384.

[71] *Ibid.*, at p. 378. The following is a paraphrase of the presentation of the facts by RaMA.

"*masur b'yad anas*" one who hands over a Jew to an oppressor, or not? And what is the law regarding the witnesses who testified against Reuven before the lord of the city?[72]

The response of the RaMA to the first question raised, whether Shimon is to be deemed a *Moser*, elicits an unequivocal response which in many ways is quite reminiscent of a similar Responsum by Rashba.[73] RaMA identifies in detail each of the elements which lead him to the conclusion that Shimon is in fact a *Moser*. Firstly, he accepts as needing no demonstration that the lord of the city is in fact an *Anas*, a violent ruler whose actions even in monetary matters would create a danger to the life of a Jew subject to his authority. The omission of argument to this effect is what must have led the publisher of the 1710 Warsaw edition to add the following footnote:

The lord of the city is the master of the city, the owner of the land of the city. He had the authority under national statutes to be involved in the resolution of conflicts between a person and his friend; and whatever he did was entirely acts of oppression/ violence ("*anas*"), like the rulers of prior centuries, until the power of the king overruled them, and higher power subdued them.[74]

Of course RaMA both earlier and later in the responsum makes reference to elements which would have led him to that conclusion. The fact is that the lord of the city accepted the truth of Shimon's assertions without the testimony of a single witness who had actually seen the alleged assault take place. The intensity and clarity of Reuven's fear of being subjected to the adjudication of the lord of the city are indicated by his repeated and public pleading with Shimon not to proceed in that direction. The implication is of the self-serving nature of the decision of the lord of the city, in imposing a huge fine of which he would be the beneficiary. Even the local non-Jewish judge who initially heard the matter had ordered that it be resolved by mediation of a Jewish court rather than supporting Shimon's preference for awaiting the arrival of the lord of the city. The implication of all of this is that there was a common awareness of the corrupt and unjust nature of the exercise of authority by the lord of the city, which certainly warrants his being viewed as an *Anas*, a violent oppressor, who in his own self-interest could do both financial and bodily damage to a Jew who appeared before him for adjudication.

Secondly, RaMA contends that it is clear that Shimon has acted voluntarily in subjecting Reuven to the power of this violent authority. He

[72] *Ibid.*

[73] See above, 3.2.5.

[74] Recorded in Siev's edition, Responsa of RaMA, at p. 378, footnote 1.

had declared his intent to bring this matter before the lord of city at a point at which Reuven had clearly and publicly indicated his willingness to resolve the controversy before a Rabbinic court.

Thirdly, Shimon's intent was clearly to cause Reuven to be injured, not just to recover what he believed was rightfully his. RaMA emphasizes that had Shimon just brought the matter before the lord of the city to gain restitution for loss or even just compensation for the injury he had suffered, he would not have been considered a *Moser*; "for we do not find in the *Talmud* any case of *Moser* unless he intended to injure his friend," and not just to regain what is rightfully his.[75] Nor is RaMA willing to let Shimon off the hook by claiming that all he wanted was compensation:

> this deceiver will not be helped by his deception, hiding behind a (false) claim, for his own mouth entrapped him when he said that Reuven should be fined in an amount equal to the number of tiles in the Synagogue roof. This made it clear that his intent was to cause injury, otherwise, why did he have to say this?[76]

Beyond this, in our case, Reuven had clearly agreed to abide by the judgement of a Rabbinic court, so if all Shimon wanted was compensation in an amount due to him, he need not have gone to the lord of the city at all.

RaMA further contends, as a fourth element, that if the initiation of the legal action in a non-Jewish venue had taken place at the very time of the assault, so that it might be viewed as a reflexive response in the passion of the moment, then he should not be considered a *Moser*, in accord with the Talmudic teaching of Rava, as "a person should not be held responsible (for what he says/does) when in distress."[77] However, this would not be applicable in a case such as ours where Shimon's submission of this matter to the lord of the city took place much later, by which time his fury should have passed, and good reason should have prevailed. In addition to which, this exemption from responsibility can only be upheld when the facts of the matter are absolutely clear, or else every claimant who wants to sue a fellow Jew in a non-Jewish court asserts that he had acted in a moment of fury. Here, in truth, no one knows what actually happened in those moments of darkness in the Synagogue, and therefore Shimon's anger at Reuven, as a matter of policy, cannot be allowed to justify his going to a non-Jewish venue for litigation of his claim.[78]

[75] *Ibid.*, at 379, citing Mordechai to *Bava Kamma*, ch. 10, para. 193.

[76] *Ibid.*

[77] Citing *Bava Batra* 16b.

[78] Siev, Responsa of RaMA, at pp. 379–380.

Fifthly, RaMA raises an objection to his own conclusion based on Rambam in *Mishneh Torah* who clearly asserts that the status of a person as a *Moser* is only possible when the person threatens to inform, not afterwards, since it is only at that prior point that he is a *Rodef*, a pursuer, who because he is a threat to the life of the person he is informing against, needs to be stopped by any means, including taking his life.[79] But here, Shimon has already executed the action of bringing the matter before the lord of the city, so while he might be financially liable, how can he be deemed to be a *Moser*? To which RaMA responds in clear antagonism to Shimon,

> Nevertheless, in this case, since this man Shimon is a habitual informer against Jews, who has always been a thorn in the side of the community, and had many times informed against the community and against individuals to the oppressors, it is simple that he has the legal status of a "*Moser*." Rambam himself wrote that if he has repeatedly informed, then we fear that he will inform against others (and thus continues to be a "*Rodef*,") ... and may therefore even be himself handed over to the non-Jewish authorities ... as (according to) the Tur ... and the Rosh.[80]

In a very sharp further comment, RaMA asserts that according to the latter authorities, even if the person was not a habitual informer, it would be permissible to hand him over to non-Jewish authorities thus endangering his own financial and physical security, and thus while it would not be permissible to simply destroy his property as punishment for his action, it would be permissible to confiscate his property and use it to compensate his victims.[81] Having thus definitively concluded that Shimon has the status of a *Masur gamur*, a "total *Moser*"[82] RaMA allows the claim of Reuven for compensation to fully stand against Shimon based on Reuven's own assertions as to the amount of the damages, without so much as an oath or other demonstration of accuracy.

None of this is particularly surprising given what we have previously seen of the Jewish law of *Mesirah*, and the demonstration of its inapplicability to usual situations of Jewish witnesses testifying even against fellow Jews in non-Jewish courts. RaMA has clearly indicated that in order for someone to be deemed a *Moser* even for initiating litigation in a non-Jewish venue against a fellow Jew, it would take a coalescence of the following factors:

[79] Ramabam, *Mishneh Torah*, *Hilchot Chovel UMazzik* 8:11.
[80] Siev, Responsa of RaMA, at p. 380 and note 19.
[81] *Ibid.*
[82] Note the implication that there might well be a lesser form of *Moser*.

1. The venue would have to be *Anas*, violent and corrupt.
2. The initiation would have to be voluntary, that is, where litigation in a Jewish venue was in fact an available alternative.
3. The intent would have to be to injure the other party by having the matter litigated before the *Anas*, as opposed to being intended simply to recover one's own property or to be fairly compensated for one's loss.
4. The intiation of the litigation would have to be done in a state of calm reflection rather than in a state of unrelieved anger or fury.
5. There is an actual threat of unlimited financial or bodily punishment to the other Jewish party in this venue (i.e. he is a *Rodef*), or there is a repeated pattern of such conduct which necessitates preemptive action in the protection of the property or lives of others in the future.

This set of elements is essentially similar to all prior determinations in Jewish llaw on this matter, in both Sefarad and in Ashkenaz,[83] and remained the mainstream position on the applicability of the law of *Mesirah* until modern times.[84]

Having thus completed his response to the first question asked of him, RaMA turns to the second question, which is of vital concern to us, "And what is the law regarding the witnesses who testified against Reuven before the lord of the city?" Surprisingly, Isserlis opens his comments on this matter by asserting that the witnesses had acted wrongfully and are therefore subject to excommunication, and are obligated to compensate Reuven for whatever injury they caused to him through their testimony.[85] This conclusion is surprising because it appears to conflict with three fundamental elements in the position of RaMA in *Shulchan Aruch*, *Choshen Mishpat*, chapter 28. There in 28:3, RaMA explicitly says that there is no financial liability so long as the witness had told the truth, which the witnesses in our case did. Further, in 28:4 RaMA had explicitly upheld the position of the *Gemara* that two witnesses were permitted to testify even in a *Magista* court and were not to be subject to excommunication, and in our case there were multiple witnesses who testified. Thirdly, the implication of RaMA's emphasis on the procedural elements of the laws of evidence in 28:3 and 4 suggested that he was deemphasizing the issue of the outcome of the adjudication in the non-Jewish court. Why then

[83] See 3.2. above.

[84] But see Chapter 7 for more contemporary treatments of this matter.

[85] Siev, Responsa of RaMA, at p. 341.

in this responsum does he place his entire emphasis on the fact that the outcome of the adjudication before the lord of the city was not in accord with Jewish law?

Actually, a careful reading of this responsum indicates that RaMA does in fact here too uphold the same positions he recorded in his *Hagahot* to *Shulchan Aruch*. However, in regard to each of those elements he is able to argue that in the case at hand there are grounds for an exception to the rule, none of which, however, are reported in his *Hagahot*. Firstly, RaMA continues to insist on conformity with the position of Mordechai that in the legislation of Rava there is liability for excommunication, but not for financial compensation. However, he points out here, Mordechai himself does recognize that there could be a basis for financial liability not only when the witness lied, but also when the Jewish defendant had witnesses who would testify in the Jewish court that he had actually paid the debt to the non-Jewish plaintiff. The witness could then be liable because he had certainly caused loss according to Jewish law, even though he had testified truthfully.[86] Similarly, argues RaMA, in an expansion of the position of the Mordechai, the Jewish judges and elders who testified concerning Reuven, and whose testimony was used in a corrupt way by the lord of the city, could be held liable for compensation not as a penalty for their testimony, but simply because they in fact caused loss to Reuven that he should not have suffered according to Jewish law.

As for the permissibility of two witnesses testifying, RaMA upholds that principle as well, indicating that there would be neither excommunication not financial liability for the testimony of two or more Jewish witnesses. However, he argues, according to the Tosephot in discussion of the case of *Hafka'at Halva'ato*, that exemption only pertains when one of two conditions pertain. Testimony by two is permissable in regard to a matter in which a Jewish court would have found the Jewish defendant liable based on their testimony, or where the Jewish defendant had suffered no actual loss.[87] But in this case, the matter under deliberation – financial liability for a fine to be paid to the government in consequence of an assault, is not even a valid cause of action in Jewish law, and therefore, their testimony would have been irrelevant and would have resulted in no liability in a Jewish court. And Reuven suffered actual loss in consequence of their testimony before the lord of the city. This explication by RaMA based on his interpretation of Tosephot, severely limits the

[86] Mordechai to *Bava Kamma,* ch. 9, para. 117.

[87] This is RaMA's interpretation of *Tosephot* to *Bava Kamma* 114a, s.v. *ve'lo amaran.*

Talmudic recognition of the permissibility of testimony by two Jewish witnesses in any non-Jewish court, and is not referred to at all in his *Hagahot* to *Shulchan Aruch*.

Isserlis then goes on to respond to three additional possible objections to his finding the witnesses financially liable. Firstly, they clearly testified only in response to the demand of the lord of the city, in which case the law applicable to them ought to be the same as that of the *Adam Chashuv*, whose case had been left unresolved in the *Talmud*,[88] but whom the *Rishonim* of Ashkenaz had clearly held was permitted to testify due to the element of coercion.[89] Again, RaMA accepts the central position, but argues that the exemption relates only to their not being liable to excommunication, leaving them subject to financial liability for any loss caused to the Jewish defendant on the grounds that the witnesses had "rescued themselves at the expense of their friend," and therefore needed to compensate him for any loss that he had suffered. In support of this contention he cites an isolated reference in Mordechai to a case in which Maharam of Rothenberg had actually imposed financial liability on parties who had each informed on the other to the civil authorities, and were then bound to testify in the non-Jewish court. However, Maharam himself had reportedly maintained that this liability was in consequence of communal legislation which imposed financial fines for such litigation in non-Jewish courts.[90] Nevertheless, RaMA argues that the liability for damages must be distinct from the communal fine, and must have been based on the actual legal liability of having caused the damage in the service of protection of oneself.[91] While this strains the language reported by Mordechai ben Hillel, the conclusion by RaMA greatly expands the financial liability for testimony by two Jewish witnesses in a non-Jewish court. Yet, no hint of this expansion of liability is reported in his *Hagahot* to *Shulchan Aruch*, *Choshen Mishpat* 28:4.

RaMA continues to confront a further problem with the position he has taken, and that is that the actions of the witnesses are only indirect causes of the economic loss of Reuven in this case, and in general the Talmudic position of Rav Ashi was sustained that in matters of personal injury or damages there is no liability for causing indirect damages.[92] His defense is that after all Rambam did maintain that there is liability

[88] *Bava Kamma* 114a. See above 4.4 for full discussion of this text.

[89] See above text at 4.4, footnotes 106–108.

[90] Mordechai to *Bava Kamma*, ch. 10, para. 195. See above, toward the end of 4.4.

[91] Responsa of RaMA, responsum no. 88, at p. 382.

[92] See discussion above at 4.4.

for indirect injury. However, long before RaMA Jewish jurists had noted the apparent contradictions within Rambam's *Mishneh Torah* as to this question,[93] and it is striking that RaMA would make this direct assertion without any equivocation. Nevertheless, RaMA gets past this problem by adding the following argument: even if this loss suffered by the Jewish party is only the indirect consequence of the testimony of the witnesses, and even if the law is that there is no liability for such indirect damage, these witnesses should still be held financially liable. To support this contention, RaMA cites Mordechai, who explains why the legislation of Rava imposed excommunication for wrongful testimony despite the fact that there is no financial liability:

> Even though all others who cause injury or damage but are not financially liable, are not excommunicated, here we do excommunicate them because they cause profit to a violent oppressor ("*Anas*") and cause loss to a Jew – that is debased; and thereby they accustom themselves to hand over ("*limsor*") money to such violent oppressors. That is why his law is more severe than that applicable to any other person who causes (indirect) injury.[94]

To which RaMA himself adds an extraordinary extension to Mordechai's reasoning:

> So here you have it, that even though there is no liability for indirect injury, nevertheless, here we excommunicate him (the wrongful witness) because it is similar to *Mesirah* (*de'dami l'mesirah*). And the law is similar in regard to compensation also, he has to pay for that same reason.[95]

Mordechai ben Hillel himself had used this reasoning precisely to explain why the witness who was not financially liable would under the legislation of Rava be subject to excommunication, because he engaged in a debased act of betrayal of his fellow Jew in the benefit of a violent oppressor, and we need to deter him and others from acting similarly, handing over the property of fellow Jews to such violent oppressors. Mordechai neither denominates the witness as a *Moser*, nor does he assert that he could be monetarily liable for his conduct. Yet RaMA uses Mordechai for both of those purposes, to assert that the crime of the wrongful witness is "similar to *Mesirah*," and that he can be held financially liable for his testimony in the non-Jewish court on the basis of his "debased" conduct.

[93] See Siev, in Responsa of RaMA, reponsum no. 88, at footnote 45 for an outline of the contradictory texts in Rambam and the variety of approaches taken to resolve the conflict.

[94] Mordechai to *Bava Kamma*, ch.9, para. 117.

[95] Responsum no. 88, at p. 383.

Yet again, no hint of this position of RaMA is present in his *Hagahot* to *Shulchan Aruch* 28:4.

The sense of the debased character of Shimon which had been evident earlier in this responsum is now reflected also in the attitude of RaMA toward the witnesses, who were themselves judges and elders of the community, but who had become partners in the injustice being perpetrated against Reuven in the hearing before the lord of the city. RaMA asks whether the very fact that these witnesses were judges and elders of the Jewish community should not entitle them to cause monetary damage to a member of the community who acts wrongfully, so that if they believed that Reuven had in fact assaulted Shimon, they should not now be held liable for causing Reuven to pay for his crime, even though it was achieved through the non-Jewish lord of the city. RaMA's response to this possible claim is sharp and angry. He says:

> Behold this claim is rotten from within, it would only be asserted by an evil person who desires to hand over Jews into the hands of violent oppressors, and would then defend himself with gobbledygook reliant upon a hollow reed. This is because even if a Jewish court had the authority to punish and to fine in order to make a fence around the *Torah*, nevertheless, to cause a loss to a fellow Jew before non-Jews is forbidden and he is liable to pay ... Certainly in our case, even if the Jewish court had the authority to fine Reuven, nevertheless, since they did so by way of handing him over to non-Jews (*derech Mesirah b'yad Kusim*) they are obligated to remove the non-Jewish authority over Reuven, and if he was injured through them, they have to pay him the damages.[96]

This extremely strong language of RaMA fails to even attempt to take account of the long Rabbinic tradition beginning with the *Mishnah* in *Gittin*,[97] and continuing through the period of the Gaonim[98] and the *Rishonim*[99] of Rabbinic courts, when lacking the capacity to enforce their judgments, precisely utilizing the non-Jewish courts to execute their judgments. His failure to even introduce this material and to distinguish it from the case at hand is indicative of his dismissive attitude toward both Shimon and the witnesses who, willingly or not, supported him in the litigation against a fellow Jew in a non-Jewish venue in which the lord of the city was clearly viewed by RaMA as an *Anas*, a violent oppressor. It comes as no surprise that this last characterization of the witnesses as

[96] *Ibid.*

[97] *Mishnah Gittin* 9:8, at 88b.

[98] See for example the *teshuvah* of Sherirah Gaon and Hai Gaon reported above at 2.3.

[99] See for example Rambam, *Hilchot Gerushin* (Laws of Divorce) 2:20, and *Shulchan Aruch, Even HaEzer* 134:5.

acting in a manner similar to *Mesirah*, also lacks any echo in the RaMA's *Hagahot* to *Shulchan Aruch, Choshen Mishpat* chapter 28.

Having explored the disparities between the positions of RaMA in the *Shulchan Aruch* – both in the areas of his silent agreement with R. Joseph Karo, and in his own distinctive statements in *Hagahot* – versus his positions in his response, it is striking to note the degree to which his latter positions are in conformity with the approaches and conclusions in the responsum of his predecessor, Rabbi Moses ben Isaac ha-Levi Mintz (Maharam Mintz) which we examined in detail earlier in this chapter.[100] While there appears to be no evidence that R. Moshe Isserlis was aware of the responsum of Maharam Mintz on this matter, there are seven parallels in both reasoning and conclusions that are quite striking:

1. Maharam Mintz restricted permission to testify truthfully in a non-Jewish court against a fellow Jew to the situation in which the specific claim would yield the same reliance on a single witness in a Jewish court.[101] RaMA restricted permission of even two Jewish witnesses to testify to the situation in which the claim being litigated would yield the same reliance on the two witnesses in a Jewish court.[102]
2. In regard to the procedural issues in the non-Jewish court, Maharam Mintz bypasses the questions of standards of reliance on single or multiple witnesses and shifts directly to the question of whether the outcome in a Jewish court would have been the same.[103]
   RaMA equally disregards the question of standards of evidence and, in two separate responsa, treats the matter purely from the perspective of whether there was actual loss caused to the Jewish litigant that he would not have suffered had the matter been litigated in a Jewish court.[104]
3. Maharam Mintz maintains that the exemptions which allow a single Jewish witness to testify would pertain only when that Jew would have been a fully eligible witness in a Jewish court, but not, for example, if he were to be considered an interested party and thus ineligible to testify in a Jewish court.[105] Similarly, RaMA holds that if the testimony of the Jewish witness would not have been

[100] See 5.1 above, citing Responsa Maharam Mintz, No. 44.
[101] *Ibid.*
[102] Responsa of RaMA, responsum no. 88.
[103] Responsa of Maharam Mintz, responsum no. 44.
[104] Responsa of RaMA, responsum no. 52 and responsum no. 88.
[105] Mintz, responsum no. 44.

conclusive in the Jewish court, because, for example, the other party had two witnesses to verify his claim of payment, then the Jewish witness would not be freed of liability.[106]

4. The basis of financial liability by a Jewish witness in such situations, according to Maharam Mintz, is not the provision of excommunication under the legislation of Rava, but is the general Jewish law principle that one who rescues himself or his property at the expense of another is liable to compensate for the loss he has caused.[107] Likewise for RaMA, the financial liability is based neither on excommunication, nor on the law of *Mesirah*, but on the principle of *Matzil atzmo bemamon chavero*,[108] "rescue of self at the expense of one's neighbor."
5. Even the exempting principle of coersion would not apply according to Maharam Mintz unless there was absolutely no way to avoid having to testify, including having previously consulted with Jewish authorities and having forewarned the Jewish party of one's intent to testify and then having limited one's testimony to saying the minimum possible.[109] RaMA expresses a similar intense reservation even in regard to a situation in which the witnesses are themselves judges and leaders of the Jewish community, that they needed to have rescued the Jewish party from the litigation in the non-Jewish court; and he even leaves open the question as to whether the evidence really confirms that they had no way out, and that perhaps they had really testified voluntarily.[110]
6. Maharam Mintz considers classifying the wrongful witness as a *Moser*, but then carefully shifts his language to indicate that the actual laws of *Mesirah* do not apply in this situation, but that the witness is to be treated "as someone debased, like a *Moser*."[111] While RaMA deals with the issue of *Mesirah* primarily in regard to a Jew who initiates legal action against a fellow Jew in a non-Jewish court,[112] he also addresses the applicability of the laws of *Mesirah* to the Jewish witnesses in the case before him. He too starts out with very strong language suggesting the applicability of

[106] RaMA, responsum no. 88.
[107] Mintz, responsum no. 44.
[108] RaMA, responsum no. 88.
[109] Mintz, responsum no. 44.
[110] RaMA, responsum no. 88.
[111] Mintz, responsum no. 44.
[112] RaMA, responsum no. 86.

the status of *Moser* to the witnesses, but then shifts to a description in which the betrayal by the witnesses is denominated as *dami l'mesirah*, similar to *Mesirah*.[113]

7. Finally it is worth noting that Maharam Mintz expressed deep animus toward the Jewish witness, Moshe. He clearly distrusted him, considered him a liar and a cheat, and one worthy of whatever punishment he could inflict upon him by his interpretations of the applicable Jewish law.[114] In almost identical manner, RaMA speaks in an extremely disparaging manner about Shimon, whom he considers to be a deceiver and a habitual informer against fellow Jews.[115] He further extends this negative attitude toward the Jewish judges and leaders whom he views as enablers, complicit in the evil being done to a fellow Jew through their testimony in the corrupt court of the lord of the city.[116]

5.4 THE TENSION BETWEEN CODIFICATION AND RESPONSA

How then are we to understand this sharp differentiation between RaMA in his *Hagahot* to the *Shulchan Aruch*, and RaMA in his own responsa? And given his positions in the *Shulchan Aruch*, how do we understand the similarity of RaMA in his responsa, to the responsum of Maharam Mintz? While there is much more to be said about this matter, I would like here to simply call attention to a few critical differences between the two genres of legal literature with which we are dealing, codes versus judicial decisions.[117]

In the history of Jewish law it is apparent that codifications of Jewish law were intended primarily for the general Jewish public rather than for the jurist or the lawyer, or for the expert in Jewish law. The code was intended to serve as the basis on which individual citizens could regulate their behavior in consonance with the will of God and the will of the Sages, who were the interpreters and executors of the Divine will. The

[113] RaMA, responsum no. 88.
[114] Mintz, responsum no. 44.
[115] RaMA, responsum no. 88.
[116] *Ibid.*
[117] For general treatment of the role of codification in Jewish law as compared to other forms of legal lliterature, see Menachem Elon, *Jewish Law*, trans. by Bernard Auerbach and Melvin J. Sykes, Philadelphia, PA, JPS, 1994, vol. III, ch. 32, pp. 1138–1148.

code, by virtue of its accessibility to all, was also able to function as the common core of required and desired behavior to which all citizens could be held accountable. Thereby, the code could serve the additional purpose of creating sufficient social uniformity to allow for a common sense of national virtues, national purpose and thus national unity. It is precisely because of the public purpose of the code in Jewish life, that even the legal portions of the Bible, let alone its historical content, are limited to what is essential for every citizen to know. For this reason, when the *Torah* waxes expansive in any particular area of law, or history, the natural question that traditional commentators feel needs to be responded to is – why was such extensive detail needed as to this particular matter?[118] For this same reason, the Sages always assumed that the public reading of the *Torah* was a centrally required institution in Jewish life, despite the absence of such legislation in the *Torah* itself, and that it must have been introduced, they said, by Moses and the Elders while the Jews were yet in the desert.[119] This assumption about the role of a code pertained not only in regard to legislation contained within the *Torah* itself, but also in regard to the first systematically organized and total codification of Jewish law, the *Mishnah*, and thereafter, to every code composed in the history of Jewish law. When codes became too extensive or too discursive, or too detailed to be seen by the public as useful in their self-governance, or too outdated in the issues that it addressed, the people voted with their feet, and abandoned the use of those particular codes.

By contrast, a second form of legal literature, the judicial decision, the responsum, was not intended primarily for public consumption. It was intended to serve as the basis for the resolution of a controversy through litigation in which the best possible justice would be achieved in accordance with the principles and precedents of Jewish law. The consumers of judicial decisions were the parties to litigation, who needed to be persuaded that justice was being done, and other jurists and legal experts for whom these judicial decisions could serve as precedents upon which they might choose to rely in future cases, and whose further opinions

[118] For an example of such an approach see Saul J. Berman, "Parashat Shekalim and the Role of the Jewish Preisthood," in R. Daniel Z. Feldman and Stuart W. Halpern (eds.), *From Within the Tent: The Haftarot*, pp. 597–607, Scharf Publication Trust of Yeshiva University Press, New York, 2011.

[119] Rambam, *Sefer Ahavah, Hilchot Tefillah* 12:1–2, and *Kesef Mishna* ad loc. See also *Tractate Soferim*, ed. by M. Higger, Jerusalem, Makor Publishing, 1950, 10:1, at pp. 209–210, footnotes to lines 6–9. See also Z.H. Chajes, *The Student's Guide Through the Talmud*, trans. by Jacob Shachter, Feldheim Pub., 2nd edition, 1960, at pp. 97 and 111–117.

might serve to refine the principles and their application in the attempt to continue to sustain just outcomes in consonance with the will of God and of the Sages. The interest of the public in judicial decisions was not the detailed knowledge of the argumentation and the sources, but the awareness that multiple competing values were being evaluated by a judge who respected the parties and their claims, who was committed to the spiritual and social urgency of upholding the values of the legal system, and who was attempting to arrive at the most fair and just possible resolution in the light of the facts of the case. It was and remains this confidence of the public in that jurist that determines whether a particular author of responsa in Jewish law becomes an influencial source of Jewish legal practice. Dr. Haym Soloveitchik contends that for Early Rishonim the attitude toward the precential value of responsa was even more limited. He explains the absence of citation of Gaonic responsa in Tosafist literature, and even the absence of collections preserving the responsa of the greatest of the Ashkenaz jurists (except for those of Rabbenu Jacob Tam), in the following manner:

> Even Rashi's responsa were not preserved in France, indeed were scarcely known by the French Tosafists, many of whom were his own descendants. Over the course of centuries, innumerable questions were naturally asked, and innumerable answers written, but these replies were viewed as *livres de circonstance*. Unlike commentary, responsa were simply not viewed as being a genre of literary expression.[120]

Thus, in contrast to the code, the responsum is a very temporal instrument, dependent upon the unique set of circumstances present in the underlying fact pattern and therefore constituting a work composed for the occasion.

Secondly, it is vital to note the relationship between codes and responsa in regard to the issue of legal diversity. In most instances a code serves the purpose of resolving debate and diversity of practice. In Jewish society, in the period subsequent to the destruction of the second Temple, sectarian divisions were very powerfully present, and internal divisions within Pharasaic legal culture were extensive and contentious.[121] In addition, the central organs of Jewish self-government were weak, as the functions of the *Sanhedrin* as legislature and also as Supreme Court were

[120] Haym Soloveitchik, *Collected Essays*, vol. I, Oxford, The Littman Library of Jewish Civilization, 2013, p. 20.

[121] See e.g. Gedalyahu Alon, *Jews, Judaism and the Classical World*, trans. by Israel Abrahams, Jerusalem, Magnes Press, 1977, ch. 5, "On The Halakhot of the Early Sages," pp. 138–145.

under attack externally by Rome and internally by the diverse schools of thought represented within its membership. The very emergence of *Mishnah* as a systematic method of study and as a means of organizing legal instructions in a coherent manner was both indicative of, and an attempt to address, the extreme diversity of opinion in matters of Jewish law, which were increasingly incapable of being resolved. The adoption of the *Mishnah* under the leadership of Rabbi Judah the Nasi in approximately 220 C.E. was an attempt to forge unity, without denying the underlying diversity out of which the need for codification had emerged. However, two consequences of this codification severely challenged its full effectiveness. Firstly, with the adoption of the code the process of its interpretation began, including the need to abstract the underlying principles which could provide the basis for applying the rules of the code to new circumstances as they arose. Secondly, given the portability of the code and its authoritative nature, Rav and Samuel were able to use it as the basis for their "States Rights" revolution – insisting that the processes of interpretation, application to novel circumstances as well as the authority for supplementary legislation could now be done locally by courts and local legislatures in Babylon, without dependence upon the *Sanhedrin* of Israel for their local authority.

This fissure meant that the very unity that had been the great promise of the *Mishnah* as the centrally adopted code was now to become the basis for ever-increasing diversity through local interpretation, local judicial decision and local legislation. Thus, the singular *Mishnah* developed around itself a separate body of study and literature in Israel, called the *Gemara* of the Land of Israel (or later the Jerusalem *Gemara*), recording the interpretations, judicial decisions and local legislation of the Land of Israel over the succeeding 200 years; and the parallel body of study and eventually literature in Babylon (Persia), called the Babylonian *Gemara*, recording the interpretations, judicial decisions and local legislation adopted in the various Babylonian academies and communities over the course of the following 400 years. Vast diversity had thus sprung from the very loins of the *Mishnah* that had been designed to produce unity, not only because of the natural development of diverse interpretations, but also because it had fed into the abandonment of the "federal system" of Jewish law in which there had been, at least in principle, a single central Legislature/Supreme Court which had authority to establish Jewish law for Jews wherever in the world they resided. This diversity pervaded the Jewish legal system, affecting not only matters of customary practice, but also requirements of "Rabbinic" law, and even of understandings of

De'Oraita, revealed laws. Every layer and every realm of law was affected by the absence of a central authority capable of definitively resolving what constituted legally required practice.

After almost a thousand years from the time of the codification of *Mishnah*, Maimonides attempted to solve the problem of diversity and disunity through his authorship of *Mishneh Torah*, only the second time in the history of Jewish law that a total and comprehensive codification was attempted and promulgated. It was a testimony both to the grandeur of his work, and to the obvious need of the Jewish public that his code swept so thoroughly through, and was adopted so extensively within, Sephardic lands. But, of course, even in those lands, the processes of interpretation of his code, and of striving to work out the underlying principles which would enable applying his code to new circumstances as they arose, began almost immediately to produce new commentaries with diverse undestandings of Maimonides' own positions. Simultaneously, the need for litigation of controversies, which had for the preceeding 500 years been producing judicial decisions, responsa, emerging from the Babylonian and Palestinian Gaonic academies, did not cease with the emergence of the new code, but the code itself became one factor in the deliberations within the responsa, as the drive for diversity continued to march forward, generating a tense, dialectical relationship between the code and the responsa. Much as the text of the code could not itself definitively resolve complex questions of law, likewise, the rulings of responsa could influence, but not automatically be transferred, into clauses of new codes. Thus, commentaries and responsa continued to produce greater and greater diversity of local Jewish law until the need for some new codification became self-evident.

In Sephardic lands, that need to periodically restore consistency and unity was satisfied by the Turim of Rabbi Jacob ben Asher, and then the *Shulchan Aruch* of Rabbi Joseph Karo. In Ashkenaz, the resistance to codification was intense and the codes of Maimonides and of Jacob ben Asher were resisted and smaller local codes composed in Ashkenaz did not gain traction. However, by the mid-sixteenth century, the *Shulchan Aruch* of Rabbi Joseph Karo struck a powerful, responsive chord amongst the Ashkenazic public which had lived with extraordinary diversity, indeed had been taught in the approach of the Tosafists to cherish the dialectic in which unresolved, diverse solutions was the ideal way to approach any question of Jewish law. Rabbi Shlomo Luria battled against the spread and use of Karo's code, not only because it embodied the law of Sephardic jurists, but also because he was methodologically opposed to the adoption of any code beyond the text of the *Talmud* itself. By contrast, Rabbi Mordechai Yaffo, recognizing the need for the resolution of diversity, decided to, and actually composed, a multi-volume code to express the positions of Ashkenazic jurists, called the *Levush*. However, due in part to general opposition to codification and in part to personal opposition to him and to his positions, his code failed to gain adherents. Rabbi Moshe Isserlis then achieved the goal for Ashkenaz that no one else had been able to achieve, through the composition of his *Mapa*, consisting of addenda, *Hagahot*, to paragraph after paragraph of the *Shulchan Aruch*, encompassing the divergent positions and practices of Ashkenaz Jewish law, as well as general explanatory comments to clarify the text when he was in agreement with it.

But, immediately after the completion of the now dual *Shulchan Aruch*, the processes of interpretation and adaptation to new situations incorporated in commentaries and novellae, and the integration of elements of the code in vast numbers of responsa resumed in a manner which rapidly restored the diversity so laboriously limited through the code. Undoubtedly, in the 550 years since the completion of the dual *Shulchan Aruch*, the level of unresolved debate and diversity in Jewish law, enhanced by the complete shattering of local geographic authority, the revolution of publishing, the Holocaust, the rise of the State of Israel, and now the internet and globalization has increased to a point far beyond that which has existed at any other time in the history of Jewish people. We are probably due again for a new codification in this dialectic cycle of narrowing and expanding legal discourse.

In the light of these factors in the divergent roles of codes and responsa in the formation of Jewish law, we can better understand the similarities between Karo's text of the *Shulchan Aruch* and RaMA's *Hagahot* on the one hand, and on the other hand the similarities between the responsa of Maharam Mintz and RaMA. Each of these forms of legal literature plays an essential but distinctive role in the way in which Jewish law governs the conduct of the Jewish people, attempts to assure the maintenance of the greatest possible standards of justice in the resolution of interpersonal conflict and sustains the dialectic between unity and diversity.

6

Further Expansion of the Duty of Testimony Against Fellow Jews in Non-Jewish Courts in the Period of the *Acharonim*

During the seventeenth and eighteenth centuries, Halakhic sources, both responsa and novellae, did not challenge the essential positions of the *Rishonim* that testimony by a Jew, against a fellow Jew, in favor of a non-Jew, in a non-Jewish court would be permissible in some situations and even mandatory in others. Such testimony would be permissible in the following situations: when offered

1. by a pair of Jewish witnesses even in a corrupt court;
2. by a single witness in an honest court;
3. by a single witness in a court which does not reach judgment based on the testimony of a single witness;
4. by even a single witness who is under threat of economic or bodily penalty for refusal to testify.

In addition, they upheld the positions of *Rishonim* in insisting that Jewish law itself would require testimony of a Jewish witness if the failure to testify would:

1. result in *Chillul Hashem*;
2. enable a fellow Jew to perpetrate a crime;
3. violate the law of the land;
4. necessitate taking a (false) oath as to his lack of information; or
5. threaten the security or the economic well-being of the Jewish community.

Of course, substantial and vigorous debate about detailed application of these rules continued, particularly around the question of whether a witness who had breached the restrictive legislation of Rava could be subject not only to excommunication, but also to liability for monetary compensation to be paid to the Jewish "victim" of his illicit testimony.

While this debate concerning the intensity of penalty was being energetically engaged in, two new foundations for leniency were being propounded by a major figure in Jewish law, to further expand the permissibility of testimony by Jews, against fellow Jews, in favor of non-Jews, in non-Jewish courts. These new expansive positions were the handiwork of Rabbi Jacob Emden.

6.1 IF THE TESTIMONY IS ITSELF NOT DEFINITIVE AND NOT DETERMINATIVE OF THE OUTCOME

The case which was referred to Rabbi Jacob Emden for his deliberation involved three Jews who had been designated to witness the signature on a note of indebtedness by a Jewish borrower from a non-Jewish lender. The matter was then being litigated in a non-Jewish court and the three Jewish witnesses were summoned to testify that the signature on the note was in fact that of the Jewish defendant. The questioner posits that their refusal to testify would create a *Chillul Hashem* as well as danger to their persons. He raises also the matter that they would be subject to oath in their appearance before the court no matter what their testimony.[1]

Rabbi Jacob Emden's initial response to the case itself is clear and unequivocal – the witnesses are permitted to testify on multiple grounds. Firstly, they have been designated, and their refusal would be a *Chillul Hashem*. Secondly, they are even more than two witnesses and therefore the constraint of the legislation of Rava does not apply to them. Thirdly, they are not permitted to take a false oath, even when combined with mental reservation in a situation of coercion.[2] These elements alone lead Emden to make a powerful assertion:

> However, since the non-Jewish court will require the witnesses to take a severe oath, by the *Torah* itself, it is most clear that we would not tell a person to sin and violate [a sin of] the greatest severity, [violation of] which rattles the entire

[1] Rabbi Jacob ben Zvi Emden (1697–1776), *She'elat Yaavetz*, Lemberg, 1884, reprinted Jerusalem, 1971, part 2, no. 51, at pp. 19b–20b.

[2] *Ibid.* He contends that such falsehood under oath, with mental reservation, would be permissible only in a situation of averting a direct threat to life. But he notes that he himself had actually forbidden such conduct even to avoid a death penalty in a case in which the defendant was actually liable, citing his own responsum no. 9 in this same volume, *She'elat Yaavetz*, part 2.

world – so that a criminal should profit! Who gave him [the Jewish defendant] permission to falsely deny liability for a debt which he owed, even if the creditor was a non-Jew! Behold the *Torah* says, "And he shall reckon precisely with he who bought him." [Lev. 25:50] (And this even at a time when we have power over them, certainly also nowadays.) And under the current circumstances, when the defendant has been sued and is subject to judgment, the principle of *Hafka'at Halva'ato*, [that is, non-liability for an indebtedness to a non-Jew due to implied waiver] is certainly not applicable.[3] In such a case all Jewish Law prohibitions apply, of robbery, illicit withholding (*Oshek*), and *Chillul Hashem*, which is of great severity, and creating danger to himself and to others. How could it even have occurred to you to help such an evildoer, for certainly one who does this is an evildoer, as you have described it in your query. Even were he a poor person, "The remnant of Israel shall not do iniquity, nor speak lies, nor shall a deceitful tongue be found in their mouth." (Zephaniah 3:13).

He could then have closed his deliberation on this matter. Enough said. Instead, Rabbi Emden then goes on to make a novel proposal that would generate a new exemption from the restrictive law of Rava. He contends that this case is quite distinct from the case of the *Talmud* and from the cases under prior discussion by the *Rishonim*. In all of those cases, Rabbi Emden asserts, the testimony of the Jewish witness or witnesses would have left the Jewish defendant with no valid defense whatsoever. In that sense, the testimony, upon its acceptance by the non-Jewish court, is fully determinative of the judicial outcome. If that outcome is not in accordance with Jewish law, he argues, then the witness or witnesses would in fact have been the direct cause of injury to the Jewish defendant – *k'maan de'avid b'yadayim dami*, "as if he had done it with his own hands."

By contrast, Rabbi Emden maintains, in the case before him the witnesses are only confirming the signature of the defendant on the document of indebtedness. Even with that fact being true and accepted as such by the non-Jewish court, there are a number of defenses which the Jewish defendant could still have to establish that he is not liable to pay. He could claim that he had already paid the debt; or he could claim that he had been coerced to sign the document. Thus, the testimony of the witnesses does not establish all of the elements necessary to prove the liability or guilt of the defendant.

This position of Rabbi Emden yields a novel exemption to the entire restriction against testimony. It implies that even a single Jewish witness would be permitted to testify, even in a corrupt non-Jewish court, so long as his sole testimony is not itself sufficient basis for finding the Jewish

[3] This echoes, and may even go further than the position of Ravad cited above in 4.1.

defendant guilty or liable. If the Jewish party has any possible defense which has not been precluded by the testimony of that witness, then the testimony is not constrained. Strikingly, Emden does not even attempt to demonstrate that the defendant in the case before him actually had sufficient counter-claims to establish his non-liability, if the court accepted the truth of the testimony of the three Jewish witnesses who confirmed his signature. The issue for Emden seems to be purely the insufficiency of the testimony in and of itself to establish liability.

It is as if Emdem was taking quite literally the *Talmud*'s report of the rationale of the Law of Rava, "Because they determine liability on (the basis of) the testimony of a single witness."[4] His use in this paragraph of phrases such as *de'avid b'yadayim* ("as if he had done it with his own hands,") and *bari hezeika*, ("the injury he causes is clear") in fact suggests that Emden is demanding much more than indirect causation of financial loss in order to determine the impermissibility of testimony. Later in this responsum, Emden makes explicit his contention that the usual standard of *Gerama*, of indirect causation would not be sufficient to constrain testimony under the Law of Rava, but that the higher, albeit still vague, standard of *Garmi* – not the totally exclusive cause, but definitely a sufficient evidentiary cause – would be necessary in order for the constraint to apply to the witnesses.[5]

6.2 THE ROLE AND SIGNIFICANCE OF THE SUBPEONA

Rabbi Jacob Emden's reinterpretation of the passage in *Bava Kamma* 113b-114a, the record of the legislation of Rava, continues into one other legal element, with striking results, despite his recognition that it bears no direct relationship to the case that is before him for adjudication.[6] Emden notes the presence in the standard printed editions of the *Talmud* before him of the phrase *ve'lo teva'o*, "and he had not been subpoenaed." He likewise notes that in virtually all records of this passage by early authorities, by the *Rishonim*, the phrase is absent. He fully accepts that the reading of the printed editions is correct,[7] and that a Jewish person

[4] *Bava Kamma* 113b-114a. See above, 2.1, line 7 of the Amoraic legislation.

[5] Emden, *She'elat Yaavetz* at p. 20a, column 1, paragraph s.v. *ve'hashta*.

[6] Emden, *She'elat Yaavetz*, at p. 20a, column 1, paragraph s.v. *Al ken...*, and the preceding sentence, at the close of the prior paragraph.

[7] *Ibid.*, at the top of column 2, he explicitly asserts that the reading of the printed text is unchallenged. He was clearly totally unaware of the absence of the phrase in all manuscripts and even the earliest printed editions. See above 2.1.3 and 4.5.

subpoenaed by a non-Jewish court to testify against a Jewish defendant on behalf of a non-Jewish plaintiff is permitted to testify as a coerced person who cannot escape the duty imposed upon him by the civil court and government. Not only is testimony permissible under circumstances of subpoena, but the witness can also not be held liable for any injury to the Jewish defendant against whom he testifies – he is not considered to be one who "rescues himself at the expense of his neighbor." This is because, says Emden, the witness is telling the truth as he knows it, affirming the liability of the Jewish defendant based on his own knowledge of the facts. This is quite a novel contention, as opposed to those prior to Emden who maintain that the basis for liability of the witness in such situations would be an evaluation by a Jewish court as to whether the witness had caused damage to the Jewish defendant that he would not have suffered had the case been tried in a Jewish court.[8] The latter, more objective, standard is rejected by Emden in favor of the subjective intent of the witness – if he honestly believed that the Jewish defendant was liable and he testified only truthfully, then he could not be held liable for the untoward consequences.

How then does Emden explain the silence of most *Rishonim* on the permissibility of testimony in the case of subpoena according to the Law of Rava? He notes that the immediately following passage in the *Talmud* is the question concerning the *Adam Chashuv*, the prominent person, who is presumed to be unable to avoid testifying, and whose testimony even as a single witness in a *Dawar* court will be assigned force as if it were the testimony of two witnesses.[9] The likely outcome of his testimony, therefore, would be liability on the part of the Jewish defendant in a manner not consonant with Jewish law. The question of whether such a prominent person ought to testify or not, is left unresolved (*Teiku*) by the *Talmud*. But, argues Emden, why should the law regulating the conduct of the prominent person be any different from that of any other Jew, as formulated in the preceding Law of Rava? That is, if the prominent person was subpoenaed, he should be permitted to testify like any regular person; and if he was not subpoenaed, why would we assume that he cannot avoid testifying – given that his role in the controversy is unrecognized? It is this apparent contradiction between the two sequential Talmudic cases, Emden maintains, that led most *Rishonim* to simply refuse to acknowledge the ruling of permissibility of testimony in case of subpoena. With that gone from the law regulating testimony by non-prominent Jews, the

[8] See Maharam Mintz.

[9] *Bava Kamma* 114a.

dilemma of the prominent person becomes clear; if his involvement in the case is unknown, he may very well be able to avoid testimony, but if he is subpoenaed, then in contrast to a regular Jew, he the prominent person, will certainly be unable to avoid testifying and thereby would certainly cause loss to the Jewish defendant. It is that dilemma which the *Talmud* declines to resolve, and leaves as a *Teiku*.

However, Emden continues (in a somewhat strained argument), that this approach is not correct, for in a case in which the witness is subpoenaed, it is actually more likely, Emden asserts, that the non-Jewish authorities would forgo forcing a prominent person to testify, but would pursue a regular Jew and compel him to testify. Therefore, he maintains, the reading of the printed text is correct, and a Jewish witness subpoenaed to testify, whether a regular Jew or a prominent person, would be fully permitted to testify and would bear no liability for losses not in consonance with Jewish law suffered by the Jewish defendant. He then continues to offer the following novel explanation of the dilemma of the prominent person to whom, according to Emden, no subpoena was issued.

The prominence of this prominent person, he says, resides precisely in the fact that he is one who pursues justice, like our Teacher, Moses. Therefore, while he was not subpoenaed to testify, he simply cannot allow the injustice to occur – he perceives himself as being obligated to stand up for the exploited, and to prevent his fellow Jew from committing a criminal act of *Oshek*, exploitation through withholding payment due. In addition, given his reputation as a person of deep religio-ethical commitment, were it to be known that he had information that could have prevented the crime, and that he withheld that information, it could produce anger, and possibly even danger or financial loss.[10] It is for that reason that the prominent person is considered to be unable to extricate himself from the responsibility to testify. So, if the non-Jewish *Dawar* court (fundamentally honest court) would treat him like anyone else and rely on his testimony as a single witness only to the extent of requiring the defendant to take an oath – as a Jewish court would do – then certainly the prominent person should testify. However, if the non-Jewish *Dawar* court would extend greater reliability to this witness, and judge the case as if he were two witnesses, with the result that the Jewish defendant would suffer loss not in accordance with Jewish law – then that dilemma

[10] Emden, *She'elat Yaavetz*, at 20a, paragraph s.v. *Elah hachi b'mai askinan*. It is striking that he omits any reference to the element of *Chillul Hashem* as further justifying the testimony by a prominent person. It is of course possible that he intends to encompass that in his reference to the possible "anger" produced by his failure to testify.

remains unresolved. In the face of that lack of resolution, Emden contends, the prominent person is free, if he so chooses, to fulfill his self-imposed obligation to pursue justice, and to testify against his fellow Jew.

The implications of Emden's positions are quite far reaching:

1. A Jew to whom a subpoena is issued to testify in any non-Jewish court, against a fellow Jew, is considered "coerced," is permitted to testify, and bears no responsibility for damage which might result to the Jewish defendant as a result of his truthful testimony.
2. Two Jews are permitted to voluntarily testify in any non-Jewish court, against a fellow Jew, and bear no responsibility for damage which might result to the Jewish defendant as a result of their truthful testimony.
3. A single Jew may volunteer to testify in an honest non-Jewish court, so long as his testimony does not, on its very face, preclude any defense whatsoever by the Jewish defendant, based on either fact or law.
4. A single Jew ought not to volunteer to testify in a dishonest non-Jewish court in a matter in which he has no interest, – "who requested this of him, who appointed him ruler and judge, to intrude in a controversy which is not his."[11] It is precisely, and solely, this situation in which the witness might be subject to excommunication and, according to Emden, contrary to the position of R. Moshe Isserlis, might even be financially liable for the loss not in accordance with Jewish law suffered by the Jewish defendant. But here too, only if the testimony itself was totally conclusive of the matter, leaving the Jewish defendant with no defense whatsoever.
5. A prominent person, that is one who is driven by his own religious and ethical conscience to prevent evil and wrongdoing, may uphold his own personal, self-imposed commitment by voluntarily offering testimony in any non-Jewish court; and the truthfulness of his testimony would prevent him from being held liable for any financial consequences to the Jewish defendant.
6. Contrary to his questioner, Emden maintains that in any of the situations in which he considers the testimony to be permissible, no prior approval by a Jewish court is necessary, "there is neither restraining law, nor judicial review."[12]

[11] *Ibid.*

[12] *Ibid.*, at paragraph s.v. *vehashta de'atinan lehachi.*

Emden makes one other final point to support his contention that the reading of *velo teva'o* was correct and that it is fundamental to the legislation of Rava that a subpoena issued by the non-Jewish court would require testimony by a Jewish witness under all circumstances. Our primary Talmudic passage had asserted that the restrictive language of the legislation of Rava would not restrain a set of two Jewish witnesses from testifying against a fellow Jew in a non-Jewish court, impliedly because the outcome of that trial would be consonant with Jewish law in that testimony of two witnesses would be conclusive in finding the defendant liable.[13] But, argue the *Tosafists*, what of the situation in which Jewish substantive law differs from the non-Jewish law, so that a Jewish court would still have held the defendant not to be liable? For example, in the case of *Hafka'at Halva'ato*, a loan from a non-Jew to a Jew for which there is no documentary evidence and which, when the creditor dies, is even unknown to his heirs. Jewish law treats such a situation as being one in which the creditor is presumed to have waived his rights to collection, as if it were a charitable contribution masquerading as a loan, or simply a gift, and even if there were Jewish witnesses to the transaction, the debt would not be ordered to be paid by a Jewish court. Yet, if those witnesses were to testify in a non-Jewish court, that court would hold the Jewish defendant liable, thus causing him a loss "not in accordance with Jewish Law." Why then should those witnesses be permitted to testify, ask the Tosafists.[14] To which the Tosafot responds, that even then, the testimony of the two Jewish witnesses in the non-Jewish court would have caused "no loss" to the Jewish defendant, because "in consequence of their testimony he would only be paying that which he truly owed."[15] That is, the Tosafists here pierce the veil of the legal fiction in recognition of the underlying justice of making the defendant pay back what he borrowed.

But, Emden argues, the case of the Tosafists must be one in which the Jewish witnesses had not been subpoenaed at all; for had they been subpoenaed, that would mean that there were persons other than the deceased creditor, such as his heirs, who knew of the debt and were suing for its repayment – in which case, even according to Jewish law the debtor would be liable. Thus, according to Emden's interpretation of the position of the Tosafists, the Talmudic permission for the two Jewish witnesses to testify must involve a situation in which they themselves, being

[13] *Bava Kamma* 114a.

[14] *Tosafot, Bava Kamma* 114a, s.v. *Ve'lo amaran elah chad.*

[15] *Ibid.*

the only persons having knowledge of the existence of the debt, reported the transaction to the heirs of the non-Jewish creditor and the court, so as to cause the initiation of the action against the Jewish defendant. Thus the meaning of *ve'lo tevao minei* is not just that the witnesses were not subpoenaed, but that the lawsuit itself had not been initiated against the Jewish defendant except as a result of the report by the two Jewish witnesses. This sounds more like a case of *Mesirah*, "informing," than just a case of testimony in a non-Jewish court, but, nevertheless, Emden insists on its full permissibility under the legislation of Rava, to be done by two witnesses even in a *Magista* court, a corrupt court, and impliedly also for a single witness in a *Dawar* court, an honest non-Jewish court.[16]

Beyond all of the limitations on the legislation of Rava imposed by the *Rishonim*, Emden has even more severely narrowed the restrictive force of Rava's Law to the single, relatively rare situation in which all eight of the following conditions pertain:

(1) A single Jewish witness,
(2) in a corrupt non-Jewish court,
(3) whose testimony would preclude any possible defense by the Jewish defendant, and
(4) who has neither a personal stake in the outcome,
(5) nor any sustained personal religious or ethical commitment to prevent injustice, and
(6) who is not subpoenaed,
(7) whose testimony would result in benefit to the non-Jewish plaintiff, and
(8) loss to the Jewish defendant which is not in accordance with Jewish law

– must refrain from voluntary testimony, lest he be subject to excommunication and possible financial liability to the Jewish defendant.

[16] *Ibid.* at 20b, paragraph s.v. *ve'ikka lemeidak*.

7

Contemporary Attempts to Revert to the Original Law of Rava: Expanding the Boundaries of Loyalty

While emptied of most of its restrictive force, the nub of Rava's legislation was retained in the literature. Strikingly, in the latter half of the twentieth century, there appears to have been a sudden resurgence of concern with the limiting force of Rava's legislation. From the early 1970s until now, the second decade of the twenty-first century, in the *Charedi* community of the United States, it has become a matter of common popular wisdom that Jewish law forbids testimony by a Jew against a fellow Jew in the courts of the United States. The usual basis for this constraint is not asserted to be the legislation of Rava, but rather the general Jewish law against *Mesirah* – informing.

Nor has this been just a popular misconception. As recently as 2010, The Central Rabbinical Congress of the United States and Canada, largely consisting of *Chassidic* Rabbis and scholars, joined by a *Charedi* court in Israel, threatened excommunication of a *Charedi* Jew who had already been convicted of tax fraud in a US criminal proceeding if he testified before a grand jury concerning other suspected co-conspirators.[1]

Why is this development now taking place? And what, if any, legal explanation can there be for this application of the law of *Mesirah*, contrary to virtually all of the history of Jewish legal discourse on this matter? Is this simply a manifestation of the isolationist orientation of the *Charedi* Orthodox community, and of its opposition to integration with any element of the pervasive secular culture by which it is surrounded? But then, what of the loyalty of the leadership of the community to the integrity of Jewish law?

[1] http://latimesblogs.latimes.com/lanow/2012/03/orthodox-rabbi-ordered-jailed.html.

7.1 THE HOVERING OF THE TERM *MESIRAH*

As we have previously demonstrated, it was clear since the early period of the *Rishonim* that even a single witness in Rava's case, were he to testify, would still not be in violation of the law of *Mesirah*.[2] However, the law of *Mesirah* remained part of the discussion in regard to the question of the nature of the excommunication to which a witness could be subject, particularly whether the excommunication was of a fixed duration or was permanent, and whether it could be lifted if the wrongful witness paid damages to his victim. The debate about this latter element was partially based on the model of the penalty of the *Moser*, albeit that the "damages" model was present as well in certain other legal situations. The result was that in numerous responsa in which determinations needed to be made as to the duration and the monetary implications of excommunication for wrongful testimony discussions of the law of *mesirah* were present.[3] Such discussion was not intended to suggest that the act of testimony against a fellow Jew in a non-Jewish court, even when wrongful, could be considered violation of the crime of *mesirah*. That possibility had long been rejected.[4] The issue was, could excommunication for the crime of *Mesirah* be used as a model for excommunication for the unrelated crime of wrongful testimony?

However, the very hovering of the term *Mesirah* within the discussion of the legislation of Rava was, I believe, a vital factor which contributed to the eventual misapplication of the law of *Mesirah* to the law of wrongful harm through testimony against a fellow Jew in a non-Jewish court. But there was yet a second, even more impactful factor which shaped the associational blurring between these two wrongs.

7.2 THE DUAL MEANING OF LEGAL TERMS

It is not unusual for a Hebrew word to have multiple shadings of meaning in different contexts. In particular there are many words which bear a general meaning and then a related but distinctive technical, legal meaning. For example the word *rasha*, which appears first in the *Torah* in Abraham's plea to God for the rescue of Sodom, in Abraham's challenge of "will you indeed sweep away the *tzadik* with the *rasha*?!"[5] The King

[2] See above, 3.2.5.

[3] As we have seen in the responsa of Maharam Mintz, above in 5.1, and in those of Rabbi Moshe Isserlis treated above in 5.3.

[4] See above, 3.2.5.

[5] Gen. 18:23.

James translation renders this verse as "Wilt thou also destroy the righteous with the wicked?" That understanding is preserved in the Jewish Publication Society of America 1917 translation,[6] and this general moral approach to the meaning of the terms *Tzadik* and *Rasha* is echoed in the The New English Bible of 1961, "wilt thou really sweep away good and bad together?"[7] By contrast, the earliest Jewish translations, into Aramaic render the phrase as "will you sweep away the innocent with the guilty?"[8] This more juridical approach to the conversation between Abraham and God suggests that Abraham takes cognizance of the fact that God has already tried and convicted the residents of Sodom and that all that remains to be done is to execute the appropriate punishment. His plea is, therefore, for the mitigation of punishment on the basis of the presence of a minimum number of innocent persons. This approach is adopted by the later New Jewish Publication Society translation of the *Torah*,[9] as well as by E. A. Speiser in the Anchor Bible,[10] and by Robert Alter in his translation of Genesis.[11]

The general moral usage of the term *Rasha* is clear in other instances. For example, in regard to Moses' chastisement of the Jewish man who raised his hand against his fellow, the *Torah* reports, "he said to the wicked one (*la'rasha*), 'why would you strike your fellow?'"[12] Similarly, in Moses' warning of the Jewish people against the hubris of thinking that their own righteousness was the reason for their conquest of the Land of Israel, he informs them that in reality, "It is not because of your virtues and your rectitude that you will be able to possess their country; but it is because of the wickedness of these nations (*be'rish'at ha'goyim ha'eleh*)."[13]

[6] Preserved unchanged in *The Pentateuch and Haftorahs*, with commentary by Dr. J.H. Hertz, one-volume edition, London, Soncino Press, 1937, 2nd edition, 1960.

[7] The New English Bible, with the Apocrypha, Oxford University Press and Cambridge University Press, 1970, published under the auspices of The Church of England and various other Protestant Denominational groups.

[8] *Targum Onkeles*, and *Targum* Yonatan ben Uzziel at Gen. 18:23.

[9] *Torah*, Philadelphia, J.P.S., 1962.

[10] E.A. Speiser, *Genesis, The Anchor Bible*, New York, Doubleday, 1964. Speiser, in his notes to Genesis 18:24, at p. 124, makes explicit his rejection of the alternative translation of "righteous ... wicked" in preference for the legal emphasis, in conformity with the usage in Exodus 22:8.

[11] Robert Alter, *Genesis, Translation and Commentary*, New York and London, W.W. Norton & Co., 1996, at Genesis 18:23. In his commentary to that verse, at p. 81, Alter takes specific note of the disparity between the legal usage and the general moral usage of both of the terms *Tzadik* and *Rasha*.

[12] Exodus 2:13.

[13] Deut. 9:4–5.

In these instances, it is clear that the term *rasha* is being used in a general sense of an evildoer, a wicked person, rather than in the technical sense of a person already convicted of a crime.

On the other hand, instances of the specific use of the term *rasha* in its technical, juridical sense of a person who was actually convicted of a crime is found in other passages in the *Torah*. For example, Numbers 35:31 forbids the acceptance of ransom (blood money) for a convicted murderer, "You may not accept ransom for the life of a murderer who was convicted of a capital crime (*asher hu rasha la'mut*), he must be put to death." Similarly in Exodus 22:8, the charge of embezzlement is to be litigated in court, and "he whom the court shall convict (*asher yarshi'un*) shall pay double to his neighbor."

The awareness of this dual usage of the term *rasha* yielded a Talmudic debate as to the correct meaning of the term in regard to one particular ground for the disqualification of witnesses. The *Torah* legislated that a *rasha* is ineligible to be a witness. Such is the central understanding of the verse in Exodus 23:1, "you shall not join hands with the wicked (*rasha*) to be an unrighteous witness."[14] But what is it that constitutes the person as a *rasha*, as an evildoer? The *Talmud* reports an Amoraic debate on this matter.[15] Rabbi Joseph maintains that a person's confession to the commission of a crime is sufficient to make him ineligible as a witness – he is, after all, an evildoer. By contrast, Rava maintains that "a person cannot constitute himself a '*rasha*'," meaning that he is only ineligible from the point in time at which he is convicted by a court of having committed a crime. The core of their debate appears to be whether the term *rasha* in this verse should be understood in the general, moral sense of an evildoer, for which purpose his own confession should be sufficient, or whether the term *rasha* is being used in this verse in its technical, juridical sense, as someone who has been convicted of a crime. This same uncertainty about the use of the term *rasha* in this verse may also be the grounds of the debate between Rava and Abbaye as to whether the disqualification of the evildoer is retroactive to the time of his commission of the crime (Abbaye), or whether it is initiated only at the point of his conviction of the crime (Rava).[16]

[14] *Bava Kamma* 72b-73a. Rambam, *Mishneh Torah*, Laws of Testimony 9:1 and 10:1–4.

[15] *Sanhedrin* 9b. See Aaron Kirschenbaum, *Self-Incrimination in Jewish Law*, New York, The Burning Book Press, 1970, pp. 50–58; and in an expanded treatment by Kirschenbaum, *The Criminal Confession in Jewish Law* (Heb.), Jerusalem, Magnes Press, 2005, pp. 143–157.

[16] *Bava Kamma* 72b-73a.

A parallel but more complicated instance of such dual meaning arises in regard to situations in which the Biblical usage of the term is singular and is of significant legal effect, but a later usage of the same term emerges for ethical or ideological purposes, and then the later meaning begins to impinge on the legal usage of the term. This is what I believe occurred in regard to the name *Amalek*. In the *Torah* itself, the name *Amalek* designates a particular nation and its population. There is not a single instance in Biblical literature in which the word *Amalek* has any possible figurative meaning. Nevertheless, by Talmudic times there is a clear development of the usage of the name *Amalek* in a figurative sense as representing persons whose intent to destroy the Jewish people is similar to that of the original *Amalek*. Thus both the Babylonian *Gemara*[17] and the *Gemara* of the Land of Israel[18] identify Haman of the Book of Esther as a descendent of Agag King of *Amalek* whom King Saul spared in violation of the command given to him by the prophet Samuel.[19]

However, this new, specifically ethical meaning of the word *Amalek* does not appear to have had any impact on the legal understanding of the two commandments related to *Amalek*, the duty to remember the evil deeds of *Amalek* and the duty to destroy *Amalek*,[20] until modern times. Thus, while medieval scholars spoke of the identification of Rome and Christianity with *Amalek*,[21] none had ever suggested that there was an actual Mitzvah to remember the evils which Rome and Christianity had perpetrated against the Jewish people. Nor had anyone ever actually suggested that the Biblical command to destroy *Amalek* in a mandated war was actually applicable to either Rome or Christianity. The occasional medieval use of Haman as a metaphor for Jesus, and Haman's hanging as an allusion to the crucifixion, was never asserted to be, as a matter of law, the fulfillment of the Biblical duty to remember the evil of *Amalek*.[22]

As far as all legal purposes were concerned, the definition of *Amalek* was clear and unequivocal: it related to the ancient nation-state known

[17] *Megillah* 13a. See also *Masechet Soferim* 13:6.

[18] J.T. *Yevamot* 2:6.

[19] I Samuel 15:1–25.

[20] Maimonides, *Sefer HaMitzvot*, Positive 189 – remembering the evil deeds of *Amalek*; and Positive 188 – destroying *Amalek* after settling the Land of Israel.

[21] Josef Stern, "Maimonides on *Amalek*, Self-Corrective Mechanisms, and the War against Idolatry," in David Hartman and Jonathan W. Malino (eds.), *Judaism and Modernity: The Religious Philosophy of David Hartman*, Farnham, Ashgate Publishing Ltd., 2004, pp. 360–362.

[22] Elliot S. Horowitz, *Reckless Rites: Purim and the Legacy of Jewish Violence*, Princeton University Press, 2006, pp. 81–106.

as *Amalek*, its citizens and their descendants. That nation-state was presumed to have disappeared with the Assyrian conquest of Israel in the sixth century B.C.E. in consequence of the very same political policy of exiling native groups through which the ten northern tribes of Israel disappeared, that is, lost their distinctive identity as part of the Israelite nation over the course of the resultant separation from their homeland and its autonomous character.[23] To the extent that the laws related to *Amalek* might pertain also to the biological offspring of *Amalek*, even in the absence of a nation-state, the idea that Sancheriv's policies resulted in the confusion of all forms of national identity meant that the descendants of *Amalek* would remain forever unidentifiable.[24]

But meanwhile, the figurative use of the term *Amalek* for non-legal purposes, to shape ethical character, to teach social responsibilities, and to help maintain ideological and philosophical purity kept growing in Jewish ethical texts and teachings. "Some rabbis allegorize *Amalek*, taking it as a euphemism for the evil inclination; others have it symbolize the enemies of Israel throughout history, yet others make it the personification of evil."[25] Anyone who has studied in *yeshivot* is quite familiar with the use of the term *Amalek* as a description of the singular evil against which the ethical teacher is attempting to arouse the passions of his students, whether it be a particular personality quality such as laziness, or a religious perspective which is barely inches outside the definition of Orthodoxy propounded by the teacher, or is some organization, Zionist or anti-Zionist, to which the teacher is ideologically or halachically opposed.

The unequivocal difference between the legal usage of the word *Amalek* and its use as a general metaphoric term was deeply and suddenly disrupted by Rabbi Chaim Soloveitchik of Brisk early in the twentieth century. According to Rabbi Joseph B. Soloveitchik, his grandfather

[23] Rambam himself takes direct note of this in his treatment of the law requiring destruction of the seven Canaanite nations, in *Sefer HaMitzvot*, Positive 187, where he argues that despite the impossibility of ever again fulfilling this commandment, after the dispersion caused by the Assyrians, nevertheless, the commandment is considered to be eternal. In *Mishneh Torah*, Laws of Kings 5:4 Rambam simply declares about those nations, "their memory is already erased."

[24] So that despite the fact that Rambam in *Sefer HaMitzvot* Positive 188 refers to the duty to destroy *zera Amalek*, the descendants of *Amalek*, Rabbi David ben Zimra was able nevertheless to encompass *Amalek* together with the seven Canaanite nations in the rule of "*Sancheriv* came and confused all the nations." RaDbZ to Rambam Laws of Kings 5:4.

[25] Stern, "Maimonides on Amalek." Quoted also in http://en.wikipedia.org/wiki/Amalek.

Reb Chaim noted a slight discrepancy in the *Mishneh Torah* in Rambam's presentation of the two sequential laws requiring first a war for the destruction of the seven Canaanite nations followed by the requirement of war for the destruction of *Amalek*. In the former, Rambam concludes the paragraph by asserting that, "their memory is already erased,"[26] as he had stated as well in his *Sefer HaMitzvot*.[27] However, in the second, which required a war against *Amalek*, Rambam omits any reference to the disappearance of that nation or people.[28] To explain that disparity, Reb Chaim Brisker enunciated a radical new legal proposition, that while the law concerning the seven Canaanite nations referred literally to those specific ancient nation-states, the law concerning the destruction of *Amalek* had a broader applicability encompassing any nation that, like *Amalek*, was engaged in an attempt to destroy the entire Jewish people. That is, Reb Chaim asserted that one particular form of figurative meaning of the word *Amalek* was to be assigned full legal force – so that under his reading of Rambam, a war against any nation attempting to destroy the Jewish people would have to be classified by Jewish jurists as a mandatory war (*Milchemet Mitzvah*), through which the commandment of war against *Amalek* would be fulfilled.

Little did Reb Chaim know that his own grandson, Rabbi Joseph B. Soloveitchik, would be called upon to make a practical decision of Jewish law in which the grandfather's novel interpretation would be of the essence.[29] As the United States entered the European theater of the Second World War, the Jewish Welfare Board (JWB), which provided for the needs of Jews serving in the US military, asked Rabbi Soloveitchik to write a response to the following question, which was essential for the guidance they needed to provide to Jewish servicemen. What Jewish law principles and rules should govern the conduct of Jewish servicemen in the US armed forces during the war against Germany?[30] Rabbi

[26] *Mishneh Torah*, Laws of Kings 5:4.

[27] *Sefer HaMitzvot*, Positive 187.

[28] *Mishneh Torah*, Law of Kings 5:5.

[29] The following account is based on a series of conversations I had with Rabbi Dr. Emanuel Rackman in the early 1970s while he served as Provost of Yeshiva University and I, a former student of his, served as Chairman of the Department of Jewish Studies at Stern College.

[30] The language of the question and the content of Rabbi Soloveitchik's response are presented here purely on the basis of my aforementioned conversations with Rabbi Emanuel Rackman. The text of the responsum that Rabbi Soloveitchik then wrote was read by Rabbi Rackman, who was then serving as a Chaplain in the US military, but is not available for scrutiny as per the agreement between Rabbi Soloveitchik and the Jewish Welfare Board. The text was to be placed in the archives of the JWB.

Soloveitchik wrote a responsum in which he explicated the distinction in Jewish law between a discretionary war (*milchemet reshut*), and a mandatory war (*milchemet mitzvah*). In a discretionary war, Jewish soldiers are obligated to maintain, as much as possible, adherence to Jewish ritual laws, such as laws of *Shabbat* and *Kashrut*, to the extent that it is only appropriate to initiate a battle in the early days of the week, in the hope that the observance of the following *Shabbat* will be able to be maintained.[31] By contrast, in a mandatory war, the *Mitzvah*, the religious legal duty of succeeding in the war, supersedes all Jewish legal ritual requirements that could interfere with the achievement of victory in the war. In which category then would the war against Germany fall? Rabbi Soloveitchik argued that given the fact that Germany was engaged in a systematic attempt to exterminate the entire Jewish people, that according to His grandfather's understanding of the position of Rambam, there is no doubt that the war against Germany was to be classified as a war against *Amalek*, and therefore unequivocally a *Milchemet Mitzvah*, a mandatory war.

Rabbi Soloveitchik clearly recognized the radical character of this legal conclusion and particularly feared the loose application of this metaphoric use of the term *Amalek* to religiously justify intense violence against any enemy toward whom passionate hatred could be aroused by the claim that particular individuals or national or ethnic or religious groups were "a contemporary *Amalek*." In particular Rabbi Soloveitchik was concerned about such hatred being aroused generally against all Arabs, or all Moslems due to the antagonism and periodic wars between Israel and Palestinians as well as some other Arab nations.[32] In response to that concern, Rabbi Soloveitchik taught and published a clarification of the position of Reb Chaim, indicating that only a nation could be considered *Amalek*, not individual citizens, and that even in regard to a nation, it could be considered *Amalek* only during the course of an actual

[31] *Shabbat* 19a; JT *Shabbat* 1:9 (Vilna ed. 23a); and Rambam, *Mishneh Torah, Hilchot Shabbat* 2:25, and *Hilchot Melachim* 6:11. See *Kesef Mishneh* and *Lechem Mishneh* to both texts in Rambam for divergent resolutions of the apparent contradiction. According to both, in the final event the restriction on intiating battle beginning on Wednesdays applies only in cases of discretionary wars.

[32] In fact an article by Rabbi Yehudah Gershuni in 1971, "Milchemet Mitzvah U'Milchemet Reshut," *Ohr HaMizrach*, Tevet 5731, pp. 104–105, appeared to argue that according to the approach of Reb Chaim, the entire Arab population, including every individual Arab living anywhere in the world, was to be considered *Amalek*, and that taking any of their lives would not constitute a criminal act of homicide according to Jewish law, but would be fulfillment of the *Mitzvah* to destroy *Amalek*.

war, to prevent the success of the attempt to exterminate the Jewish people, but that with the end of the war the status of *Amalek* attached to that nation would come to an immediate end.[33] This approach reduces the sharp edges of Reb Chaim's teaching by essentially equating this form of the war against *Amalek* with a straightforward war of self-defense.

What is apparent in this analysis of the evolution of the meaning of the term *Amalek* is that a term that has a clear and unequivocal Biblical meaning can eventually develop a figurative layer of meaning at variance from the juridical meaning, for use in ethical, social and political teaching not intended as law. However, a point in time may arrive when the power of the figurative meaning becomes so strong, or so potentially important in the life of the community, that an attempt may be made to assign juridical force to the figurative meaning of the term. The dynamic of such a development could then become identical to the situation in which from the outset the *Torah* itself had used the term with two different meanings, as in the case of the term *rasha*, with intense debate resulting as to which understanding of the term is "correct" in the context of the particular law under discussion.[34]

7.3 THE DUAL MEANING OF THE TERM *MESIRAH*

Early in Rabbinic literature, the terms *Moser* and *Mesirah* began to transcend their original legal usage, and began to be used in a more generic manner as an indication of breach of moral responsibility for the protection of a fellow Jew. An early classic and extreme instance of this underlying expansion of the usage, despite the absence of the critical term itself, is found in a Talmudic *Aggadah* to the Book of Joshua, chapter 7. When God informs Joshua that the reason for the loss of the war at the city of

[33] See Joseph B. Soloveitchik, *Kol Dodi Dofek, Fate and Destiny*, New York, KTAV, 1992, at pp. 92–95, footnote 25. In this note, Rabbi Soloveitchik ascribed the essential distinction to his father, Rabbi Moshe Soloveitchik. See also discussion of this matter by Rabbi Gil Student and others in the blog, www.torahmusings.com/2012/02/contemporary-amalek.

[34] While far beyond the purview of this study, it is worth exploring a parallel process that appears to have occurred in regard to the law prohibiting the drinking of wine made or handled by a *Goy*, the law of *stam yeynam*. In its origin the term *Goy* clearly had reference to a non-Jew. However, there existed a Rabbinic philosophical assertion that a Jew who violates the *Shabbat* has engaged in such total denial of God as creator, and of the covenant between God and the Jewish people, as to be considered equal to a non-Jew (a *Goy*). Eventually the question was bound to be raised as to which form of *Goy* was the one whose manufacture or handling of otherwise kosher wine would make the wine impermissible as "*stam yeynam*" – general non-Jewish wine. See Zevin, *Encyclopedia Talmudit*, vol. XXIV, columns 395–399.

Ai was that someone had stolen from the "devoted property" of the city of Jericho, the *Aggadah* asserts that Joshua asked God to reveal the identity of that person so that he could be punished and the property could be destroyed. God, in response to that request, says the *Talmud*, refuses to directly identify the person who stole from the *Cherem* at Jericho, lest He (God) be viewed as a *delator*, an informer.[35] This was despite the fact that Joshua was the duly constituted leader of the Jewish people, and his actions would certainly be just – in fact would be precisely what God had ordered him to do. Why then does the *Midrash* invent this conversation between Joshua and God? Purely as a matter of textual exegesis, the reason for the amplification responds to the problem of why God insists that Joshua use a lottery to determine who the criminal is, when God could simply have directly told Joshua the name of the criminal. This *Midrash* is clearly presuming that its audience will best understand the Divine reluctance in terms of the problem of being an informer – the sheer horror of turning a Jew over to the authorities for punishment, even to duly constituted and just authorities, was a betrayal of loyalty that even God Himself was reluctant to do.

The earliest explicit use of the term *Mesirah* in this manner, as a standard not required by the law itself, but one which was aspirational as a higher level manifestation of loyalty to a fellow Jew, appears in a passage in the Jerusalem *Talmud* that we have already cited.[36] In that case, Rabbi Joshua ben Levi had handed over to the Romans a Jew who had taken refuge with him, in order to rescue the city of Lod from threatened destruction. The prophet Elijah then ceased manifesting himself to the Rabbi, who then fasted and prayed. When Elijah reappeared, he explained his absence by saying, "am I to reveal myself to one who hands others over (*le'Mesorot*)?!" Rabbi Joshua defended his conduct by correctly asserting that he had in fact acted in accordance with the law, by handing over an individual specifically named by the oppressor in order to save an entire community from destruction. To that Elijah responded, saying, "Is this then the Law for the Righteous (*Mishnat Chassidim*)?!!"[37] This greater, but not legally required standard of loyalty is reflected as well in other sources we have seen above,[38] such as the critical comment

[35] *Sanhedrin* 43a. For the use of the term *Delator* as an equivalent of *Moser*, as a threat to life, see JT *Peah* 4b (Vilna edition)(Venice edition Y. *Peah* I: mid 16a.), making reference to Psalms 57:5.

[36] JT *Terumot* 8:10, at 47a; discussed above at 3.2.2.2.

[37] *Ibid.*

[38] See above, 3.2.3.2.

of Rabbi Joshua ben Korcha to Rabbi Eleazar the son of Rabbi Shimon (bar Yochai) who served within the Jewish community as a police officer for the Roman authorities.[39] Similarly, again in identical words, this time in the mouth of the prophet Elijah, was the criticism of Rabbi Ishmael ben Yossi, who also served as an officer of the Roman government to arrest Jewish criminals.[40] The Talmudic passage eventually upholds the legal standard as against the supererogatory, more protective standard proposed in the name of Elijah.[41]

This tension between the legally required standard of protective loyalty owed to fellow Jews under the law of *Mesirah*, which would only constrain handing them over to oppressors for unjust treatment, and the supererogatory standard proposed in the name of Elijah, which would extend protective loyalty even to Jewish criminals and those who represented a sustained threat to the peace and security of the Jewish community itself, was always resolved in the legal literature in favor of the more limited legally required standard.[42] The fundamental awareness that excessive loyalty to evildoers could destroy the ethical fabric of the community was recognized early in Rabbinic literature, as in the teachings, "The punishing of the wicked is an act of mercy to the world,"[43] and "Whoever pities where he should be cruel will ultimately be cruel where he should pity."[44]

Nevertheless, later rabbinic ethical literature sustained this non-legal, supererogatory usage of the terms *Moser* and *Mesirah* in a manner quite distinct from its legal use. As a legal term, *Moser* continued to describe the distinctive criminal disloyalty of handing over an innocent Jew to a non-Jewish or Jewish oppressive authority or criminal who would subject him to unjust treatment involving confiscation of his property and possible taking of his life. But as a general ethical term, the word *Moser* was used to describe any undesirable manifestation of disloyalty to a fellow Jew involving "snitching" to any authorities.

Eventually, this popular usage of the terms *Moser* and *Mesirah* began to infringe upon their technical, legal meanings. Thus, in the twentieth century, as Rabbis in relatively democratic lands began to explore the

39 JT *Bava Metzia* 83b.

40 *Ibid.* 83b–84a.

41 See above at end of 3.2.3.2, the analysis of Rambam, *Mishneh Torah*, *Hilchot Yesodei HaTorah*, 8:9–11.

42 Rambam, *ibid. Shulchan Aruch, Choshen Mishpat,* 28:5. See above 5.2.

43 *Midrash Tannaim*, Deut. 13:18.

44 *Kohellet Rabbati*, 7:33.

applicability of the laws of *Mesirah* to their particular contexts, some tended to shift over from the technical legal usage of the term to the popular ethical use of the term – resulting in a blurring of the elements of the crime needed according to earlier Jewish law, and a vast expansion of the potential application of the term.

Rabbi Michael Broyde presents a careful analysis of the variety of positions taken by contemporary decisors of Jewish law on the question of applicability of the laws of *Mesirah* in democratic societies.[45] The article divides finely between five current positions, but in doing so, I fear, it obfuscates the dominance of a single approach which is in complete consonance with the traditional understanding that the law of *Mesirah* exists only in a situation of handing over a fellow Jew to an *Anas* – to a violent oppressor.[46] A careful reading of Broyde's article and review of the related sources indicates clearly that such is the position of the following contemporary, that is twentieth-century, authorities: Rabbis Eliezer Waldenberg.[47] Shlomo Zalman Auerbach,[48] Yoseph Shalom Elyashiv,[49] Yitzchak Shmelkes,[50] Yaakov Yeshaya Blau,[51] Shmuel Wozner,[52] Yoseph Eliyahu Henkin,[53] Joseph B. Soloveitchik,[54] Yoel Teitelbaum,[55] and Moshe Feinstein.[56]

Broyde is quite correct in distinguishing between diverse underlying theories which justify the position, particularly the difference between simply the absence of unjust threat to life (i.e. absence of *Anas*), as opposed to the presence of an affirmative duty resting upon Jews in democratic societies to comply with the law of the land under the principle of *Dina de Malchuta Dina*. Nevertheless, one would be hard put to identify almost any other single really significant substantive matter of Jewish

45 Michael Broyde, "Informing on Others for Violating American Law: A Jewish Law View," posted at www.jlaw.com/Articles/mesiralaw2.html, no date. Also published with some modifications as "Informing on Others to A Just Government," *Journal of Halacha and Contemporary Society*, 41, 2002, pp. 5–46.

46 *Ibid.* at III.A. and his notes 43 and 44 re. position of the *Aruch haShulchan*.

47 *Ibid.* at his note 45.

48 *Ibid.* at his notes 15 and 48.

49 *Ibid.* at his note 48.

50 (1828–1905) *Ibid.* at III.C. and his note 58. Albeit he would consider the possibility of tort liability for damages resulting from even indirect injury.

51 *Ibid.* at his note 59.

52 *Ibid.* at III.D. and his notes 63 and 64.

53 *Ibid.* at his notes 78 and 81

54 *Ibid.* at his notes 79 and 81.

55 *Ibid.* at his notes 80 and 81.

56 *Ibid.* at his notes 77 and 81. I will deal with Feinstein's distinctive position in greater detail below.

law on which all of those authorities agree in practice, even when they disagree about the rationale of their positions. Broyde is clearly stretching in order to discover a position which dissents from this consensus, and he turns to two emotionally evocative, but poorly reasoned positions, both of which shift the meaning of the term *Moser* from its historical juridical meaning to the ethical meaning assigned to it on those occasions in *Talmud* in which a higher, aspirational standard is evoked in the name of the prophet Elijah.

Such a development is, for example, evident in the treatment of the contemporary application of the Laws of *Mesirah* published by Rabbi Ezra Batzri in 1981.[57] In a footnote, Rabbi Batzri makes the following assertion:

> Do not be astonished by the rules in this chapter, and think that they are inapplicable nowadays since governments are enlightened and Democracy is their guiding principle. This could be thought true only by the very naïve; since even in democracies, in truth when there is a matter of concern to the government, it is treated as exceptional to the normal protocol, as happens when matters relate to security of the state. **All rules of informing are applicable even currently.** Anyone who knows and understands and sees beyond what is externally visible, will understand that only the external appearance has changed – but the essential characteristics [of government] have not changed. **Even if they bring all matters to court, it is clear that, through interrogation and the police, government can destroy people and in many places they do, in fact, destroy people.**[58]

Rabbi Broyde summarizes Rabbi Batzri's position as follows:

> Rabbi Batzri posits that even when the external justice system seems to work, nonetheless the executive and judicial systems is [*sic*] so deeply fraught with exceptions, and extra-judicial misconduct, and coerced confessions, that one must assume injustice will occur and thus informing on a fellow Jew remains generally prohibited, as always.[59]

What is strikingly absent from this brief treatment by Rabbi Batzri is any recognition of the relative meaning of the term *Anas* ("oppressor"),

[57] Rabbi Ezra Batzri, *Dinei Mammonot*, Jerusalem, Haktav Institute, 1981, vol. IV, ch. 2, para. 5, footnote 1, at pp. 86–87. Rabbi Ezra Batzri, born 1937, is Head of the Rabbinical Court of Jerusalem.

[58] The translation is, with slight modifications, that of Rabbi Michael Broyde in "Informing on Others for Violating American Law" at www.jlaw.com/Articles/mesiralaw2.html, pp. 8–9.

[59] *Ibid.* Strikingly, Rabbi Broyde notes his own ambivalence about this assertion of Rabbi Batzri, at *ibid.*, footnote 52: "This writer posits, but acknowledges that he cannot prove without a doubt, that this basic argument is factually incorrect in America." However, he later takes sharp issue with the general conclusion of Rabbi Batzri.

which is already treated in prior Rabbinic literature, in the *Talmud* itself, and certainly since the time of the Gaonim. Does Rabbi Batzri not have to take account of the position of Rabbi Eleazar son of Rabbi Shimon, who saw room for arresting Jewish criminals in cooperation with the Roman government of the late second century in Israel; a position which the *Gemara* upholds, even against the protest of Rabbi Joshua ben Karcha?[60] Does Rabbi Batzri truly consider the courts of modern democratic states to be more corrupt and violent that the Persian *Dawar* courts, which the Gaonim in the tenth century of the Common Era considered to be appropriate settings in which Jews could initiate legal actions against fellow Jews in the absence of available enforcement procedures through Jewish courts?[61] Did Rabbi Batzri not feel that he had somehow to contend with the position of Rabbi Yechiel Michel Epstein, author of the *Aruch haShulchan* in the late nineteenth century, who argued for the inapplicability of the laws of *Mesirah* in relation to just governments, such as in Britain, or for that matter even in Czarist Russia?[62] Indeed, Rabbi Batzri offers nothing more than a passionate argument for the evil of governments, devoid of any Jewish legal argumentation whatsoever.

A similarly extreme abandonment of the juridical use of the term *Mesirah* is found in a responsum of Rabbi Mordechai Yaakov Breisch. He attempts a brief justification of his position that the full laws of *Mesirah* continue to be applicable in modern democratic states, but then leaps to the holocaust as evidence of the eternal applicability of the Talmudic teaching that "once a Jew has fallen into the hands of idolators, they have no mercy upon him" and, adds Breisch, "there is nothing more to be said about this."[63]

The positions of Rabbis Batzri and Breisch are essentially outliers in the contemporary treatment of this question, and in reality represent a radical, though possibly unconscious shift in the use of the terms *Moser*

60 *Bava Metzia* 83b–84a.

61 See above, 2.3, and text of responsum of Hai Gaon and Sherirah Gaon.

62 Rabbi Broyde, *ibid.* at footnote 44, presents an excellent case for the proposition that if the hand of the Russian censor was present in this text of *Aruch haShulchan*, it was only as to the addition of the government of the Czar, not as to the essential proposition that the rules of *Mesirah* were not applicable to just governments. See the recent contribution to this discussion by Marc Shapiro, "Self-Censorship in the *Arukh ha-Shulhan*, ArtScroll's Latest Betrayal, and Other Assorted Comments," December 10, 2014, at http://seforim.blogspot.com/2014/12/self-censorship-in-arukh-ha-shulhan.html.

63 Rabbi Mordechai Yaakov Breisch, *Chelkat Yaakov*, Jerusalem, 1950–1965, vol. III, no. 96, at p. 208. And see Rabbi Broyde, "Informing on Others," note 91, for his enlightening comment on the non-juridical nature of Rabbi Breisch's argument.

and *Mesirah* from their juridical use, which has remained the dominant usage, to a supererogatory usage which has roots in Talmudic *Aggadah*, and has emotionally persuasive energy, but no legal force.[64] To better understand this shift in usage, we need to examine the position of Rabbi Moshe Feinstein, which shares some characteristics with the position of Rabbis Batzri and Breisch, while preserving a greater degree of integrity with the use of the term *Mesirah* in the history of Jewish law.

7.4 *MESIRAH* IN THE RESPONSA OF RABBI MOSHE FEINSTEIN

To appreciate the distinctive position of Rabbi Moshe Feinstein in regard to the application of the law of *Mesirah* to democratic governments, it is helpful to pay attention to an undated responsum published as number 29 in the seventh volume of his collected responsa, *Iggerot Moshe*. The text is as follows:[65]

That it is forbidden to *Torah* Institutions to take from the government more than is allowed by its established regulations.

This is in regard to the kindness of our government, of the United States of America, to which our Blessed God brought us, in His great mercy on the saved remnant of all the countries of Europe, and on the remnant of the great scholars of *Torah* and their students, where we established the old *Torah* Centers of Europe, and also new ones. And since this Government of Kindness (*malchut shel Chessed*), the whole purpose of which is to benefit all the residents of the nation, has initiated various programs to aid students of all schools in the country, to enable them to learn and to grow in their studies, so that *Torah* institutions also receive great aid for their students; certainly all Rabbinic Heads of *Yeshivot* and the Administrators, and the students recognize all of the goodness of the nation, and extend blessings of peace to the nation, and fullness of blessings to all who lead it.

However, certainly we are admonished by our Blessed God who commanded us in His Holy *Torah* to avoid taking more than the governmental regulations established to be given; even when it is possible to receive more through certain officials who desire to be of benefit not in accordance with the established regulations. And most certainly it is forbidden to lie about the number of students, and other matters of that sort; for beyond the fact that this would constitute violation of the crime of theft, there are other great prohibitions therein – of speaking lies

[64] Despite periodic deliberations on the possibility of assigning such force to the position of Rabbi Joshua ben Korcha, as noted in Broyde, "Informing on Others," at note 94. For my treatment of the position of Rambam in regard to this issue, see above, 3.2.3.2.

[65] Rabbi Moshe Feinstein, *Iggerot Moshe*, vol. VII, New York, 1985, *Choshen Mishpat*, part 2, no. 29, at p. 244.

and fabrications, and deception, and also the desecration of the Divine name and the disgrace of the *Torah* and those who study it. In the entire world there is no authority for permitting such actions. Just as the Holy One Blessed Be He hates theft in the world, likewise the Holy One Blessed Be He hates the support of the *Torah* and of those who study it through theft. Such actions also cause the "pursuit" (*rodef*) of the Great *Torah* scholars and their students, who are exceptionally punctilious to avoid even the slightest suspicion of theft or other wrongdoing.

The Rabbinic Heads of *Yeshivot* and the Administrators who fear Heaven, are not, God forbid, under suspicion of violating the prohibitions against theft, or of speaking lies and fabrications, or of deception, nor of (violation of) the Law of the Land, through any possible authorization of the permissibility of such actions, for they know the severity of these prohibitions and of the consequent severe Heavenly punishments in this world and in the next. Such actions are contrary to the entire purpose of the establishment of the *Yeshivot*, and of the teaching of the students therein to be truly in fear of God, and to be especially punctilious in financial matters.

Nevertheless, we find it appropriate to arouse awareness of this matter, so that special attention may be paid to it also in regard to donors who offer their contributions for the support of *Torah*, that they should not cause theft or financial loss to the nation in violation of the laws of the *Torah* as well as the laws of the government; that they not be entrapped even unintentionally in these great sins.

To all who are especially careful in these matters, may Blessings of Good be visited upon them. And may they be successful in their *Torah* institutions to increase students who fear Heaven, which is also a great blessing for the Nation, for it is known and the public is aware that students of the *Yeshivot* are exceptional, thank God, from amongst all the citizens, in their good character and their good deeds.

Three elements of the position of Rabbi Feinstein in the above text are worth noting. Firstly, his identification of the United States government as *Malchut shel Chessed*, a Government of Kindness, which is specifically the converse of the essential condition for deeming an act of informing as prohibited – that the entity to which the victim is informed upon be an *Anas*, a violent and lawless criminal or government. Secondly, Rabbi Feinstein deems the law of the land to be fully applicable to Jews.[66] Thirdly, he recognizes that the violation of both Jewish and national law forbidding theft, lies and deception would also constitute violation of the distinctively Jewish law crimes of *Chillul Hashem*, desecration of the Divine name, and *Bizayon HaTorah*, the disgrace of the *Torah* and of those who study it.

In the light of these teachings it would be astonishing if Rabbi Feinstein were to take any position but that of Rabbis Epstein and Waldenberg in

[66] Rabbi Feinstein takes the identical position in the immediately following responsum, Iggerot Moshe at no. 30; and also at no. 62, at p. 284.

denying the applicability of the law of *Mesirah* in a democratic nation. Yet in three separate responsa, Rabbi Feinstein appears to be in full agreement with Rabbi Breisch, and is viewed by Rabbi Broyde as having at least implied "that the prohibition against informing remains identical in a just society."[67] I believe that a careful reading particularly of the two responsa published in Rabbi Feinstein's lifetime suggest a very different, sensitively nuanced position which is not in accord with that of Rabbi Breisch, nor that of Rabbi Batzri.

The first responsum of Rabbi Feinstein on this matter was written in 1961.[68] The question involved an employee of a Kosher meat factory who forged the *kashrut* seal of his employer and attached them to non-kosher meat which he sold as kosher, thus not only causing Jews to eat non-kosher food, but also committing criminal fraud and causing financial injury to his employer. The question submitted to Rabbi Feinstein is somewhat unclear, but apparently asks whether the injured party could initiate a lawsuit against the employee in a civil court, or was required to litigate the matter in a Rabbinic Beit Din. Rabbi Feinstein asserts that it is not permissible to "hand over a fellow Jew to a non-Jewish court" (*LeMosero leArkaot*), even if the outcome would be identical to that which would be arrived at in Jewish law, consonant with *Shulchan Aruch, Choshen Mishpat* 26:1.[69] He further asserts that the civil court would hold the thief financially liable in a manner beyond the standards of Jewish law, and that such litigation would also result in criminal prosecution that would result in imprisonment, which is certainly not consonant with Jewish law:

> and then one must be fearful of the prohibition against informing (*yesh lachush leissur masur*), for it is forbidden to hand over a Jew to gentiles both bodily, and as to his property, even if he was an evil-doer and a sinner as is found in *Shulchan Aruch, Choshen Mishpat* 388:9. However, when it is clear that the Jewish judges cannot stop him, then it is permissible, after he is warned, to bring him before a non-Jewish court (*Arkaot*). This matter is even more severe than just a monetary matter, where if it is not possible to rescue (one's property) in a Jewish court, it is permissible, with the authority of a Beit Din, to go to a non-Jewish court and to litigate the matter in accordance with their laws, as is found in *Choshen Mishpat* 26:2. A fortiori here, where the purpose is to prevent him from causing persons to

[67] Rabbi Michael Broyde, "Informing on Others," at p. 18.

[68] Rabbi Moshe Feinstein, *Iggerot Moshe*, vol. IV, *Choshen Mishpat*, part 1, New York, 1963, no. 8, at p. 22.

[69] Based on *Gemara Gittin* 88a, where the teaching of Rabbi Tarfon precludes litigation between Jews in non-Jewish courts. This teaching is completely unrelated to the law of *Mesirah*.

violate prohibitions (of *Kashrut*), in addition to the second element of preventing fraud, which is a monetary claim.[70]

While Rabbi Feinstein twice uses the word *Moser* in this responsum, clearly the substantive law he is treating is that of litigation in a gentile court based on *Shulchan Aruch*, *Choshen Mishpat*, chapter 26. He does not actually assert that submission of the matter to the non-Jewish court would constitute *Mesirah*, but rather it would constitute violation of the prohibition against the submission of litigation between two Jews to a gentile court. That is why the standard for permissibility upon which he ultimately relies is whether justice can be achieved through a Jewish court – if not, then the matter can be submitted to the gentile court despite the penalties which would be imposed upon the defendant. What then is the role of his introduction of the need to "be fearful of the prohibition against *Mesirah*" (*yesh lachush leissur masur*)?

As we have seen in the responsum concerning defrauding the government, Rabbi Feinstein clearly does not view the governments of the United States as *Anasim*, as violent and criminal, and therefore does not consider it possible to apply the rigors of the law of *Mesirah* to them. However, in the situation before him there was no civil legal duty resting upon the Jewish injured party to report the fraud to any agency of government – the injuries were monetary and spiritual. Therefore, for Rabbi Feinstein, if those matters could be handled internally, within the Jewish community, by recourse to Rabbinic courts, then the situation should be viewed as no different from any matter of civil litigation between Jews which, as a matter of Jewish law need to be litigated before a Rabbinic court and not brought before gentile courts. But as is the case with matters of use of gentile courts, as opposed to matters involving *Mesirah* to an *Anas*, if either the monetary matter or the spiritual matter could not be dealt with adequately in the Jewish court, then, as in *Shulchan Aruch, Choshen Mishpat* 26:2, the matter could be submitted to the gentile court, despite the difference in outcome, and the harsher result for the Jewish defendant.[71]

Thus Rabbi Feinstein's references to *Mesirah* were in fact not indicative of his actual application of the laws of *Mesirah* to American governments, but represented rather the use of the term in its non-juridical sense, as a call to greater loyalty to fellow Jews in situations where that would be possible without loss to the Jewish injured parties, and without

[70] Feinstein, *Iggerot Moshe*, vol. IV, at p. 22.

[71] In this reading I respectfully differ with Rabbi Michael Broyde, "Informing on Others," at p. 18.

violation of the law of the land. Indeed this is apparently why Rabbi Feinstein does not explicitly refer to the "informer" as a *Moser*, but instead uses the circumlocution of, "then one must be fearful of the prohibition against *Mesirah*" (*yesh lachush leissur masur*).

It is precisely this same approach that I believe is manifest in the second of these responsa, the tax auditor case, written by Rabbi Feinstein in 1962.[72] This short responsum begins as follows:

> In the matter of one who wants to be an auditor for the government such that on occasion one will encounter the tax returns of one who has cheated, and he will detect the fraud, [and will thus report it to his superiors] and will be like one who informs the government, (*k'mesaro lehamemshalah*) and they will punish this person more than he is liable according to Jewish law. It seems logical to me (*hanachon l'aniyat da'ati*) that since anyone who examines tax returns will encounter the fraud, and even if this person declines the job, others will take the job and discover the fraud, one sees from this that the one who commits the fraud suffers no loss whether this person takes the job or not and another is there, and thus the one who cheats loses nothing whether or not this person takes the job and without a loss there is no prohibition.[73]

Here too, as in the previous responsum, Rabbi Feinstein avoids actually referring to the auditor as a *Moser*, even in his initially making the case for why his accepting such employment would be Halachically problematic. He rather uses a circumlocution, that he "will be like one who informs the government," (*k'mesaro lehamemshalah*). While he is making an analogy to the law of *mesirah*, it is clear through this entire responsum that he is not actually applying the law of *Mesirah*. Thus, after expressing the concern that the auditor might be considered to be "like a *Moser*" (*k'moser*), he offers a logical argument for why the auditor should not be considered such, because if he were not in that job, someone else would be doing that work and fraud would be found out and punished. Therefore, logic dictates that the auditor would not be causing the tax evader any loss that he would not be suffering even if this particular auditor was not doing that work. While Rabbi Feinstein then suggests an analogy to this within the law of *Mesirah*, in reality this is a perfectly novel proposal and one that is quite strange. Is it really a perfectly reasonable argument to make in regard to a criminal act of theft or assault that if the admitted perpetrator had not done it, someone else would have and therefore the perpetrator should not be found guilty? On the other hand, as we have

[72] Feinstein, *Iggerot Moshe*, vol. IV, *Choshen Mishpat*, part I, no. 92, at p. 158.

[73] Trans. by Rabbi Michael Broyde, "Informing on Others," at p. 19. Transliterations in parentheses are added by me.

seen, the absence of loss to a supposed victim is grounds for full exoneration of someone who testified truthfully against a fellow Jew in an honest non-Jewish court in favor of a non-Jew.[74]

Rabbi Feinstein continues to argue that the occasions of discovery of fraud are rare, and that once the auditor is employed in that capacity he is actually under a legal duty under the law of the land to report any discovery of fraud, and so is to be viewed as if he were being coerced to inform. Beyond which, Rabbi Feinstein concludes:

> Even absent the element of coercion, he would be duty bound to testify for he is like one who had been designated by the government to serve as a witness when he is subpoenaed, as is established in (*Shulchan Aruch, Choshen Mishpat*) chapter 28, par. 3, for the reason that there would be *Chillul Hashem*, desecration of the Divine Name, if he were not to testify.[75]

Here Rabbi Feinstein unequivocally and explicitly turns away from the use of the law of *Mesirah* toward the binding character of the law of the land, and the recognition of the duty to testify against a fellow Jew in a situation in which refusal to do so would constitute a desecration of the Divine name.

From all of the foregoing it appears clear that Rabbi Moshe Feinstein understood that the Talmudic laws of *Mesirah* that had remained applicable through medieval times and even into modern times under oppressive governments was distinctively not applicable within democratic societies such as the United States. However, he was deeply aware of the existence of another layer of the term *Mesirah*, a supererogatory layer, which demanded not legal compliance but moral attentiveness to the well-being of fellow Jews even when they were guilty of crimes or other wrongdoing. That second layer embodied a distinctive loyalty to fellow Jews in situations in which there was no overriding demand by government and no competing consideration within Jewish law itself that would require the protective urge to be set aside. For that reason Rabbi Feinstein was able to repeatedly speak in his responsa of *Mesirah l'arkaot*, "informing to the courts," rather than what would have been appropriate in a true juridical *Mesirah* case, namely *Mesirah le'Anas*, "informing to an oppressor."

In yet another responsum of Rabbi Feinstein appearing in volume 8 of *Iggerot Moshe*, which was published posthumously,[76] this same

[74] As both Rashi and Tosafot note immediately in commenting on the legislation of Rava in *Bava Kamma* 113b–114a. See above, 2.2.2.

[75] Feinstein, *Iggerot Moshe*, vol. IV, *Choshen Mishpat*, part I, no. 92, at p. 158.

[76] Feinstein, *Iggerot Moshe*, vol. VIII, 1996, *Orach Chaim* 9:11, at pp. 16–17. This volume was fully edited and somewhat amplified by Rabbi Feinstein's grandson, Rabbi

fundamental approach is further utilized. The question involved a person who had stolen *Torah* scrolls and silver *Torah* accoutrements from a synagogue, and whether he could be reported to the civil authorities. Here, as earlier, Rabbi Feinstein formulates the issue in Jewish law as whether the accused can be "handed over to the governmental courts and to the police," *lemosro le'arko'aot hamedinah ve'laMishtarah*. There is no reference in the responsum to those authorities as *Anasim*, as "violent oppressors." His stated concern in handing over the accused is that the civil authorities could impose forms of punishment such as imprisonment, which is not provided for in Jewish law, while a Jew should not cause a fellow Jew to be subjected to any penalty but one that could result from adjudication under Jewish law. This special manifestation of loyalty to a fellow Jew, he goes on to say, could be overridden by a threat to the community, or even to a single individual who might need to avoid being implicated in the evildoing of the accused. While drawing on sources related to juridical *Mesirah*, Rabbi Feinstein is clearly dealing with a situation in which there exists no legal duty to inform the civil authorities of the theft, and his understanding of the supererogatory layer of *Mesirah* would expect that the matter should be taken care of within the Jewish community. But again, as would be the case in the matter of testimony in the gentile courts, if justice could only be achieved or injury avoided by submission of the accused to the non-Jewish authorities of the democratic government, it would be unequivocally permissible to do so.

Unequivocally, Rabbi Feinstein belongs to that long list of contemporary Jewish jurists mentioned above who would not apply the juridical form of the law of *Mesirah* to the legal system of democratic societies such as the United States. Nevertheless, he does attempt to promote the non-juridical form of *Mesirah* as a virtue that should be adhered to as much as possible. In this sense, Rabbi Feinstein consciously shapes the term *Mesirah* into a multi-vocal term, much as a similar development had taken place in relation to the term *Amalek* in Rabbinic literature,

Mordechai Tendler, and grandson-in-law, Rabbi Shabbtai Rapaport, as the editors themselves indicate in their introduction to the volume. While the responsum was dated as having been written in 1980, one never knows, of course, what changes or subtle variations Rabbi Feinstein might have made if the material had been carefully reviewed by him prior to publication. For this reason, there is always some hesitancy in the ascription of distinctive positions to Rabbi Feinstein based on responsa in this volume. However, in this instance, it appears to me to be clear that the position in the published text in volume 8 is substantially the same as the position which he had taken in the prior published material which we have seen above.

and as in Biblical usage the term *Rasha* was a multi-vocal term that bore both the legal meaning of "a convicted criminal" and the general ethical meaning of "an evildoer." In this new supererogatory form of the concept of *Mesirah*, the operative model used by Rabbi Feinstein was in fact the literature concerning testimony against fellow Jews, in favor of a non-Jew, in a non-Jewish court. In that context, as we have extensively seen in the course of this book, there are many circumstances in which such testimony is permissible, and a group of situations in which there exists a Jewish law duty to testify.

These two factors, the mere hovering of the term *Mesirah* within the discussion of the legislation of Rava, and the availability of the non-juridical usage of the term in place of its technical, legal meaning, lent false credence and apparent legitimacy to the attempt to assign unjustified legal force to the claim of *Mesirah* when such usage served only the ideological and economic interests of the Orthodox community, or even more narrowly served to prevent individual members of the Jewish community from being held accountable for their illegal conduct.

8

Conclusion: Reflections on Loyalty and Law

The term "loyalty" has a long and varied history, and a multitude of shades of meaning.[1] The sense in which I use the term, and what I consider to be its core meaning, is that loyalty is an emotion which entails an enduring urge or desire to protect from harm and to enhance the well-being of persons, either individually or collectively. The use of the word loyalty to describe a relationship to ideals, truths, virtues or institutions is an extension of the same core meaning in that it represents the feeling or belief that those particular truths, virtues, values or organizations are those which are ultimately most protective and most enhancing of, that is, most beneficial to, the individuals or collectives toward whom one has feelings of loyalty.

If loyalty is an inner feeling, an emotion, what business is it of the law? Most legal systems do not presume to regulate emotions themselves, but do take cognizance of emotions as motives for behavior, while only the behavior itself remains what the law actually regulates in the interest of the protection and well-being of society as a whole. By contrast, Biblical law has a somewhat broader agenda within which it does undertake the direct regulation of both beliefs and emotions as well as of speech and actions.[2] It does so firstly for their own sake, in assuring that people believe in that which is true, and in attempting to shape personality qualities that are noble and self-enhancing.[3] But additionally Biblical law

[1] For a short bibliography of approaches to the term loyalty, see http://en.wikipedia.org/wiki/Loyalty. For a book-length treatment of the significance of the term for legal thought, see George P. Fletcher, *Loyalty, An Essay on the Morality of Relationships*, New York, Oxford University Press, 1993.

[2] Maimonides in Rambam, *Sefer HaMitzvot*, Principle (*Shoresh*) no. 9.

[3] Rambam, Maimonides, Guide to the Perplexed, Book III, chs. 27 and 31. See the outstanding treatment of these issues in Josef Stern, *Problems and Parables of Law:*

regulates beliefs and emotions as inner states, precisely because they are essential motivating factors in both conduct and speech, which are the two dimensions of outer behavior which the law must regulate in order to achieve its social purposes. After all, law is the primary social instrument through which emotionally driven speech and behavior are regulated – either prohibited, or mandated or left discretionary – in order to maximize the beneficial effects on the protection and enhancement of the well-being of all the members of that society.

Thus, the emotion or inner virtue of loyalty is embodied and evoked in Jewish law in the variety of ways in which the law regulates the affirmative and negative duties of individuals and in the ways in which the law limits its own mandates. So, for example, the exceptional nature of the virtue of loyalty to family members is manifest in the fact that of the thirty-six capital crimes in the *Torah*, the majority relate to breaches of family loyalty as in adultery, incest or offenses between parents and children.[4] In similar manner, the determination of Jewish law that family members of a particular degree, whether by birth or marriage, are not eligible to testify concerning each other,[5] is not premised on the actual emotional relationship between those persons that could result in false testimony, but on the law's desire to support family solidarity and loyalty.[6]

But Rabbinic law has a powerful interpretive preference to construe Biblical legislative language describing the governance of emotions as constituting rather the governance of behavior or speech that manifests the existence of that inner emotion. Thus the Biblical command, "Honor your father and mother"[7] is deemed by the *Talmud* to be fulfilled through the performance of acts of service to parents, such as feeding or dressing them, rather than just through experiencing the inner feeling of respect.[8] Similarly, the Biblical command of "Each person should fear mother and father"[9] is not viewed in Talmudic law as requiring the emotion of fear, or even of awe, but as requiring persons to refrain from directly contradicting that which parents have said, and to refrain from sitting in the chair which the parent customarily occupies.[10] Under ideal

Maimonides and Nachmanides on Reasons for the Commandments, Albany, NY, SUNY Press, 1998, ch. 1, pp. 1–13, and ch. 6, pp. 109–160.

4 *Mishnah Sanhedrin* 7:4 and 9:1.

5 Rambam, *Mishneh Torah*, Book of Judges, Laws of Testimony 13:1.

6 Cf. *ibid.* at 13:15.

7 Exodus 20:12.

8 *Kiddushin* 31b. Rambam, *Shoftim, Hilchot Mamrim* 6:3.

9 Lev. 19:3.

10 *Kiddushin* 31b. Rambam, *Shoftim, Hilchot Mamrim* 6:3.

circumstances, loyalty within the family is to be achieved both in conduct and in the achievement of the underlying emotions of respect and awe; but the law places emphasis upon the speech and conduct, without excluding the emotional governance, while recognizing the insufficiency of the inner virtue if it is contradicted, or even just not expressed, in speech and action. Loyalty as an emotion therefore translates in Jewish law into principles and rules which either require or forbid particular behavior or speech.

In the Biblical governance of interpersonal relations there appear to be five domains of responsibility toward others which are the legal product of the desirability of loyalty. The domains so governed are: the interest in life itself; the protection of health; the safeguarding of property; the sensitivity toward emotional well-being; and the sustaining of spiritual integrity. They each begin with an essentially universally applicable principle that a person ought not to cause harm to that particular well-being interest of others. While many laws of the *Torah* fit into each of these domains, a single illustration of each will suffice to show the power with which Biblical legislation manifests these concerns. In the same order as the interest domains above, we could note: the prohibition against homicide;[11] the criminalization of assault;[12] the prohibition against theft;[13] the prohibition against the verbal oppression of the immigrant, orphan and widow;[14] and the prohibition against enticing another person to sin.[15] The very universality of the application of these constraints indicates that they are rooted in a loyalty of the greatest breadth – the loyalty to fellow humans because of the shared quality of having been created in the Divine image.

Each of these domains, however, share a further layer of responsibility derived from a narrower loyalty, one which is applicable to a less extensive set of persons than the duties in the first layer. They are the duties of rescue applicable to each of those interests, which pertain either solely in the relationship with fellow Jews, or to almost all persons, but to the exclusion of some limited set of persons. They would be illustrated by the following duties of intervention, in which the *Torah* criminalizes the sense of indifference which would lead to failure to act, again in the same order of the five interests: the duty to rescue a person whose life is

[11] Exodus 20:13. Rambam, *Sefer HaMitzvot*, Negative no. 289.
[12] Deut. 25:3. Rambam, *Sefer HaMitzvot*, Negative no. 300.
[13] Lev. 19:11 and 13. Rambam, *Sefer HaMitzvot*, Negative nos. 244 and 245.
[14] Exodus 22:20–23. Rambam, *Sefer Ha Mitzvot* Negative no. 252.
[15] Lev. 19:14. Rambam, *Sefer HaMitzvot* Negative no. 298.

endangered;[16] the duty to build a parapet around a flat roof;[17] the duty to restore lost property to its owner;[18] the duty of government to grant military exemption to a newly married person in a discretionary war;[19] and the duty of chastisement to deter sinful conduct.[20] The criminalization of inaction, which is at the root of all of these duties, is a step that many legal systems, such as that of the United States, are reluctant to take.[21] Yet, for the *Torah*, this second step is an essential element of loyalty owed at least to all fellow Jews, and sometimes to most humans, with active idolators[22] being the usual class of persons toward whom one might be freed from these exceptional duties of rescue.[23]

Much as loyalty within the family is viewed in Jewish law as a virtue to be honored, similarly loyalty to fellow Jews is seen as a valued emotion which underlies many distinctive legal duties legislated within the *Torah* itself and which is further intensified in Rabbinic law and teachings. It is therefore not surprising that the essential legislation of Rava, threatening excommunication for testimony against a fellow Jew in a non-Jewish court, was justified by Rashi on the grounds that such testimony could cause injury to the Jewish party that he would not suffer were the matter to be adjudicated according to Jewish law.[24] This was Rashi's approach precisely because he could not identify an actual criminal offense committed by the witness, nor any ground in Jewish law to hold him liable under principles of damages. What Rashi is in effect telling us is that restricting such testimony had not been justifiable by prior

[16] Lev. 19:16. Rambam *Sefer HaMitzvot*, Positive no. 247.

[17] Deut. 22:8. Rambam *Sefer HaMitzvot*, Positive no. 84.

[18] Exodus 23:4. Rambam *Sefer HaMitzvot*, Positive no. 204.

[19] Deut. 24:5. Rambam *Sefer HaMitzvot*, Positive no. 214, Negative no. 311.

[20] Lev. 19:17. Rambam *Sefer HaMitzvot*, Positive no. 205.

[21] Steven H. Resnicoff, "Jewish Law and the Tragedy of Sexual Abuse of Children:The Dilemma within the Orthodox Jewish Community" *Rutgers Journal of Law and Religion*, 13(2) 2012, pp. 1–90, at pp.1–3. Available at SSRN: http://ssrn.com/abstract=2072116.

[22] The question of whether idolators should be defined by their theology, or by their corrupt conduct, is an extensive debate in the history of Jewish law and thought, and is beyond the parameters of this work. Careful attention needs to be paid in this regard to the work of Jacob Katz, *Exclusiveness and Tolerance*, Oxford University Press, 1961, and the recent work of Moshe Halbertal, *Between Torah and Wisdom: Menachem ha-Meiri and the Maimonodean Halakhists in Provence*, Magnes Press, 2000, and "'One Possessed of Religion': Religious Tolerance in the Teaching of the *Me'iri*," *Edah Journal*, 1, 2000, pp. 1–23; and Adiel Schremer, Brothers Estranged.

[23] There is yet a third layer of responsibilities pertaining to each of these domains, which demands attentiveness to the enhancement of the particular interest. However, I leave that for elaboration in another context.

[24] See above, 2.2.2.

Jewish law, and that the legislation of Rava was introduced to expand the legal restrictions reflective of the underlying virtue of personal loyalty to a fellow Jew, in the protection of his material well-being. As an attempt to expand the legal duty of loyalty, as we have amply demonstrated above, it was then read as narrowly as possible by subsequent *Amoraim* and Gaonim, as well as by the vast majority of *Rishonim* and *Acharonim*.

For this fundamental reason, as previously noted,[25] until the mid-twentieth century, dominant Halakhic sources, both responsa and novellae, continued to uphold the essential positions of the *Rishonim* that testimony by a Jew, against a fellow Jew, in favor of a non-Jew, in a non-Jewish court would be permissible in some situations and even mandatory in others. Such testimony would be **permissible** in the following situations: when offered

1. by a pair of Jewish witnesses even in a corrupt non-Jewish court
2. by a single witness in an honest non-Jewish court,
3. by a single witness in a court that does not reach judgment based on the testimony of a single witness,
4. by even a single witness who is under threat of economic or bodily penalty for refusal to testify.

In addition, Halakhic sources upheld the positions of *Rishonim* in insisting that Jewish law itself would **require** testimony of a Jewish witness if the failure to testify would:

1. result in *Chillul Hashem*,
2. enable a fellow Jew to perpetrate a crime (i.e. undermine justice),
3. violate the law of the land,
4. require the witness to suffer financial loss or physical threat, or to take a (false) oath as to his lack of information, or
5. threaten the security or the economic well-being of the Jewish community.

Rabbinic Sages had thus on one hand upheld the desirability of acting with due loyalty to fellow Jews in the complex situation in which non-Jewish law would be governing the relationship with others; while simultaneously acknowledging that this novel extension of loyalty would not stand when it came into conflict with a variety of other confirmed Jewish values.

[25] See above at the conclusions of chs. 5 and 6.

The emergence of large Jewish communities in democratic lands has added another layer of significance to this delicate balancing of loyalties. Since in the dominant contemporary position, Jewish law would not recognize the application of its earlier law of *Mesirah* to the interface between Jews and democratic governments and their fundamentally just judicial organs, the subtle legal approach of Rabbi Moshe Feinstein essentially transposed the same balancing of loyalties manifested in Jewish legal treatment of the question of testimony into the treatment also of the issue of informing or handing over (*Mesirah*.) Thus, he preserved the supererogatory virtue of loyalty to fellow Jews through the reluctance to inform or hand them over, while simultaneously recognizing the overriding character of the other virtues such as avoidance of *Chillul Hashem*, achievement of justice, adherence to the law of the land, avoiding injury or falsehood, and protection of the security and economic well-being of the Jewish community.

On the one hand, the sustained loyalty and passionate defense of fellow Jews which is manifest in the reluctance to subject them to the legal process even of just non-Jewish governments and courts could be seen as quite admirable, and worthy of respect. After all, even the most fair legal system is still subject to aberrational decisions by both judges and juries which could result in injustice.[26] And everyone knows that the prison system of even the most moral society can create risks of abuse and profound unpleasantness which are not part of the "just punishment" ordered by the courts.[27] Indeed such deficiencies, such disparities between ideal justice and the justice which is actually available in human courts are deeply evident even within contemporary Rabbinic judiciaries in Israel[28] and in the United States.[29] One need only review the literature of Jewish law over the past half-century in both Israel and the United States in regard to the *Agunah* problem to recognize that even Jewish law and well-intentioned Rabbinic Courts, lacking full civil enforcement authority,

[26] Thane Rosenbaum, *The Myth of Moral Justice: Why our legal system fails to do what's right*, New York, Harper Collins, 2004.

[27] As this is written, the *New York Times* reports that the Justice Department has joined "a class action suit against new York City's Correction Department" for what the Justice department has described as a "deep seated culture of violence" in the jail system. *New York Times*, "An Enemy of Reform in New York Jails," January 2, 2015, p. A20. See also, Michael Broyde, "Informing on Others" at his note 57.

[28] Susan M. Weiss and Netti C. Gross-Horowitz, *Marriage and Divorce in the Jewish State: Israel's Civil War*, HBI Series on Jewish Women, Waltham, MA, Brandeis University Press, 2012, closing chapter, "Human Rights Violations in Israeli Rabbinic Courts."

[29] See e.g. Breitowitz, Between Civil and Religious Law, pp. 14–19.

cannot regularly assure that justice will be done and that chained spouses will be freed from their unjust imprisonment at the hands of an enraged and or evil abuser.[30] And if these refined instruments cannot constrain spouses who are otherwise good and normal people, is there really any expectation that such Rabbinic Courts, certainly lacking the capacity to impose criminal penalties or to enforce compensatory payment of fines, could bring justice in cases of child sexual abuse? Truly, Rambam himself, who clearly believed that the Jewish legal system and the organs of justice that the *Torah* created were the best that any human society could have, nevertheless recognized that injustice would of necessity be present even in this divinely ordained system due to the limitations of human implementation and the necessity for rules that regulated society by generality. Only God's personal issuance of every judicial decision could assure perfect justice in every case.[31]

In every generation in which a Jewish community co-existed in one or another form of partnership with non-Jewish society, Jewish Sages recognized that when the Jewish community and Jewish courts could not produce Jewish justice, some joint collaborative effort with non-Jewish government was both necessary and justifiable. Thus, the *Mishnah* understood that when Jewish courts lacked enforcement powers, they needed to welcome the enforcement procedures of non-Jewish courts to assure that the orders of the Jewish court were complied with.[32] And later in the Talmudic period, Rabbi Eleazar ben Shimon served as an officer of the Roman government to enforce criminal law, despite the objection of purists.[33] The *Tannaim* understood that non-Jewish justice was better than no justice, and that some social order was better than no social order. And likewise, the Gaonim Hai and Sherira recognized that when Jewish courts could not enforce their judgments against members of the Jewish community, then not just the Jewish litigant, but even the scholars and the leaders of the community must join in the process of gaining a fair outcome by directly appearing before basically honest non-Jewish courts, despite knowing that the outcome would not be precisely the same as that which would have been arrived at according to Jewish law.[34] The Gaonim

[30] *Ibid.* at pp. 1–4 and 277–279. Also, Shlomo Riskin, *Women and Jewish Divorce*, Hoboken, NJ, KTAV Publishing, 1989, at pp. 134–142; and Basil Herring and Kenneth Auman, *The Prenuptial Agreement: Halakhic and Pastoral Considerations*, Northvale, NJ, Jason Aronson Inc., 1996.

[31] Rambam, Maimonides, Guide to the Perplexed, Book II, ch. 40 and Book III, ch.34.

[32] *Mishnah Gittin* 9:8.

[33] *Bava Metzia* 83b.

[34] Lewin, *Otzar HaGeonim* to *Bava Kamma*, sec. 291, at p. 100. See above, 2.3.

understood that doing no justice because you cannot achieve ideal justice destroys the fabric of honesty of the Jewish community. When Rabbi Asher ben Yehiel arrived in Spain and discovered that Jewish courts were using capital punishment and bodily mutilation, his initial outrage was assuaged as the local scholars explained to him that the price of some Jewish autonomy in criminal matters was the periodic use of extremely harsh punishments that kept the non-Jewish culture persuaded that the Jews were serious about controlling criminality.[35] Rabbenu Asher understood and agreed that the Jewish community was not self-sufficient and that the opinions of the broader society needed to be respectfully taken into account as a mutual social order was maintained.

In every period there was also the voice of the purist, whether Rabbi Joshua[36] or the Prophet Elijah,[37] which voice continued to resonate through the centuries as the voice of the patriot, the true believer, reminding us that striving for pure Jewish justice should allow no compromise, no collaboration with imperfection – perfect or nothing. But that voice was rejected as a matter of law, despite its preservation as an aspiration. So, when Rambam wants to preserve the consciousness of the aspirational element in not handing Jews over to oppressors, he still cannot read even Elijah as insisting on total resistance, he can only read him as demanding delay and exploration of alternatives before submitting to the imperfect reality.[38]

It is precisely this balance that Rabbi Feinstein attempts to preserve in his response on the applicability of the laws of *Mesirah* within democratic society. On the one hand, the aspirational urge is very powerful, to protect fellow Jews from being subjected to the criminal enforcement procedures of the general society, which are often more severe than those that would be applied within Jewish law itself. On the other hand, that aspiration is limited by the overarching values of the Jewish legal system itself, which have been recognized and refined in the context of dealing with testimony against fellow Jews in non-Jewish courts – the avoidance of *Chillul Hashem*, the achievement of justice, adherence to the law of the land, avoiding injury and falsehood, and protection of the security and economic well-being of the Jewish community.

A similar, albeit more societally engaged, response to this balance was manifested to me in a conversation with Rabbi Joseph B. Soloveitchik in

35 Farber, "Extra-Legal Punishments in Medieval Jewish Courts," at pp. 212–217.

36 *Bava Metzia* 83b.

37 JT *Terumot* 8:10, at 47a. See above, 3.2.2.2.

38 Rambam, *Mishneh Torah, Hilchot Yesodei HaTorah* 5:5. See above, 3.2.3.

1973. I asked Rabbi Soloveitchik whether the extensive level of sexual abuse found in American local and state prisons should result in a need to view any Jew imprisoned in such institutions as a captive, a *shavui*, toward whom we would then have an overriding duty of redemption, of *pidyon shvuyim*. The Rav's response was that if the Jewish person had been properly charged, tried, convicted and sentenced to imprisonment in an American court, then he was definitely not to be considered a captive in the hands of oppressors.[39] Of course, he added, the situation of sexual abuse in prisons is quite disgraceful, and needs to be addressed – but it has to be dealt with as a general societal issue, not as a vehicle for raising questions about special benefits or privileges for Jewish prisoners.

The aspirational voice calling for the protection of fellow Jews from indignities that they would not be subjected to under the ideal administration of Jewish law should never be dismissed out of hand. Such calls can sometimes meaningfully alert us to injustice and unfairness that call for remediation in the particular instance, or in the general conduct of social governance. However, it is essential to be cognizant of the way in which such claims to upholding prophetic standards could lead us to betray the history of Jewish legal interpretation and balancing of ethical interests. The legislation of Rava, in its magnification of the duty of loyalty to the material well-being of an individual Jew in his relationship to a non-Jewish government was not allowed in the subsequent unfolding of its application through the centuries to undermine the well-established prioritization of other values, in particular: the maintenance of justice; the avoidance of *Chillul Hashem*; the duty to the spiritual well-being of fellow Jews by not being enablers of their criminal conduct; the duty of obedience to the law of the land; the protection of one's own economic and physical well-being; the avoidance of falsehood; and the protection of the reputation and economic security of the Jewish community. We need to sustain that balance of loyalties.

[39] Michael Broyde, "Informing on Others," ch. 7 at footnote 16 cites a position taken by Rabbi Shlomo Zalman Auerbach, which was identical to this first part of the position of Rabbi Soloveitchik.

References

Books and Articles

Albeck, Chanoch, *Mavo LaTalmudim*, Tel Aviv, Dvir Co., 1969, pp. 504–522.
"Lekheker HaTalmud," *Tarbiz*, 9, 1938, pp. 163–178.

Alon, G., *Jews, Judaism and the Classical World*, trans. by Israel Abrahams, Jerusalem, Magnes Press, 1977, ch. 5, "On The Halakhot of the Early Sages," pp. 138–145.
Mehkarim Betoldot Yisrael, (Heb.), HaKibutz Hameuchad Pub. House, 1958, vol. II, pp. 121–147, and particularly at pp. 144–145.

Alter, Robert, *Genesis, Translation and Commentary*, New York and London, W.W. Norton & Co., 1996.

Amir, Abraham Shaul, *Institutions and Titles in Talmudic Literature* (Heb.), Jerusalem, Mossad Harav Kook, 1977, pp. 18–37

Amital, Yehuda, "Rebuking a Fellow Jew: Theory and Practice," in Jacob J. Schacter (ed.), *Jewish Tradition and the Non-Traditional Jew*, Northvale, NJ, Jason Aronson Inc., 1992, pp. 119–138.

Batzri, Ezra, *Dinei Mammonot*, Jerusalem, Haktav Institute, 1981, vol. IV, ch. 2, para. 5, footnote 1, at pp. 86–87.

Berman, Saul J., "Adam Hashub: New Light on the History of Babylonian Amoraic Academies," *Dine Israel*, 13–14, 1988, pp. 123–154, 174, 183.
"Parashat Shekalim and the Role of the Jewish Preisthood," in R. Daniel Z. Feldman and Stuart W. Halpern (eds.), *From Within the Tent: The Haftarot*, New York, Scharf Publication Trust of Yeshiva University Press, 2011, pp. 597–607.

Blidstein, Gerald, "Rabbinic Legislation on Idolatry," unpublished Doctoral Thesis, Bernard Revel Graduate School, Yeshiva University, 1968, particularly at pp. 122–130.

Breisch, Mordechai Yaakov, *Chelkat Yaakov*, vol. III, no. 96, Jerusalem, 1950–1965, p. 208.

Breitowitz, Irving A., *Between Civil and Religious Law: The Plight of the Agunah in American Society*, Westport, CT, Greenwood Press, 1993, at pp. 5–40.

Broyde, Michael, "Informing on Others for Violating American Law: A Jewish Law View," available at www.jlaw.com/Articles/mesiralaw2.html, no date. Also published with some modifications as "Informing on Others to a Just Government," *Journal of Halacha and Contemporary Society*, 41, 2002, pp. 5–46.

Buber, S., *Tanhuma Buber*, Vilna, 1885, reprinted 1946, New York, Sefer Press, at pp. 9–10; and *Shoftim*, sec. 1, p. 14a.

Cahn, Edmond N., *The Sense of Injustice*, New York University Press, 1949, pp. 11–27, at p. 24.

Chajes, Z.H., *The Student's Guide Through the Talmud*, trans. by Jacob Shachter, Feldheim Pub., 2nd edition, 1960, at pp. 97 and 111–117.

Chambers, Marcia, "Ex-Bergman Aide Declines To Talk." *New York Times*, April 30, 1975, p. 81.

Daube, David, *Collaboration with Tyranny in Jewish Law*, London, Oxford University Press, 1965, at pp. 18–39 and 69–83.

DeVries, Benjamin, "Halachic Categories" (Heb.), *Bar Ilan Annual*, II, 1965, pp. 77–83.

Mechkarim Besafrut HaTalmud, Jerusalem, 1968, at pp. 188–193 and 195–196.

Elman, Yaakov, *Authority and Tradition: Toseftan Baraitot in Talmudic Babylonia*, New York, Yeshiva University Press, 1994, pp. 275–281.

"Middle Persian Culture and Babylonian Sages: Accommodation and Resistance in the Shaping of Rabbinic Legal Tradition," in Charlotte Elisheva Fonrobert and Martin S. Jaffe (eds.), *Cambridge Companion to the Talmud and Rabbinic Literature*, Cambridge and New York, Cambridge University Press, 2007, pp. 165–197.

Elon, Menachem, *Jewish Law*, trans. by Bernard Auerbach and Melvin J. Sykes, Philadelphia, PA, JPS, 1994, vol. III, ch. 32, pp. 1138–1148.

Epstein, J.N., "Fragments of Debei R. Ishmael to Leviticus" (Heb.), in Samuel Krauss and Joseph Klausner (eds.), *Festschrift for Samuel Krauss*, Jerusalem, R. Mass, 1936, pp. 19–35, at p. 25.

"A Grammar of Babylonian Aramaic" (Heb.), Jerusalem, Magnes Press, 1960, at pp. 61, 63.

Farber, Zev, "Extra-Legal Punishments in Medieval Jewish Courts," in Yamin Levy (ed.), *Mishpetei Shalom, A jubilee Volume in Honor of Rabbi Saul (Shalom) Berman*, New York, Yeshivat Chovevei Torah Rabbinical School, with Ktav Publishing House, 2010, pp. 191–232, at pp. 216–217.

Fletcher, George P., *Loyalty, An Essay on the Morality of Relationships*, New York, Oxford University Press, 1993.

Fraenkel, J., *Rashi's Methodology in his Exegesis of the Babylonian Talmud* (Heb.), Jerusalem, 1975, at p. 195.

Friedman, Shamma, "Perek HaIsha Rabba," in H.Z. Dimitrovsky (ed.), *Mechkarim U'Mekorot*, New York, Jewish Theological Seminary of America, 1977, at pp. 283–304, 346 and 378.

Frimer, Dov, "Israel, the Noahide Laws and Maimonides: Jewish-Gentile Legal Relations in Maimonidean Thought," *Jewish Law Association Studies* 2, 1986, pp. 89–102.

Gershuni, Yehudah, "Milchemet Mitzvah U'Milchemet Reshut," *Ohr HaMizrach*, Tevet 5731, 1971, pp. 104–105.

Ginsburger, M. (ed.), *Pseudo Jonathan*, Berlin, 1903.

Ginzberg, Louis, *Genizah Studies in Memory of Dr. Solomon Schechter (Ginzei Schechter)*, vol. II, New York, J.T.S., 1929, pp. 127–128, item no. 137.

Goitein, S.D., *A Mediterranean Society, vol. II, The Community*, Berkeley, CA, University of California Press, 1971, at pp. 86 and 367–368, 395–402 and 607, n. 25.

Goodblatt, David M., *Rabbinic Instruction in Sasanian Babylonia*, Leiden, E.J. Brill, 1975.

Groner, Tsvi, *The Legal Methodology of Hai Gaon*, Chico, CA, Scholars Press, 1985, at pp. 118–119.

Gulak, A., *Le-Heker Toledot ha-Mishpat ha-Ivri bi-Tekufat ha-Talmud*, Jerusalem, Ha-Sifriyyah ha-Mishpatit, 1929, at p. 58.

Halbertal, Moshe, *Between Torah and Wisdom: Menachem ha-Meiri and the Maimonodean Halakhists in Provence*, Jerusalem, Magnes Press, 2000.

"One Possessed of Religion": Religious Tolerance in the Teaching of the Me'iri" *Edah Journal*, 1, 2000, pp. 1–23.

Heller, Marvin J., "Earliest Printings of the Talmud," in Sharon Lieberman (ed.), *Printing the Talmud: From Bomberg To Schottenstein*, Yeshiva University Museum, 2006, pp. 61–78, at p. 74.

Herring, Basil and Auman, Kenneth, *The Prenuptial Agreement: Halakhic and Pastoral Considerations*, Northvale, NJ, Jason Aronson Inc., 1996.

Hertz, J.H., *The Pentateuch and Haftorahs*, one-volume edition, London, Soncino Press, 1937, 2nd edition, 1960.

Hildesheimer, Esriel Erich, "Die Komposition der Sammlungen von Responsen der Gaonen," in Joseph Wohlgemuth (ed.), *Judisce Studien*, Frankfurt am Main, 1928, pp. 177–269.

Horowitz, Elliot S., *Reckless Rites: Purim and the Legacy of Jewish Violence*, Princeton University Press, 2006, pp. 81–106.

Hyman, A., *Toldot Tannaim VeAmoraim*, vol. III, London, Express Printers, 1910, at p. 847.

Jewish Encyclopedia, Managing Editor Isadore Singer, article entitled "Jacob ben Asher," at vol. 7, pp. 27–28, Funk and Wagnalls Co., New York and London, 1904.

Kasowski, Chaim Josua, *Thesaurus Talmudis*, New York, Jewish Theological Seminary of America, 1954, vol. I, pp. 121–125 and 207–208; vol. XV, pp. 228–251; vol. XXXI, pp. 57–60.

Katz, Jacob, *Exclusiveness and Tolerance*, Oxford University Press, 1961.

Kirschenbaum, Aaron, *The Criminal Confession in Jewish Law* (Heb.), Jerusalem, Magnes Press, 2005, pp. 143–157.

"The Good Samaritan and Jewish Law," *Dinè Israel*, 7, 1976, at pp. 10–12, particularly notes 15 and 16, and pp. 7–85, particularly pp. 28–59.

Self-Incrimination in Jewish Law, New York, The Burning Book Press, 1970, pp. 50–58.

Klein, Hyman, articles in *J.Q.R.* 38, 1947, pp. 67–91; 43, 1953, pp. 341–363; 50, 1959, pp. 124–146; in *Journal of Semitic Studies*, 3, 1958, pp. 363–372; and in *Tarbiz* 31, 1962, pp. 23–42.

Kochen, Madeline, *Organ Donation and the Divine Lien in Talmudic Law*, Cambridge University Press, 2014, pp. 195–201, at p. 196 n. 53 and p. 200.

Leibson, Gideon, "Determining Factors in Herem and Nidui During the *Tannaitic* and Amoraic Periods" (Heb.), in *Shenaton HaMishpat HaIvri*, Jerusalem, Institute for Research in Jewish Law, vol. 2, 1975, pp. 292–342.

Lewin, B.M., *Otzar Ha-Geonim* to *Bava Kamma*, Jerusalem, 1943, at 92b, at pp. 69 and 100.

Mantel, Hugo, *Studies in the History of the Sanhedrin*, Cambridge, MA, Harvard University Press, 1961, at p. 239.

Melammed, E.Z., "*An Introduction to Talmudic Literature*" (Heb.), Jerusalem, 1973, at pp. 435–436.

The New English Bible, with the Apocrypha, Oxford University Press and Cambridge University Press, 1970, published under the auspices of The Church of England and various other Protestant Denominational groups.

The New York Times Editorial Board, "An Enemy of Reform in New York Jails," *New York Times*, January 2, 2015, p. A20.

Onkeles, ed. by A. Berliner, Berlin, 1884.

Rabbinovicz, *Dikdukei Soferim* to *Berachot*, 1882, Introduction, pp. 101, 104–105.

Dikdukei Soferim to *Bava Kamma* 113b, at p. 281, n. 8; 114a, at p. 281, n. 20.

Rabinovitch, Nachum, *Commentary to Rambam's Mishneh Torah, Yad Peshutah*, Jerusalem, Maaliyot Press, 1990.

"Jews Are Responsible for One Another," in Jacob J. Schacter (ed.), *Jewish Tradition and the Non-Traditional Jew*, The Orthodox Forum series, Northvale, NJ, Jason Aronson, Inc., 1992, pp. 177–204, at pp. 179–180 and notes 6–7.

Rakover, Nahum, *Mesirut Nefesh* (*Sacrificing Life: Giving Up One to Save the Many*), (Heb.) Jerusalem, The Library of Jewish Law, 2000, at p. 25.

Rapaport, Abraham A., "The Informer in Jewish Literature (Until the End of the Geonic Period)," unpublished Doctoral Thesis, May 1952, Bernard Revel Graduate School of Yeshiva University, New York, at pp. 120–126.

Resnicoff, Steven H., "Jewish Law and the Tragedy of Sexual Abuse of Children: The Dilemma within the Orthodox Jewish Community," *Rutgers Journal of Law and Religion*, 13(2), 2012, pp. 1–90, at pp. 1–3.

Revel, Dov, "Adam Chashuv" (Heb.), *Ner Maaravi*, 1, 1924, pp. 7–21, at pp. 12–13.

Riskin, Shlomo, *Women and Jewish Divorce*, Hoboken, NJ, KTAV Publishing, 1989, at pp. 134–142.

Rosenbaum, Thane, *The Myth of Moral Justice: Why our Legal System Fails to Do What's Right*, New York, Harper Collins, 2004.

Rubenstein, Jeffrey L., "The Rise of the Babylonian Rabbinic Academy: A Reexamination of the Talmudic Evidence," *JSIJ* 1, 2002, pp. 55–68.

Schacht, Joseph, *An Introduction to Islamic Law*, Oxford, Clarendon Press, 1964, pp. 132 and 192–195.

Schremer, Adiel, *Brothers Estranged: Heresy, Christianity and Jewish Identity in Late Antiquity*, Oxford and New York, Oxford University Press, 2010, pp. 131–141.

Shapiro, Marc, Comments on Michael Broyde, "Informing on Others for Violating American Law: A Jewish Law View," in *Self-Censorship in the Arukh ha-Shulhan, ArtScroll's Latest Betrayal, and Other Assorted Comments,* available at www.jlaw.com/Articles/mesiralaw2.html.

Shilo, Shmuel, "Maimonides on Dina de Malchuta Dina (The Law of the State is Law)," *Jewish Law Annual*, I, 1982, pp. 146–167. See particularly pp. 150–154, and note 25 on p. 151.

at pp. 150 and 151. Based on Rambam, *Hilchot Zechiya Umattanah* 1:15.

at p. 148, based on Rambam, *Hilchot Gezelah* 5:18.

at 150, based on Rambam, *Hilchot Gezelah* 5:14.

Siev, Asher, (ed.), "Introduction," in *Responsa of Ramah*, Jerusalem, 1971, pp. 27–29.

Sifra de bei Rav, Jerusalem, 1959, p. 104a, to *Emor*, *Perek* 8, sec. 9.

Sklare, David E., *Samuel Ben Hofni Gaon and his Cultural World*, Leiden, E.J. Brill, 1996, at p. 74, n. 24.

Soloveitchik, Haym, *Collected Essays*, vol. I, Oxford, The Littman Library of Jewish Civilization, 2013, p. 20.

Soloveitchik, Joseph B., *Kol Dodi Dofek, Fate and Destiny*, New York, KTAV, 1992, at pp. 92–95, n. 25.

Speiser, E.A., *Genesis, The Anchor Bible*, translation and notes, New York, Doubleday, 1964. Notes to Genesis 18:24, at p. 124.

Spicehandler, Ezra, "*Bei Dawar* and *Dina D'Magista*: Notes on Gentile Courts in Talmudic Babylonia," *HUCA* 26, 1955, pp. 333–354.

Stern, Josef, "Maimonides on *Amalek*, Self-Corrective Mechanisms, and the War against Idolatry," in David Hartman and Jonathan W. Malino (eds.), *Judaism and Modernity: The Religious Philosophy of David Hartman*, Farnham, Ashgate Publishing Ltd., 2004, pp. 360–362.

Problems and Parables of Law: Maimonides and Nachmanides on Reasons for the Commandments, Albany, NY, SUNY Press, 1998, ch. 1, pp. 1–13, and ch. 6, pp. 109–160.

Tractate Soferim, M. Higger (ed.), Jerusalem, Makor Publishing, 1950, 10:1, at pp. 209–210, footnotes to lines 6–9.

Weiss, Avraham, *Mehkarim BeTalmud* (Heb.), Jerusalem, 1975, pp. 225–226, 231–237

Weiss, Susan M. and Gross-Horowitz, Netti C., *Marriage and Divorce in the Jewish State: Israel's Civil War*, HBI Series on Jewish Women, Waltham, MA, Brandeis University Press, 2012, Closing chapter, "Human Rights Violations in Israeli Rabbinic Courts."

Weisz, D. Max, *Seridim Min HaGenizah*, Budapest, 1924, p. 29.

Wohlman, M., Bet Mishpat Magista, in *Hamishpat*, vol. IV, 1930–1931, pp. 114–116.

Zevin, Shlomo Josef, Rabbi, *Encyclopedia Talmudit*,

vol. I, *Adam Chasuv*, pp. 175–180.

vol. II, s.v. *Ones*, p. 162.

vol. V, pp. 337–339.

vol. VI, *Gerama b'Nezikin*, columns 461–497, at 485–497.

vol. XVII, *Chillul Hashem*, columns 340–360.
vol. XXIV, columns 395–399.
Zunz, *Haderashot BeYisrael* (Heb.), H. Albeck (ed.), Jerusalem, Mossad Bialik, 1947, at p. 111.

Post Talmudic Jewish Legal Sources

Asher, Jacob ben (1270–1340), *Kitzur Piskei HaRosh* Constantinople, 1575, *to Sanhedrin*, ch. 3, law 4
Shavuot, ch. 4, law 15
Bava Kamma, ch. 10, law 14.
Tur, *Choshen Mishpat*, 22, 28.
Ashkenaze, Betzalel, *Shita Mekubetzet* to *Bava Kamma* 113b, s.v. *VehaRam za"l Misarkesta.*
Chananel ben Chusiel (990–1053), Commentary of Rabbenu Chananel to *Bava Kamma* 114a, in Lewin, *Otzar Ha-Geonim.*
Emden, Jacob ben Zvi (1697–1776), *She'elat Yaavetz*, Lemberg, 1884, reprinted Jerusalem, 1971, Part 2, No. 51, at pp. 19b-20b.
Epstein, Yechiel Michel (1829–1908), *Aruch Hashulchan*, *Choshen Mishpat* 28:8.
Falk, Joshua ben Alexander Hacohen (1555–1614), Drisha to Tur, *Choshen Mishpat*, ch. 28, at n. 13.
Sefer Meirat Einayim to *Shulchan Aruch*, *Choshen Mishpat*, 28:2 and 28: 3, at n. 21.
Feinstein, Moshe (1895–1986), *Iggerot Moshe*, vol. IV, *Choshen Mishpat* Part 1, New York, 1963, no. 8, p. 22, no 92, p. 158.
Iggerot Moshe, vol. VII, New York, 1985, *Choshen Mishpat* Part 2, No. 29–30, 62.
Iggerot Moshe, vol. VIII, 1996, *Orach Chaim* 9:11, at pp. 16–17.
Gaon, Hai (969–1038), in Lewin, *Otzar Ha-Geonim*, *Bava Kamma*, Responsa p. 100.
in *Sefer Hamekach Vehamemkar*, ch. 32, para. R, p. 67a.
Gaon, Yehudai (Gaon of Sura 757–761), *Sefer Halachot Pesukot*, Codex Sassoon 263, ed. S. Abramson, Jerusalem, 1971, at p. 82.
Grossnass, Aryeh, in Responsa Lev Aryeh, London, 1973, vol. II, no. 39.
Harkavy, A.E., *Zichron la-rishonim*, vol. I, Berlin, 1887, reprinted under new title, *Teshuvot HaGaonim – Harkavy*, Jerusalem, 1966, no. 213, p. 111.
Heller, Aryeh Leib Hacohen (1745–1812) in *K'Tzot Hachoshen* to S.A. Ch.M.
Hacohen, Alexander Suslin *Sefer HaAgudah*, to *Bava Kamma*, sec. 137 and quoting R. Eliezer MiTulla, at sec. 155, edition of Elazar Brissel, Jerusalem, 1970.
Karo, Joseph ben Ephraim (1488–1575), *Beit Yosef* to Tur, *Choshen Mishpat*, Laws of Judges, sec. 2.
Beit Yosef to Tur, *Choshen Mishpat*, ch. 28, s.v. *Bameh devarim amurim*, s.v. *V'eino chayav.*
Kesef Mishneh to Rambam, *Hilchot Talmud Torah* 6:14:6 s.v. *Mi Shelo Kibbel.*
Kesef Mishneh to Rambam, *Hilchot Talmud Torah* 6:14 at no. 20.

Kesef Mishneh to Rambam, *Hilchot Yesodei HaTorah* 5:5, at s.v. *Vechen im amru lahem.*

Shulchan Aruch, *Choshen Mishpat*, New York, Otzar Halacha Inc., 1960, ch. 28, paras. 3–4.

Shulchan Aruch, *Even HaEzer* 134:5.

Kayyara, Shimon (first half of the eighth century) (Behag-Baal Halachot Gedolot), *Sefer Halachot Gedolot*, Tel Aviv, 1962, sec. 43, at p. 177.

Kohut, Alexander (ed.) (1842–1894), *Aruch Completum of Nathan ben Yehiel of Rome (c. 1035–1106)*, vol. III, pp. 31–32, p. 386b, vol. V, pp. 78–79.

Kook, Abraham Isaac Hakohen (1865–1935), *Responsa Mishpetei Kohen*, Responsum no. 144, sec. 15–16, at pp. 336–340.

Lieberman, Saul, *Tosefet Rishonim*, vol. I, p. 242 and vol. II, p. 186.

Tosefta Kifeshutah, vol. VIII, New York, Order Nashim, 1973, at pp. 785–791.

Tosefta Kifeshutah, *Ketuboth*, pp. 266–268.

Tosefta Kifeshutah, *Moed*, pp. 1241–1242.

Tosefta Kifeshutah, Seder Zeraim, Terumot 7:20, at pp. 420–421, Jewish Theological Seminary of America, New York, 1955.

Tosefta Zeraim, *Terumot* 7:20, at pp. 148–149.

Luria, Shlomo ben Yehiel (1510–1573), *Yam Shel Shlomo*, to *Bava Kamma,* ch. 10, sec. 23, last column.

Maharam Mintz, Moses ben Isaac ha-Levi Mintz (1415–1480), *Teshuvot Maharam Mintz*, Cracow, 1617, Number 44, at 42a-43b.

Maharam of Rothenberg, Meir ben Baruch of Rothenberg (c. 1220–1293), *Responsa of Maharam MiRottenberg*, vol. I, ed. Bloch (Parma manuscript), no. 58; and vol. II, ed. Rabbinovicz (Levov edition) no. 58.

Prague edition, sec. 1022, para. no. 81, cited in Zevin, *Encyclopedia Talmudit*, supplement to article s.v. Cherem deRabbenu Gershom, at p. 772.

Mari of Marseilles, Isaac ben Abba (c. 1122–1193), *Sefer HaIttur*, Warsaw, end of Part I, sec. 8, at pp. 32b–33a, Kabbalat Ha'edut, p. 62b.

Meiri, Menachem (1249–c. 1310), Beit HaBechirah to *Bava Kamma*, last comment to 113a, s.v. *Gedolei Hamepharshim* and 113b.

Sanhedrin 72b, at p. 271.

Mordechai ben Hillel (c. 1250–1298), *Hagahot Mordechai to*

Bava Kamma ch. 9, para. 117.

Bava Kamma ch. 10, para. 157, 193, 195, 212.

Moses of Vienna, Isaac Ben (1200–1279), *Or Zarua, Piskei Bava Kamma, ch. 10, sec. 450, s.v. Katav Mori.*

Piskei Ri'az, to Bava Kamma, ch. 10, Law 2, para. 19, at p. 189.

Raavan, Eliezer ben Nathan of Mintz (1090–1170), *Sefer Raavan*, Part 2, end of Tractate *Bava Kamma*, at pp. 194–195.

RaMA, Moses ben Israel Isserlis (1520–1572), Responsa of Rama, no. 88, ed. Asher Siev, Jerusalem, 1971, at pp. 341, 378–384 and no. 86, pp. 354–377.

RaMaH, Meir HaLevy Abulafia (1170–1244), Yad Ramah to *Bava Kamma* 114a, s.v. *ve'lo amaran.*

Rambam, Moshe ben Maimon (1135–1204), *Hilchot HaYerushalmi LehaRambam, Berachot,* ch. 3, p. 27, ed. and commentary by Saul Lieberman, New York, JTS, 1958, sec. 100.

Maimonides Guide of the Perplexed, trans. Shlomo Pines, University of Chicago Press, 1963, Book II, ch. 40 and Book III, chs. 27, 31 and 34.

Mishneh Torah, Frankel Edition, Jerusalem, 2001.

To'en Venit'an 1:2.

Sefer HaMitzvot, trans. Ibn Tiobbon, revised by Chaim Heller, 2nd edition, Mosad Harav Kook, Jerusalem, New York, NY, 1946.

Responsa of Rambam, ed. Jehoshua Blau, Jerusalem, Mekitzei Nirdamim, 1960, vol. I, no. 210, at pp. 371–373. and no. 299, at p. 687.

RaN, Nissim ben Reuven Gerondi (1320–1376), Responsa of R. Nissim, no. 73, Koenigsberg, 1831.

Rashba, Solomon ben Adret (1235–1310), Commentary to *Bava Kamma* 113a, s.v. *Ha d'amrinan bebar Israel.*

Commentary to *Gittin* 46a.

Responsa of Rashba, Pietrokov, reprinted Jerusalem, 1960, vol. VII, no. 160.

Teshuvot She'elot LeHaRashba, First Edition, Rome, circa 1470. Introduction by Shlomo Zalman Havlin, Jerusalem, Jewish National and University Press, 1976, responsum no. 160.

Ravad, Abraham ben David Posquieres (c. 1125–1198), *Sefer Chiddushe HaRavad al Masechet, Bava Kamma*, ed. Shmuel Atlas, Jerusalem, Feldheim Pub., 1963, 2nd edition, at 113b and 114a.

Responsa Sha'are Zedek (Gaonic Responsa), ed. Hayyim Modai, Salonika, 1792, at p. 846, no. 4, Part IV, Sha'ar 7, no. 4.

Rosh, Asher ben Yechiel (1250–1327), *Asheri to Bava Kamma*, 113b–114a, ch. 10, secs. 14 and 27–28.

Sanhedrin 24a, at ch. 3, secs. 4–5.

Sardi, Samuel ben Isaac (c. 1185–1256), *Sefer HaTerumot*, of Sha'ar 62, part I, at p. 342a.

Shabbatai Hakohen (1621–1662), Siftei Cohen, (ShaKh), to Sh. A., Ch. M.

Sirkis, Joel ben Samuel (1561–1640), Bayit Chadash (BaCH),
to Tur, *Choshen Mishpat*, ch. 28, s.v. *Umah sekatav HaRosh.*
to Tur, *Even HaEzer*, ch. 115, s.v. *Umah shekatav vedavka.*

Sofer, Moshe (1762–1839), *Responsa Chatam Sofer*, to *Choshen Mishpat*, no. 23.

Vilna Gaon, Elijah ben Shlomo Zalman (1720–1797), *in Biur HaGra*, to *Shulchan Aruch, Choshen Mishpat* 28:4, at notes 27 and 28.

Waldenberg, Eliezer, (1915–2006), *Responsa Tzitz Eliezer*, vol. XIII, no. 101, Jerusalem 1985.

Index

"handingoren" (meshirah) 192

"informing" 191

"inaction" – criminalization thereof = Jewish / not USA 216

"justice" (univ. human) 218, 219, 220, 221
215

vs Feinstein (orthodox) 212

* Not anti-nonJewish gov 204, 207
depends democ soc as different 210

loyalty 215
+ criminalization of inaction 216

Resche 12, 13

war + observance 198

'weeds' 11, 15